MOSHE SAFDIE

In memory of Philip Matthews, our colleague and friend

MOSHE SAFDIE

Edited by Wendy Kohn

A.D. ACADEMY EDITIONS

ACKNOWLEDGEMENTS

EDITOR'S NOTE

Like the architecture within its pages, this monograph represents the attention, wisdom and care of many individuals. At Academy Editions in London, the dedication and patience of John Stoddart, Andrea Bettella, Maggie Toy, Mario Bettella, Nicola Kearton, Iona Baird and Alistair Probert helped make this book a reality. At the McGill University Safdie Archive in Montreal, Irena Murray and her colleagues contributed substantially to creating the chronology and staff list. Special thanks in particular are due to photographers Timothy Hursley, Steve Rosenthal and Malak who generously contributed their work to ours; to the late Jerry Spearman for his indelible images of Habitat and Michal Ronnen Safdie, whose images of models and buildings captured over many years fill the following pages; to Paul Goldberger, Peter G Rowe, Witold Rybczynski and Michael Sorkin for the words of resonance and meaning that have broadened this volume; to Laura Norton, Caroline Rogers and Lisa Green who helped assemble and organise a steady stream of images and information; to Sarah Radding, Jay Berman, Maura Fernandez-Abernethy and the drawing team who contributed more than revealing drawings.

Finally, my deep gratitude goes to the extraordinary group of professionals at Moshe Safdie and Associates. The entire Boston office accepted its role as consultant and construction site for this project with justified bemusement and exceptional grace. I would like to thank the many colleagues and friends whose knowledge and insight have enhanced this monograph, without whose support and perspective this project could not have been realised, and to whom I am very grateful.   *Wendy Kohn*

All illustrative material is courtesy of the architect unless otherwise stated.
Cover credits: Photographer: Michal Ronnen Safdie. Contributing artist (prism design): Charles Ross. **Photographic credits:** Aeroplan Ltd pp72-73; Albatross Aerial Photography, Duby Tal, Moni Haramati pp100-01; Joan Almond p89 (above right); Arnott Rodgers Batten Ltd p42 (above); NGC Photo Services, Rob Fillion pp178 (below right), 179; David Harris pp80, 88 (below), 89 (above left); Graetz Photography pp44-45; Michael Guran pp312 (below), 313 (above), 314 (below), 315 (below); Ya'Acov Harlap p87 (below); Timothy Hursley pp2, 14, 17 (above, centre), 24, 27 (above right, centre right), 28 (upper right, lower right), 29 (below right), 30, 33 (centre right, below right), 38-39, 41 (above), 48-50, 51 (above), 52 (below right), 53, 54 (above), 55 (above), 56, 144, 145 (above), 146 (above), 147 (above left), 152, 157 (above left, above right), 159, (above), 161 (centre right), 162, 164-66, 167 (above), 168 (above), 172, 173 (below right), 176-77, 178 (centre right), 180, 181 (above right), 182 (above), 183-84, 185 (above, below left), 186 (above, below left), 187 (above), 188, 190, 192 (above), 194 (centre right), 195 (above), 197 (above), 198-99, 208, 210-12, 214, 215 (above right, centre right), 216 (above right), 217-19, 230-35, 263 (above), 264 (above), 265 (above), 266-67, 268 (above), 270 (above, below), 271 (below left), 272 (above right, below right), 273 (above, below), 274-77, 284, 285 (above), 286-87, 288 (above), 290 (above, below), 291 (above left, below left), 292-98, 299 (above), 300-01; Wendy Kohn p52 (above left); Malak pp12 (below right), 13 (below right), 155 (above), 156 (above), 158 (above), 160, 161 (below right), 163 (above), 170-71, 173 (above right, middle right); Philip Matthews p141 (above); William P McElligot pp27, 209 (above); Brian Merritt pp189 (above), 193 (above), 194 (above left, centre left, above right), 195 (below), 196; Grant Mudford pp262, 269 (above), 271 (above left, centre left); Ofek Aerial Photography Ltd p316; Cymie Payne p140; Steve Rosenthal pp33 (above right), 98 (above), 200, 201 (above), 202 (above, below right), 205 (above), 206, 238, 239 (above), 240, 241 (above right), 242, 244, 245 (above), 278, 279 (above), 280, 282 (above), 283 (above left); Michal Ronnen Safdie pp7, 9 (below right), 18, 21 (above right, below right), 22 (above right, below right), 23, 27 (below right), 28 (below right), 72-75, 77 (above right, centre right, below right), 78, 79 (centre right), 81, 86, 88, 89 (above left), 92-98, 103-05, 107-10, 112-20, 121 (below), 122-31, 134-36, 148-51, 191 (centre right), 207 (above), 215 (below right), 216 (centre right, below right), 220-21, 222, 224-25, 227-29, 241 (below right), 243, 246-57, 259, 261, 320, 322, 324 (above), 325 (above), 329; Moshe Safdie pp9 (above right), 11 (below right), 12 (above right), 13 (above right), 52 (above right), 147 (below left), 161 (above right); Pierre Soulard p154 (above); Jerry Spearman pp40, 46 (below right); Studio Shuki Kook p106; Justin Wonnacot p178 (above right). **Illustration credits:** Carlos Diniz pp68 (above); Gene Dyer pp136 (above left, above right), 137 (below), 318, 319 (above, below), 321 (above); Michael Guran pp153 (above), 204 (above), 223 (above); Steve Oles pp281 (above left, below left). **Original sketches by Moshe Safdie:** pp23 (below left), 41 (below), 37 (above), 66 (above right), 79 (left), 83 (below), 85 (below right), 103 (centre right), 105 (below right), 107 (below), 111, 118 (below left), 119 (centre left, below left), 128 (above right), 131 (below), 132 (above), 125 (above), 147 (above right), 153 (below), 155 (below right), 158 (below right), 163 (below), 169 (right), 173 (left), 174 (left), 175, 178 (above left), 181 (above left), 182 (below left), 185 (below right), 187 (below), 189 (below), 191 (above right), 193 (below), 197 (below right), 201 (below), 202 (below left), 203 (left), 204 (below), 205 (below), 207 (below), 209 (below), 213 (right), 222 (above), 223 (below), 226, 227 (centre, below), 247 (right), 253 (below right), 257 (below), 258, 260, 263 (below), 264 (below), 265 (below), 271 (above right), 279 (below), 282 (below), 283 (centre right, below right), 285 (below), 288 (below), 291 (below right), 307 (right), 311 (right), 312 (above left), 313 (below), 314 (above), 324 (below), 325 (below left).
MSA monograph production: Archives: Lisa Green, Laura Norton, Caroline Rogers, Alicia Kennedy; Drawings: Sarah Radding, Jay Berman, Maura Fernandez-Abernethy, David Burnett, Mark Gordon, Uwe Brandes, Jeff Jacoby, Peter Jelley, Caroline Hu, Jeung Seok Hyun.

Cover: Refracted light, Class of 1959 Chapel, Harvard Business School
Frontispiece: Library Square, Vancouver

First published in Great Britain in 1996 by
ACADEMY EDITIONS
An imprint of

ACADEMY GROUP LTD
42 Leinster Gardens, London W2 3AN
Member of the VCH Publishing Group

ISBN 1 85490 453 1

Distributed to the trade in the United States of America by
NATIONAL BOOK NETWORK, INC
4720 Boston Way, Lanham, Maryland 20706

Printed and bound in Singapore

CONTENTS

INTRODUCTION

WENDY KOHN

Timelessness, in the view of Moshe Safdie, is the most meaningful quality one can ascribe to a building. His design process, however, focuses unrelentingly on the daily life of the architecture: the way spaces will be used; the building's performance in its climate; the real desires of the prospective inhabitants. In many ways this dichotomy characterises the essence of his work: a struggle and mediation between the universal and the specific, the ideal and the real.

Open-eyed in his approach to site, scale, building materials and programme, Safdie's deep inspirations, his precedents and passions, derive most often from broad mythological imagery – the Garden of Paradise, the Tower of Babel, the Light of Heaven. The resulting architectural form possesses both the immediacy of a specific tectonic solution and the timelessness of a familiar image.

Monumental, dramatic, ceremoniously public: these are qualities generated by bold ideas and accentuated in photographs of Safdie's buildings from Canada to Los Angeles to Israel. But while this dominant strain – the large-scale order and resoluteness, the Big Ideas of geometry and emphatically intersected platonic forms – sounds throughout the work, it is continuously accompanied by minor chords that rise and fall through intricately sculpted skylights, carefully studied apertures and rhythmically layered walls. The apparent singularity of Safdie's work provides structure for the strong and sure pleasure of walking, climbing, standing, sitting and contemplating in the complete environment of a real place.

It is Safdie's insistence upon the *experience* of architecture – the wordless, phenomenological, universally perceptible qualities of space and form – that most impresses those who visit his buildings. Safdie is convinced that true invention occurs only at the moment when an architect recognises all of the contradictions inherent in the design of buildings, and meets their challenges. No decision in the design process stands without his conviction that the space, volume, light and texture of the building is known and has been crafted. Safdie's eye explores and inhabits models made at every stage and at every scale: he carries them in and out-of-doors, photographs and amends and transforms them with fluid intensity. In the evolution of a design, Safdie maintains a continuous dialogue between recurrent sketchbook explorations and these small moments in construction. His finished buildings embody the vitality of this exchange.

In one of his most recent projects, Safdie joins the muscular, ordered, elliptical shell of Library Square with a sculpted, sloping urban plane in the city of Vancouver. Smoothly connecting two major avenues, the built surface of the block is moulded with landings, gradual stairs and wells for light below. On site, the urban floor becomes not plinth, but organic foundation: it is of the building as the library is of the city, as an institution and as urban architecture. The building's big 'square-in-circle' idea is maintained on the exterior only in partnership with these urban inflections, and on the interior, only with the complete collusion of spatial interstices like odd-shaped shafts for air and enormous earthquake joints. The city block of Library Square subtly fuses an urban building with an urban grid, and gracefully intersects the space of the public library with the space of its city.

In Habitat '67, his early *tour de force*, Safdie first established this characteristic symbiosis of ideal order and constructed specificity. In image, Habitat is an orderly ziggurat of cantilevered boxes, but from beneath, a Piranesian tangle of many-storeyed columns propping up the elegant honeycomb. There is hardly a structural element of Habitat that is not habitable: elevator shafts and fire stairs are columns; sheltered outdoor corridors are beams; houses with beautifully detailed interiors and planted gardens are walls, floors and roofs. Habitat is both a playground jungle-gym and a plausible piece of city that might easily extend along any axis – up, out or across. Experienced as a real place to live in a big city, it is both soaring and humanly scaled.

Standing on a roof garden at Habitat, surrounded by air and city, the complex effortlessly re-forms one's expectations of an urban home.

This is architecture as an event. Designed to be experienced, Safdie's buildings depend on the interaction of their three built dimensions with the both infinite and instantaneous quality of time. These places require the immediacy of movement through space, which gives rise to the 'trajectories' (as described here by Peter Rowe) of outdoor trellised walkways, angular skylit promenades and grandly curving passages. These spaces require a particular time of day, a specific angle of the sun. They require many individuals moving in a stop/start rhythm. Safdie's great and consistent achievement is an architecture that is simultaneously geometric and organic. His built work is strong enough to construct precious moments of the world 'as desired' (in Safdie's words) and malleable enough to adapt to the world 'as found'.

In his essay for this volume, Witold Rybczynski comments that Safdie is not a theorist, despite his almost constant output of articles and books. That Safdie believes it is possible to make judgements about what are the appropriate bases for design, what is the proper role of an architect in society, what is *moral* in architecture, renders his message incongruous with recent decades of academic theory. It is also because he has realised such an abundance of major projects, especially in the last decade, that it would be hard to consider any of his statements as only theoretical; the 'proof' is before our eyes.

It is my hope that this volume will be apprehended not as a conclusion, but as a provocation; not as a summary, but as a selection; not as a lesson, but finally as an invitation – to take a book up to the reading arcade of Safdie's Library Square, walk the trellised skywalks of Hebrew Union College or swing open the thick, double-height copper door of Harvard's Class of 1959 Chapel on a sunny day and touch the cool, curved concrete walls splashed with prismatic light.

THE MEDIUM AND LANGUAGE OF ARCHITECTURE

MOSHE SAFDIE

Originality in itself cannot be the criterion for measuring excellence in architecture. Only originality born in the resolution of truly architectural issues contributes to great design. In this imperative, does architecture differ from painting, sculpture, music and literature? Whether it is even possible to compare these types of artistic expression to architecture cannot be decided without attempting to define what constitutes the medium and language of architecture itself.

I believe that architecture is unique among art forms: similar in aspects of structure, poetry and invention, but different fundamentally. Three basic and essential elements constitute this distinction: first, *purpose* – the manner in which architecture accommodates life; second, *tectonics*, derived from the Greek *tektonikos* – the materiality of architecture and the technology of building; and third, *place* – architecture, unlike many other art forms, is rooted in time and place. These are the essential constituent parts of architecture: the means by which we translate architectural aspirations into habitable, durable and vital buildings.

One must ask what relation purpose, tectonics, and place bear to the totality of design. Clearly, any attempt to state universal rules is misguided. The ancients shared this mistrust of systematic solutions. On the contrary, they were forever postulating what were the basic elements of building and emphasising the necessity to balance them in the total work of architecture. Purpose, tectonics, and place evoke Vitruvius' 'commodity, firmness and delight'. Palladio, in turn, urged that the resolution of these three Vitruvian elements should render them virtually synthesised in the completed building. For me, design has been a search to produce a compelling spatial geometry in complete harmony with the formal imperatives of the programme, generated by a cohesive resolution of all the building's systems, and naturally rooted in its site.

Purpose

Speaking of purpose is like exulting the virtues of motherhood. Since the term 'function' has been debased to mean merely 'utility', I speak here of purpose as function in its profound sense: as the life intended for a building. D'Arcy Thompson defined the science of morphology as 'the study of forms which are so concomitant with life that they are seemingly controlled by life'.[1] Ideally, these words also apply to architecture. Fundamental to the medium of architecture is a continuous search into the meaning of programme. In my mind, true insight grows out of an understanding and resolution of the spatial organisation of human activity and behaviour.

Today we seem to differentiate between functionalism and art. The functionalist is pedestrian and dull, while the artistic is imaginative and challenging. In this cultural mind-set, the purpose of a building

has little relationship to its spatial richness. *Ergo*, the art of architecture has taken root in aesthetic explorations independent of purpose and materiality. This inversion is the cause of architecture's current chaotic condition: a popular misconception has been embraced by the profession.

As an example, one might compare Louis Kahn's Salk Institute for Biological Studies (1965) to Peter Eisenman's proposal for a Biocenter in Frankfurt (1987). At face value, the programmes are similar: both are meant to be places for research. The formal distinctions between the two designs, however, do not simply manifest the resolution of similar problems by dissimilar architects; nor do they merely testify to the two decades that separate their work. Rather, the two projects reveal absolutely contrasting fundamental values.

Kahn focused his entire being on an attempt to understand the creative process of scientists. Seeking to penetrate the mind-set of creative research, Kahn spoke of the qualities of calmness that breed contemplation. He was obsessed with the interdependence of communal work and individual work, with the balance between privacy and community.

Eisenman declares his project emerged out of an interest in the mathematical theory of fractals, a field that has inspired his formal explorations. I have studied Mandelbrot's fractals and, I must confess, I have difficulty appreciating the connection. But this difference of opinion is secondary. Eisenman has many interests – including the spheres of linguistics, mathematics and philosophy – that have led him to connections and applications to architecture. What is significant is the genesis of a science complex based not on the activity of research and the environment most conducive to it, but on what I believe is another agenda: a preoccupation with linguistics, and not with the life of the building itself.

Tectonics

Form derives from structure. I mean this in a more global way than the Miesian definition of structure. This deeper meaning of structure as not only the skeleton, but also the skin, arteries and veins of a building, implies that structure has a soul. Lancelot Law Whyte created a framework for the exploration of form in nature, but it applies equally and significantly to form in architecture. 'Form is both deeply material and highly spiritual', he wrote. 'It cannot *exist* without material support. It cannot be properly *expressed* without involving some supra-material principle.'[2]

For the appreciation of this relationship between architecture, materials and the process of construction in our time, we are forever indebted to Louis Kahn. In his term 'servant and served spaces', Kahn encapsulated the uniqueness of building in the 20th century: that the myriad air handling, mechanical, lighting, environmental control and data transmission systems had suddenly become real and requisite components of building. To me, their materiality is central. This is a clear and important difference between the world of stage sets and the architecture of real life.

The comprehension of the coming together of the parts of a building is a prerequisite to authenticity in a work of architecture. Gothic cathedrals have repeatedly reminded me that this is possible. In *The Gothic Cathedral,* Otto von Simson describes the cathedral of Chartres: 'Its design, authoritative and austere, offers nothing that one would attribute to personal invention or individual fancy. Indeed, we can no longer distinguish between structure and appearance, between the technical and the aesthetic accomplishment. The beauty of the edifice consists of the crystalline clarity of its structural anatomy. And these two aspects of the cathedral have in turn become inseparable from its symbolic character.'[3] Christopher Alexander, asked about the search for the quality of timelessness in buildings, responded that this particular authenticity is achieved when 'man allows nature to reveal itself through a building'.[4] Auguste Perret asked, 'Will the building make a beautiful ruin?'

Place

To appreciate the profound difference between architecture and other art forms, one need only consider the dilemma of a painter whose canvas is to be permanently juxtaposed with canvases painted by others, to be appreciated always as part of an assemblage; or a composer whose music is to be heard simultaneously and exclusively with the music of others.

Unlike other art forms, architecture is always perceived in a physical context. Experientially, the work of architecture and its setting are one. Architecture conceived as an addition to the existing urban fabric is the *sine qua non* of urbanism. This is also equally true of architecture set in the open landscape – a building cannot be experienced as independent of the land in which it is rooted.

A building's language cannot be resolved without taking a position on the issues of continuity versus disruption, of unity versus dissonance. The attitude of Le Vaux in designing one of several wings of the Louvre was fundamentally different from that of Frank Lloyd Wright in designing the Guggenheim Museum in New York City. One can either invent based on a recognition of similarities and differences – a recognition of what constitutes formal, experiential and cultural relationships in a particular place and time – or one can act as if in a vacuum. To me, the latter involves extreme *hubris*.

The Personal and the Shared

At any given moment, one's interests might focus on platonic solids or fractal geometry, aleatory music, Eastern philosophy or the theories

Tombs near Persepolis, Iran. Photograph by Moshe Safdie, 1975

Yeshiva Porat Yosef

of Lacan or Deleuze. Architecture is intrinsically the product both of a shared culture and the ideas of an individual. While teaching, I found myself constantly seeking to distinguish those ideas that can be considered collective concepts, which might form a shared theory of architecture, from those that were intrinsically personal, emerging from my own background, interests and obsessions. This search is, I believe, fundamental to our ability as architects to assess, judge and react to the multitude of possibilities continually presented to us. Intellectual preoccupations cannot overshadow the quest to understand and explore the essential elements of architecture. But the lessons learned in the process of discerning the shared, through the lens of the personal, can be, for each of us, deeply meaningful.

'I am part of all that I have met', wrote William Blake. My own work has been dominated by five personal themes: gardens, steps, sites, building blocks, and ritual and procession.

Gardens

From the beginning of my designs for buildings, I have been obsessed with the notion of the garden as the ideal place of being, undoubtedly sparked by the images of the Garden of Eden as Paradise – the human environment in its ideal state. I grew up in Haifa, a Mediterranean hill town overlooking the Baha'i Gardens, a place of pilgrimage and the burial place of the founder of the Baha'i religion, a sect whose name for God is *Jamal* – Arabic for beauty. Reflecting a cultural heritage of centuries of Persian and Moorish gardens, the Baha'ists proceeded to create their holiest grounds in their image of the Garden of Paradise. As a boy, I wandered through the Baha'i Gardens along walks of multicoloured river pebbles. The grounds were set off with white marble pavilions placed amid olive and cypress trees, rich plantings of jasmine and bougainvillea, and multiple axes that accommodated the hilly topography. This glimpse of Paradise recurred for me later whenever the ideas of building and garden became one – in Hadrian's Villa at Tivoli and in the garden-building island of Lake Maggiore.

Every culture has evolved its own image of Paradise, its own quintessential garden. As we have built and urbanised, the notion of garden has been extended three-dimensionally. I was nourished on images of the Hanging Gardens of Babylon through viewing the many fantastic illustrations made over time, but mostly through images conjured in written texts, with my own fantasies extending the land skyward.

When I first read Ebenezer Howard's *Garden Cities of Tomorrow,* I was struck by the seemingly universal desire to live in a house in a garden, the underlying impetus of suburbanisation. As cities have intensified, their residents have continued to dream about houses with gardens while living in high-rise apartments. Moved by this plight, I responded with Habitat as a possible modern-day hanging garden

– a high-rise city that seeks to satisfy our primeval desire for a garden. Ever since, each institution and building I have designed has recalled, in some way, a search for a connection to this idea.

Steps

For generations, painters have depicted Jacob's dream: his struggle with the Angel, the ladder ascending and then disappearing into the clouds. It was, perhaps, this image that was first sparked in my mind in 1968, when students from San Francisco State College asked me to design a building that they could climb on and enter from any direction. I have marvelled ever since at the concept of climbable buildings and landscapes, in the designs of others as well as my own.

As I have travelled, buildings that extend earth into sky, descend to the depths of the earth, or ascend without apparent limit have sparked my imagination. I climbed the steps, rising as if to infinity, of the astronomical observatories in Jaipur and New Delhi, and walked down the steps of India's many water temples, into the earth. I have visited the terraced and stepped temples and pyramids of the Aztec, the Zapotec and the Maya. At the Temple of Isis in Aswan, steps disappear down into the waters of the Nile. On the Mediterranean island of Santorini, clusters of houses and steps become one.

This theme generated the designs of the Western Wall precinct in Jerusalem, the Quebec Museum of Civilisation and the International House at the University of California in Los Angeles. In each case, the stepped building itself became a connector, part of the ground: in Jerusalem, between the Temple Mount, the Wall and the Old City; in Quebec, between the river and the upper city, and at UCLA, between the upper and lower campuses.

Sites

Le Corbusier proclaimed, 'the plan is the generator'. First, however, *the site* must be the generator of the plan. If the site generates the plan, then the urban experience of architecture will be based inherently on a relationship to its context. As a design, it will be holistic. This raises the question of the attitude of the architect: is the building perceived as a patchwork, an invisible mending, a mosaic, or a statement of contrast and contradiction?

My own attitudes have been conditioned by my work in Jerusalem. There, for the first time, I was confronted with building a great institution, the Yeshiva Porat Yosef, in the heart of the historic fabric of the Old City. Unlike the Romans or the Omayyads, who destroyed and rebuilt whole sections of Jerusalem, I felt awe and respect for the architectural heritage of that place. Could one design a building that belonged there and yet was of today? Could one relate to the particular scale, colours and textures of Jerusalem stone, and to the exuberant, soft, feminine forms of the city's domes and vaults? Could one do so without mimicking or producing a stage set of the historic?

I resolved this paradox by designing a building in which traditional and contemporary construction methods work in counterpoint to one another. The prevailing geometries of the surrounding architecture echo through the structures, but their uses are new. 'Will you give us a modern or traditional building?' asked the client. 'If I succeed, you will not be able to answer the question', I responded.

I remembered this experience profoundly more than ten years later, as I designed the Museum of Civilisation and the National Gallery in Canada. Facing the steep Nordic copper roofs and dormers of Quebec City and the exuberant theatrical neo-Gothic Parliament and cathedral of Ottawa, I found myself fascinated by the geometric versatility and diversity of the city. 'What is the essence of these 19th-century structures', I wondered. 'What are the rhythms, proportions and geometries that one might evoke in counterpoint and dialogue?'

More recently, in Vancouver, I recognised the virtue of contrast, of syncopation, as a means of responding and commenting. For me, design rooted in place fundamentally requires an effort to create structures that recognise the musical key of their surroundings. Only then can one realise the full potential for harmony as well as dissonance, for the *divertimenti* most meaningfully heard as part of a whole.

Building Blocks

The ultimate manifestation of the materiality of architecture is, for me, expressed in children's building blocks. As generations of builders set beam upon column, brick upon brick, roof tiles over joists, so too the uninhibited child assembles pieces that, like the beams and columns of a building, contain their own discipline. Whether the set of blocks consists of a limited number of related geometric pieces simply assembled or cleverly interlocked like Lego, each set follows its own rules of assembly. Each has an order, mysteriously encoded, which yields attractive results regardless of the child's talents.

Primitive buildings always manifest a similar methodical assemblage of simple parts. As these vernacular building forms evolved – be they the brick domes and vaults of mud architecture or the intricate wooden pieces in a Japanese temple – their development was guided by a search for the ideal shapes and materials for particular climates, topographies and ways of life.

The desire to break things down into parts, to build into individual components their own technique of assemblage, and to conceive geometries capable of permutations and combinations have all guided my work. In the paintings of early Cubism, landscapes or human faces and bodies are divided and recombined to become whole once again. Yet, the new whole emerges as more than the sum of individual parts. I have sought an equivalent in the modes of contemporary construction and architecture.

Hanging Gardens of Babylon, 19th-century engraving

Quebec Museum of Civilisation. Photograph by Moshe Safdie, 1987

Procession and Ritual: The Cardo Maximus

Regular, gridiron cities allow one to orient oneself by reference to numbered lateral and longitudinal streets. I have always been impressed, however, to discover how a circuitous ancient place such as the Old City of Jerusalem can also afford a clear sense of orientation in a completely different manner. An intricate maze of alleys and passages, the city is given structure by the intersection of two principal arcaded streets.

The alignment of Jerusalem's medieval markets was established by the Romans and Byzantines through a grand, colonnaded street, the *Cardo*, that extended from the northern gate to the southern entrance of the city. Along this spine of urban life every major public building took its place. The result was a hierarchical urban structure that still orients and orders several millennia later. More significantly, such monumental spines and gateways created a sense of procession that was an indispensable part of the experience of both sacred and secular life. Greek and Roman cities, and later, restructured 19th-century cities (the Paris of Haussmann's *boulevards* and the Vienna of the *Ringstraße*), each in its way strived to create an appropriate hierarchy. The colonnade around the Palais Royale, the porch around the Louvre and the Galleria Vittorio Emanuele in Milan each constitutes a component of hierarchical structure. As contemporary building complexes become increasingly large, these types of processional networks must be appreciated, invoked and expanded.

In Conclusion: Hubris versus Humility

On first seeing a photograph of the collapsed Nimitz Freeway in Oakland, California destroyed by the autumn 1989 earthquake, I was shocked to realise that here was a 'structure' that embodied, via extraordinary natural violence, the closest real-life manifestation of architectural Deconstructivism I had seen. I do not make the analogy with human tragedy lightly, but I am convinced that the striking physical resemblance found here begs several fundamental questions. Why have some artists and architects endeavoured to perpetuate, magnify, document, even celebrate the violence surrounding us?

We live in an age of *hubris*. I mean this both in the ancient Greek connotation of 'violence', and in the modern sense of the word – a supreme arrogance with respect to our world. Our century has been marked by greater destruction of human life than any preceding century. Increasing local violence, especially in our cities, has been amplified by omnipresent media. We experience this violence not only as destruction, but as disjuncture, discontinuity and disassociation. Artistically, we have tended to take these conditions for granted, even to glorify them.

The ancient Greeks could not have comprehended such an acceptance of destruction. To them, the term *hubris* stood for a mental-

Karnak, Egypt. Photograph by Moshe Safdie, 1985

National Gallery of Canada

ity that encouraged violence; it was a condition we were meant to resist. Human endeavours in philosophy, in the arts, in architecture and in literature were all meant to counter *hubris*.

In architecture, we have recently sought to create – in the imagery of violently colliding forms – analogies to the random spatial experience associated with explosion and collapse. Disruptions we observe in nature when systems move out of equilibrium have provided profound inspiration. To be sure, the world has always been filled with violence. Nevertheless, and perhaps in response, I feel increasingly committed to a search for calmness and serenity in my own work. The more surrounded I become with acts of *hubris*, the greater my search for serenity – its opposite, and, I hope, antidote. As an architect, I feel committed to seek out the Greeks' antithesis to *hubris* – in a search for the dignity of human life.

He who seeks truth shall find beauty;
He who seeks beauty shall find vanity.
He who seeks order shall find gratification;
He who seeks gratification shall be disappointed.
He who considers himself the servant of his fellow beings
    shall find the joy of self-expression.
He who seeks self-expression shall fall into the pit of arrogance.
Arrogance is incompatible with nature;
Through nature, the nature of the universe and the nature of
    man, we shall seek truth.
If we seek truth, we shall find beauty.[5]

Rajasthan, India. Photograph by Moshe Safdie, 1979

Habitat '67

Notes

1 D'Arcy Wentworth Thompson, *On Growth and Form*, Cambridge University Press (Cambridge, England), 1959 (originally published 1917).

2 Lancelot Law Whyte, *Accent on Form*, Greenwood Publishing Group (Westport, Connecticut), 1973.

3 Otto von Simson, *The Gothic Cathedral*, Princeton University Press (Princeton and London), 1962 (reprint of 1956 edition).

4 Stephen Grabow, *Christopher Alexander: The Search for a New Paradigm in Architecture*, Oriel Press (Stockfield, Northumberland, Boston, Massachusetts), 1983.

5 Moshe Safdie, from *The Language and Medium of Architecture*, Harvard University Graduate School of Design (Cambridge, Massachusetts), 1989.

Habitat '67

HABITAT AND AFTER

MICHAEL SORKIN

Habitat gave clarity to one of Modernism's main befuddlements: the styles of equality. We know that Modernity has both technical and political vectors, that it was enabled by ideas of both science and rights. This conjunction produced a predictable consequence: the attempt to measure the dimensions of rights. For architecture, there were a number of implications. Perhaps foremost, housing became the privileged site of architectural Modernism – only logical since shelter is *the* fundamental right in architectural terms. Mass housing maps a relationship of social breadth, encapsulating a theory of equality: it specifies.

If Marx's great contribution was to clarify the economic engine of history, to show the informative underpinning of economy in virtually every cultural expression, housing provided the spatial analogue for the polemic about economic equality. As Modernity produced its 'new man', his domain was surely to express his rights *vis-à-vis* property. More, housing was to be a principal organ in shaping his attitudes and character. Rationalism and economism were not the only pillars of Modernity, a teleological psychologism was also a staple of the age, another scientific notion of 'man-environment' relations that further flavoured architecture with a spirit of determinism.

This atmosphere of scientific precision entered the housing question via several axes. One was quantitative, the ongoing debate about the *existenzminimum*, the quantum of shelter, a suitably hygienic, dignified and functional unit of housing that would guarantee and describe this basic right. To this day, this discussion has devolved into insanely asymptotic dimensioning, a measuring of rights by inches. Of course, in a conservative climate in which housing is considered a privilege and not a right, this same obsession with measure is inverted, deformed into a question of excess rather than entitlement.

The therapeutic aspects of the crusade for housing grew, however, not simply from the dimensional or volumetric aspects of equality but also from the character of the space itself. High Modernist housing tended to retain the Calvinist parsimony of character that offered both a kind of chaste, disciplinary atmosphere and the putative rationality of visibility, the sure knowledge that the characteristics of one's own dwelling would be clearly repeated in those of one's neighbours.

The medium for the creation of these interacting sets of relations was geometry. The association of the grid with the supreme philosopher of rationality, Descartes, reinforced the apparent logic of orthogonality. High Modernism is certainly characterised by its zeal for the right angle, for the clarifying therapy of social relations made geometrical. Perhaps no more succinct statement of the impulse is to be found than Idlefons Cerdà's explanation of his plans for the enlargement of Barcelona: 'the squared block is the clear and genuine expression of mathematical equality which is the equality of rights and interests, of justice itself'. Squared forms in repetition assumed not simply the aura but the substance of democracy.

This conjunction has been pursued insanely, the putative democratic content of the grid serving as a cover for the sciences of discipline. What are we really to make of the schemes of Hilberseimer, Gropius, Le Corbusier, of the thralled housing authorities of New York or Chicago, and their exaltation of what, retrospectively, can only be seen as landscapes of alienation and incarceration? Then again, this fantasy of infinite parity is Modernity's Janus. What do a billion Chinese in Mao suits tell us . . . tell them? That all men are equal? That all men are miserable? That no one is in chains? That everyone is in chains?

Modern architecture tends to be read at one extreme or another, as either the good-faith experiment of generations gripped with the desire to put the world right or the delusional communism of dupes and fellow-travellers. The real situation, naturally, is more complicated. We are past the point where such uniform readings are the only ones available and can now look back at an architecture that has long embraced both nuance and productive contradictions. Le Corbusier's are emblematic. As theorist, his contribution is all mechanism and megalomania, universal principles and an architecture of mesmerising replicability. As practitioner, his production speaks of values that spring from sources quite different, of sculptural modulation and the inflections of eccentricity.

All that crisp white architecture produced by the Modern Movement is, however, not just a fantasy of purity and reflectivity but of a very particular place in the sun. One of European Modernism's deepest roots is Mediterranean: the prismatic, sun-dappled, modularity of the hill towns of Italy and the villages of North Africa. The accidental, 'natural' cubism of such places inspired the movement, both for its dramatic sculpturality and high-key chiaroscuro, its primary simplicity, and for its accretive genesis, for the way in which a set of simple volumes acquires, in growth, a labyrinthine complexity. The isolation of Modernism from this primary source is one of its sad ironies.

Perhaps one of the reasons for this is Modernism's much remarked elevation of space over mass and its preference for the legibility of the object over that of the ensemble. Scientific Modernism was, in this sense, anti-organic, seeking constant objects in constant relations, an interstice as 'squared' and predictable as the objects that hemmed its edges. This constant lack of tension, this insistence on an absolutely continuous and non-contradictory reading is at the heart of Modern architecture's failure to produce a habitable urbanism. Its devotion to perfection left no room for the structures of apparent anomaly that the natural world is so brilliant at producing, structures that, indeed, form one of the fundamental consistencies of nature.

Which brings me to Habitat, to Moshe Safdie's repatriation of Modernism to this neglected point of origin. Biography, of course, is an unreliable guide but a convenient source of metaphor, and Safdie's is perhaps too apt. Mediterranean-born and relocated to icy rationalist climes, his architecture – at its own origin – is one of reconciliation. There is something unusually North American about the synthesis. From the start, Safdie has been conscious of his comminglings, happy both in the patterns of village life and in the gleamy technicality of construction. Indeed, it is the frank imagibility of the ensemble that sets Habitat apart: the image of the village is the medium by which the product of the factory is individuated.

Safdie has invoked the analogy of the automobile industry in describing the project. His use of this comparison, though, seems to be more about mechanisation than individuation, the efficiencies of indoor, assembly-line construction rather than the possibilities for a mechanised entry into the territories of variety. But, the life-cycle of the American car also suggests a formal mode: the styling of a taste- and function-sensitive envelope that offers possibilities for the accumulation of an aesthetic of excess in the susceptibility of the car to customisation, addition and individual whim. One of the joys of Habitat is precisely this. It has accreted all the physical extensions – the awnings, draperies, potted plants and deck furnishings – of individual occupancy.

Habitat impresses precisely for its openness to such alterations. The relatively mute and prismatic forms of the stacked boxes are especially fine for their failures of coercion, their subtle under-expression. Simple openings, plain surfaces and copious terraces are exactly the territories of self-expression so well advanced in the North American suburbs. If the Habitat *parti* were to become more general, one would expect the individuation of its elements to become still more particular. Habitat's tragedy, of course, is that it has remained so singular, so iconic. The result is a kind of theft of latitude: one doesn't mess with a work of art. A community of Habitats would, one expects, be daubed in competing colours, encrusted with vines, hung with shutters, re-glazed with sash, wildly morphed into the flamboyance of form and image of a bourgeois *favela* (the great sixties addition to the lexicon of democratic architecture's sources). If only . . .

This paradigm of unspecified extension (as opposed to various overbearing 'kit of parts' fantasies that were more or less contemporaneous with it) is Habitat's most important conceptual contribution. It is also here that Habitat's most resonant analogy with the city lies. Safdie was explicit in the urbanistic rationale for Habitat, the idea of combining urban scale and density with the family-object of the suburban pattern. The appeal of the suburbs is a compound of safe homogeneity, open space and fresh air, and – perhaps paramount – a sense of territoriality that extends beyond the walls, the bufferings of a proprietary spatial envelope. Safdie's canniness is in the calibration of the dimensions of this hemming space, in providing an envelopment (not just of the terrace but of the airspace that surrounds the suspended pods on all sides) that is usefully assertive in making a place which each dweller can call his or her own.

It would thus be a mistake to associate Habitat too closely with the culture of pods that grew concurrently with it. Habitat's capsules were always a means rather than an end. One can't emphasise enough how pervasive (and pervasively ambiguous) the fantasy of the module was in those days. Habitat is a line-strider, disposed between the close-packed nightmare of endless monads, the high-stacked, universally-equipped, crouch-height pods of Japanese love hotels, and various delirious filing cabinet fantasies of the hive on the one hand and, on the other, the benign seriality of the idea of a house for everyone, delivered by a technology harnessed for good.

Of course, Habitat was also a victim of a loss of faith. Opened at the apogee of the technological slaughter of Vietnam, it fell afoul both of a society that was favouring guns over butter for its capital investments as well as a more generally rising conviction that large-scale 'heavy' technology was the answer to nothing benign. An irony, this, as Habitat was one of the first of the 'mass-produced' projects to engage a problematic beyond cost, to incorporate a meaningful theory of contemporary collectivity. *For Everyone A Garden* is the title of one of Safdie's books and the argument which it (and Habitat) embraces is transformative: architecture should take as its ambition the provision of a fragment of paradise for everyone, not just the regressive calculus of the minimum turf of daily existence.

The series of unrealised projects which followed Habitat, including a variety of sisters and brothers initiated in the flush of enthusiasm for the new system, then abandoned by failures of commitment to the necessary scale of its industrial aspect, are sad witness to a general decline of the sciences of optimism, their displacement by the decade-and-a-half of suspicion and venality that followed the collapse of the sixties. Of particular poignancy is the unbuilt project for a student union at San Francisco State College, scene of some of the most vigorous student activism of the time (presided over by the ridiculous repressions of its president, SI Hayakawa). The Student Union project pointed the way to Habitat's logical advance, refining the module, embodying a much more activated notion of use input, and – most dramatically – realising Habitat's destiny as artificial topography, an inhabited mountain, its outer surface almost completely negotiable: a beautiful direction.

It is another of Habitat's historical ironies that the first instance of the construction of a seminal idea was also the end of the road. This is a characteristic Habitat shares with a nearly contemporaneous project which both crystallised and finalised another set of ideas dear to architectural Modernity: the Pompidou Centre also stood for a juncture between technology and freedom but reconciled them in terms of potential rather than individuation. Here was another of the *beaux-idéals* of Modernity: the anticipating void; the idea of 'equipotentiality'; the location of the idea of malleability in the absence of intervention; the space of all possibilities awaiting freedom's own (unspecified) creativity; space which in its non-particularity could be (potentially) all things to all people.

The well-serviced shed attempted to do much of the same conceptual work as the metastasising pod. At Pompidou, football-field-sized spaces, open and untrammelled, were supported by the migration of all structure and services to the building perimeter or to deep 'servant' (technology also takes care of the class system) interstices between floors. These voids were to await the defining particularities of an endlessly shifting flow of use. This is a fantasy that clearly has its limits, too coy about its own modulations and necessarily deeply invested in the specific tectonics of its long-spanning strategies. The pressure is for the greatest possible leap to liberate the greatest possible set of potentials. Size is crucially bound to possibility in this expressive economy.

Habitat suggests a more nuanced strategy for the collaboration of structure and complex possibility. In Safdie's initial design, Habitat isolated its dwelling pods from the structure which supported them, a 'plug-in' in the lingo of the time. In this incarnation, the form of the dwelling cliff-faces was very much subordinated to the heroic tectonics of the apparatus of support, taking on a mega-scaled rhythm and regularity. In the reduced scheme eventually built, however, the means of support has been incorporated into the pods themselves, yielding a far richer and more eccentric statical condition. To me, this is one of the beauties of Habitat: the complexities of its loading and the fiendish negotiated transfer of the forces that stabilise the structure. Here is a fine metaphor for the culture of cooperation that informs the city of real choice: each element plays its singular part in a structure that is sustained by a complex negotiation between its citizens/components.

We are once more at a moment in architecture in which the sources of form have become a vexed subject, in which the bases of architecture's authority are in dispute. Habitat provides what remains a remarkably coherent set of arguments about the origins of form, invoking both rationalism's orders of objectivity in construction and purpose but leavening their mathematical reduction with a vision of life. For Safdie, abstraction is a medium for solving the problems of housing a vibrant daily existence, not an end-all means for *representing* the character of modern living. It is logical, too, that Safdie's best post-Habitat work signals a more literal return to Modernism's repressed Mediterranean influence, inspired by the glowing simple modularities and complex ensemble of Jerusalem.

Habitat '67

Habitat '67

San Francisco State College Student Union

Old City of Jerusalem, view from Mt of Olives

REBUILDING JERUSALEM

PAUL GOLDBERGER

Moshe Safdie's work in Jerusalem is less an architectural oeuvre than a saga. A saga that is very much the story of the city itself since the 1967 war: a struggle to make peace between East and West, between modesty and bold gestures, between the past and the present. The story this work tells is no more complete than Jerusalem is, and it moves back and forth between the triumph of architecture completed, the frustration of projects compromised, and the disappointment of work postponed.

Safdie has not remade the city, despite the considerable sweep of his work there: his impact has been tremendous, but only small sections of the city have been reshaped entirely according to his designs. In some ways it would be more accurate to say that Jerusalem has remade Safdie, since in the nearly 30 years since he began his work there, the city's intense politics, its increasingly multi-ethnic culture, and its determination to respect the scale, if not the forms of its past, have all had a significant effect on his work. His projects have become less diagrammatic as the years have gone on, more concerned with finding ways in which new architecture can complement rather than replace the texture of the existing cityscape. While he came into Jerusalem believing that a neighbourhood like Mamilla, which lies in front of the Jaffa Gate beside the Old City, could be completely reshaped, he has come now to be more concerned with weaving together new and old strands of the urban fabric at a scale that relates comfortably to what has come before, as the final designs for his sprawling Mamilla project demonstrate.

Safdie's priority has always been the spirit of the city, and if his way of expressing that spirit has shifted slightly over the years, his passionate response to Jerusalem – not to mention his profound understanding of the city – have remained unchanged. His vision of the city is striking, perhaps unique, in that he sees it both as an architect and as an enlightened citizen. His architectural sensibility does not overwhelm all other concerns and lead him to impose a set of arbitrary forms unrelated to the city's needs, yet neither does his fascination with the city's politics and culture lead him to put aside his architectural judgement. If there is anything that can be said about all of his Jerusalem work, it is that it is driven by the desire to balance his reaction to the particular conditions of this city with his larger architectural impulses; Safdie designs in response to Jerusalem, but he designs in response to Safdie as well.

Safdie's professional involvement with Jerusalem began when he was invited there in 1967 to design a version of Habitat. The Habitat Israel project was never built, but Safdie's frequent visits to the city led to an invitation to step in and take over the design for Yeshiva Porat Yosef, a rabbinical college rebuilding its original home overlooking the Western Wall in the Jewish Quarter of the Old City. It was his first attempt to evolve a middle ground between the stark, geometric

and frankly tectonically-inspired work he had been producing in North America and the more textured, rich and eccentric forms of traditional architecture in Jerusalem.

While the Yeshiva was never completed as designed – the contentious clients, having thrown aside a previous architect in favour of Safdie, then proceeded to alter his scheme while it was being built – it nonetheless provided the conceptual basis for much of Safdie's work throughout the Jewish Quarter, as well as the Mamilla project just outside the gates. Safdie's many projects within the Jewish Quarter, primarily residential but also commercial and institutional, used the extraordinary, glowing Jerusalem stone and echoed the scale and texture of the original buildings of the Old City. But their partial half-sphere acrylic bubble domes, terraces and continual motif of half-round arches made it clear that this was not archaeological architecture committed to replication as the only means of respecting the past. Safdie attempted here to meld his fondness for basic geometries and his Modernist instinct with what might be called a Post-Modernist urban sensibility: this work accepts, even celebrates, the value of respect for urban context, but sets out to do it without literally replicating historical form.

Safdie's own house at the north end of the Jewish Quarter, where he was his own client, proved a more successful laboratory than the Yeshiva. Here, overlooking the Western Wall in this three-storey structure that Safdie reconstructed from a ruin, is the first sliding transparent dome he designed, a form which was to become something of a trademark for him in Jerusalem. It makes splendid sense functionally, permitting spaces to act as open roof terraces in summer and as enclosed winter gardens in other seasons, and it is easy to see how Safdie felt that these shapes provided a welcome allusion to the traditional architecture of the Middle East. Still, the round, transparent quarter spheres have a kind of sleekness that is at odds not only with the older architecture they attempt to recall, but with the rougher, boxier forms of the buildings of which they are a part. The result can be slightly discordant, and from the exterior gives the buildings an air of theatricality, almost jauntiness.

Such are the risks of attempting a middle ground between historic replication, which, whatever its other shortcomings, tends to steer clear of the pitfall of a slightly forced playfulness, and industrialised Modernism, which makes no gestures towards history and context whatsoever. Indeed, a recurring shortcoming of much of Safdie's early work in Jerusalem is its inability to make a convincing case for the fact that Safdie's goal of combining Modernism and Post-Modernism might be capable of yielding new architecture that resembles something other than a shotgun marriage. While from the beginning Safdie was steadfast in his belief that he was following the right path philosophically, his forms did not always reflect this certainty with buildings in which the modern and traditional elements are synthesised into a fully resolved harmony.

A splendid exception to this is what can probably be called Safdie's most successful project in Jerusalem: the campus complex for the Hebrew Union College. Here, just a few blocks away from the Mamilla project, Safdie produced a small campus that gracefully echoes the scale and spirit of traditional architecture, yet has a crispness to it that marks it as being of this moment. There are arches and loggias, arcades, courtyards and piazzas which have gently overlaid what is, at base, a set of Modernist buildings skilfully shoehorned into an oddly shaped urban site. Most of the details, particularly the windows, are more conventionally modern than those in the Jewish Quarter, and there are sleek walls of glass and metal neatly woven behind the Jerusalem stone of the loggias and facades.

For all the mixture of periods seen here, the overall effect is self-assured and serene. The proportions are almost always better than those in most of the Jewish Quarter buildings – there are no continually repeating half-round arches, but much more subtle rhythms to the facades, and a wonderful sense of layered texture. Yet for all the complexity here, there is less of a sense of visible effort to this project than to some of Safdie's other work in Jerusalem. It takes a moment to realise why this is so: part of the magic of this project is its quiet grace, a restraint that makes you wonder, on first entering, whether there is anything special at all. The Hebrew Union College, unlike Safdie's work in Mamilla, does not grab the visitor on first look – it is a building of second glances, of repeated encounters, that offers up its architectural pleasures gently over time. It is designed to be walked through, not merely looked at: it is processional architecture in the best sense of the word, its qualities unfolding as you move through it.

In the case of Hebrew Union College, unlike the Jewish Quarter, the context was not particularly powerful – a messy streetscape with monuments like the King David Hotel and the Jerusalem YMCA not far away, but undistinguished commercial structures directly adjacent. The important buildings on the block gave Safdie a level to aspire to, but made no immediate demands in terms of form, and allowed him, in a sense, to relax as he could not do in the Jewish Quarter where far more was prescribed. Indeed, it is hard not to sense that some of the more theatrical details of the buildings in the Jewish Quarter and Mamilla come from the architect's fear, perhaps unspoken, that the power of the context would deny him sufficient chance to leave his mark, and that the bold shapes of repeating arches and domes were the only way out, a shout to be heard over the heavy din of history. At the Hebrew Union College there would have been no such fear, no worries that future generations would fail to perceive what Safdie had done. The result is a striking and telling paradox: in the situation in which the context made fewer demands, Safdie designed more modestly.

Modest is not the first word that comes to mind when discussing either Safdie's Mamilla urban renewal project or his proposal for the ceremonial area surrounding the Western Wall at the edge of the Jewish Quarter. Mamilla is now under construction, in somewhat reduced form: the Western Wall project is as yet unrealised. Both projects represent Safdie at his most ambitious, and while each contains to some degree the diagrammatic and theatrical qualities that can sometimes characterise his work, each project emphatically demonstrates the depth of his knowledge of Jerusalem and the conscientiousness with which he takes up the sociological as well as the architectural challenges that face an architect in this city.

First, Mamilla. This was almost Safdie's Waterloo, a vast project for the complete rebuilding of the neighbourhood between the central business district and the Jaffa Gate to the Old City that in its initial form was sharply attacked as too big, too automobile-oriented, and too indifferent to the traditional street pattern of the city. The programme for Mamilla includes condominiums, a hotel, a parking garage, a bus garage and terminal, public gardens and a pedestrian marketplace. Safdie was originally asked by the City in 1972 to design 232,250 square metres of utilities for the 101,170-square-metre site. When environmental and planning groups objected, he cut the project back to roughly half the original size and increased the number of structures to be rehabilitated rather than replaced.

The political winds that buffeted the Mamilla project, and delayed its construction for nearly 15 years, ultimately served both it and its architect well. Safdie was wise enough not to fight to preserve the original design; indeed, his own thinking was evolving rapidly at the same time that the project was undergoing public review, and it is fair to say that what ended up being built is less an unwelcome compromise than a happy representation of his own more enlightened thinking. Certain basic aspects of the original plan, however, did not change significantly: the Mamilla neighbourhood lies in a valley between the Old City and the central business district, and Safdie's chief urban goal was to restore a sense of connection to this area, to open up the valley, the form of which had been denied by the pattern of the old neighbourhood. Safdie ran a major boulevard through the valley, providing an automobile connection between the central business district and the Old City, and terraced up structures on each side of it. On one side the bus terminal is buried under public gardens, which themselves serve as a promenade to connect the Jaffa Gate with the existing central business district via the new pedestrian shopping street, which thankfully is left uncovered. (There was pressure, which was resisted by Safdie, to cover it and turn it literally into a mall.) On the other side of the boulevard, facing the Old City, are several blocks of condominiums whose architecture is a more dramatic version of Safdie's Jewish Quarter projects, with bigger and bolder neo-oriental details and some units set on bridges sailing over pedestrian walkways, like Middle Eastern versions of the Ponte Vecchio. (The bridge units sold first.) At the far end, tying in with the existing business district, is a seven-storey luxury hotel.

If anything distinguishes the final design from the earlier version, beyond a reduction in height, it is a greater sense of connection to the existing cityscape: this is a project that endeavours to weave into the fabric of the city, not to deny it. Overall, Mamilla's programme and its design represent an attempt to deal with several conflicting needs: that the Old City be connected literally to the rest of Jerusalem and not be set aside as a kind of theme park; that the pressures for traffic and vehicular movement between the Old City and the rest of Jerusalem be accommodated; that the special quality of the Old City and its Walls, landscaped as a national monument since the 1967 war brought the Old City under Israeli control, be respected; and, that a commercial centre of gravity be provided in a part of Jerusalem midway between the Jewish business district towards the west and the Arab district towards the east to counterbalance the continued economic segregation of the city. It is a tall order, demanding a synthesis of traditional, pedestrian-oriented urban density and automobile-oriented expansiveness, and Safdie endeavoured to respond to all sides of this complex equation.

The programme for Mamilla was at least partially driven by economics. For the Western Wall, the issue was religious and civic: what would be the most appropriate way to express the importance of this sacred site of Jewish history, and to accommodate the crowds who come to pray there? The basis of Safdie's elaborate proposal, commissioned in 1974 and revised in 1982, was the excavation of another 9 metres of the Wall, exposing it to a lower level and earlier period of history, and the conversion of the immense open space in front of it into a terraced amphitheatre. Safdie's belief was that this would allow a sense of intimacy for those close to the wall, which is technically only a foundation but is the only remaining portion of the Second Temple, and is frequently a site of prayer and pilgrimage. At quiet times visitors would approach the Wall by stepping down towards it, level by level, while at busier times during holy days, the terraces would accommodate the much larger crowds and give them a greater sense of connection to the Wall than that presently offered by the amorphous and ugly open plaza in front of it. That plaza, the result of the hasty demolition (after the 1967 war) of houses that once went right up to the Wall, offers nothing except open space and robs the Wall of what had once been a stunningly powerful sense of emergence out of a dense urban neighbourhood.

The Safdie plan, commissioned by the Municipality of Jerusalem and the Corporation for the Development of the Jewish Quarter, cannot replace that remarkable juxtaposition of tight, ancient city and monu-

Private Residence

Hebrew Union College

Mamilla Center under construction

mental artifact. Some degree of open space is required to provide room for the crowds that, since 1967, have flowed continually, night and day, to the Wall. But Safdie's plan at least offers some degree of enclosure, and responds intelligently to the varying needs the space in front of the Wall must fulfil at different times while also offering the potential for a magnificent processional approach. The very care of the design, however, for all its virtues, creates a certain sense of artifice that is at odds with the sombre, powerful, almost cosmic presence of the Wall itself. Unfortunately, discussions about the Safdie plan are destined to remain academic, at least for the moment: it has fallen victim to political differences between various religious factions, the city and the national government over control of the site, and it is unlikely to be realised for some time, if at all.

Considerably more likely to be realised is Safdie's ambitious plan for the area around the Damascus Gate, the entry to the Arab Quarter of the Old City. Here, for what is now a roughly triangular open area, he has proposed a large open space, sloping gently downwards to reach the level of the gate, which is slightly below the current street level. The space would be a public piazza and marketplace, in effect allowing the functions of the Old City to spill through, weaving into the fabric of the existing city outside the gates. Pedestrians would pass under an automobile street to approach the Damascus Gate; here, again, Safdie has dealt with a complex urban design in three-dimensions, and chosen to solve it in terms of levels, the segregation of automobile and pedestrian traffic, and the provision of monumental public space that would be infused with energy and activity.

Safdie's two memorials at Yad Vashem, the Children's Holocaust Memorial of 1987 (designed in 1976), and the Transport Memorial of 1994, make clear his profound commitment not only to the memory of the Holocaust, but to the responsibility of architecture to strengthen and support that memory. In each case Safdie has conceived a simple, almost theatrical gesture and executed it with such a sure hand that it is deeply moving, without being melodramatic. The Children's Memorial is a dark room, set within a rocky, landscaped mound so that entering it is like entering a cave. An entry vestibule has photographs of children who were victims of the Holocaust, and then the main room consists of nothing but darkness, broken only by what seem like millions of tiny flickering lights, reflecting one into the other like thousands of stars in a night sky. A recorded voice repeats the names of children who were killed in the Holocaust and the sense is of blackness, deep and limitless, yet illuminated by tiny points of hope.

The Transport Memorial, marking the trains that took victims to concentration camps, consists of an actual car taken from an Auschwitz-bound train. Safdie has placed it on a track that projects out from a stone wall, as if it were moving away from us towards the

David's Village, Mamilla

Western Wall Precinct design

Damascus Gate Precinct design

neighbouring forest. The train is at the edge of the track, which ends abruptly in open space, so that it looks as if the train car is rushing towards a void, racing headlong into nothingness.

The stunning emotional impact of these memorials renders them different, at least superficially, from Safdie's other work in Jerusalem. Yet they surely do not emerge from a different view of what architecture is, or what it can mean. Both the memorials, in their intense drama, and the urban projects, in their search for a viable form of contextualism, are ways of seeking connections, ways in which Safdie has tried to make his architecture a part of the larger life of the city and, beyond this, to tie it to the history of the Jewish people. The forms may be abstract, but the meaning is not. This is the architecture of wholeness, Safdie is telling us – an architecture that aspires to express the fullness of Jerusalem and of the experience of the Jewish people.

Yad Vashem Holocaust Transport Memorial

Damascus Gate Precinct, sketch by Moshe Safdie

Yad Vashem Children's Holocaust Memorial

Skirball Museum and Cultural Center

TRAJECTORIES, TRACES AND TROPES

PETER G ROWE

Moshe Safdie has designed in many different regional and national settings, encountered many different site conditions and dealt with many different use programmes in a body of work that has spanned almost three decades. His projects vary in size from fully-developed proposals for new communities and large-scale mixed-use complexes to intricate small-scale restorations of historical districts and designs for relatively small institutions.

Nevertheless, all the work recognisably belongs to Moshe Safdie. It is consistent, and underlying this consistency are at least three long-standing commitments. One is a particular kind of Modernist spatial organisational strategy; another is a direct, broad and unsentimental attitude towards context, and a third is a considered preference for regular geometric forms. Together, all three constitute the persistent trajectories, traces and tropes of Moshe Safdie's work.

Trajectories: A Modern Organisational Sensibility

Even a casual perusal of Safdie's projects quickly reveals the sensibilities of a modern urbanist at work. Unlike the traditional urban spaces of, say, Rob Krier or Camillo Sitte, which consist of well-defined figural plazas and squares seemingly cut out of a unified building mass, Safdie's approach is distinctly modern. More precisely, it is very much aligned with the practices of Team 10, involving formal devices like grids and spines, and a strong emphasis on movement and the 'connectivity' of important external as well as internal spaces.[1]

Invariably, buildings are conceptualised as precincts that order and aggregate a series of well-defined spaces. Conversely, urban districts are treated as well-linked building complexes, again with a precise spatial articulation of each component. The programme for the building, or complex of buildings, is either clarified into distinct spaces or recombined to form larger yet coherent complexes. The former approach is clearly evident in Ottawa City Hall (1988-94), and the latter in the Mamilla Development project, Jerusalem, for which design work began in 1974. In effect, buildings and precincts become one and the same.

Often, the functional analysis of both programme adjacencies and circulation sequences underlies the final form of the plan. In the Skirball Museum and Cultural Center in Los Angeles, California (1986-95), this is particularly apparent. Here, following topographic contours and skirting the base of a comparatively steep hill, various elements of the building are housed relatively separately. To adjust the alignment of circulation and to link buildings together physically, formal and organisational elements such as entry pavilions and rotundas join the principal building complexes of an academic centre, an American Jewish heritage museum, and a communications centre. These adjacent functions and their built forms appear to generate a clear but sequential circulation route through the project.

Ottawa City Hall, in which a strong circulation armature links various distinct building components, displays the inverse of this approach. The overall pattern is in the shape of a strong, slightly curved axis leading from an entry pavilion to a major council chamber, perpendicular to which is a subordinate orthogonal grid of internal and external passageways. The unbuilt proposal for the Superconducting Super Collider Laboratory (1992-94), also possesses a strong linear and serial spatial organisation with many of the same characteristics. These hierarchically clear connections and connectors strongly recall layout and planning principles of the late sixties and early seventies.

Safdie's approach to the organisation of institutional building differs fundamentally from other approaches of recent times. In comparison, IM Pei's East Wing of the National Gallery of Art in Washington, DC (completed 1978), and Frank O Gehry's Air and Space Museum in Los Angeles, California (completed 1984), are both large sculptural objects, and not aggregations of parts. Furthermore, Safdie's work avoids the figurative and typological references which predominate in the recent work of Hans Hollein at the Museum of Modern Art in Frankfurt and in Rafael Moneo's recent scheme for the Museum of Roman Art in Merida, Spain.[2] In its well-ordered hierarchy of rooms, Safdie's National Gallery of Canada in Ottawa, Ontario (1983-88), superficially appears to make strong typological references to Schinkel's nineteenth-century Altes Museum in Berlin. Nevertheless, Safdie's much stronger formal articulation of the galleries and other areas within the overall plan probably undermines such an interpretation. The essential spatial arrangement of the National Gallery, seen less referentially, is that of a formal circulation spine, or pair of spines, which regulate a less formal gridwork of spaces.

In Safdie's hands, this organisational sensibility has several advantages. Complex programmes – a distinctive feature of most contemporary institutions – can be accommodated readily. In Ottawa City Hall and the Skirball Museum and Cultural Center, for instance, there are no obvious attempts to force the programmes into predetermined forms, rather, elements are deployed across each site in a seemingly effortless manner. Vital issues of scale and hierarchy among various building components likewise appear to have been resolved without too much difficulty. Big spaces, ceremonial public areas, and back-office spaces are neither confined nor appear out of place in the City Hall, the National Gallery of Canada, or the Hebrew Union College in Jerusalem (1976-present). Variable site topography and orientation can also be accommodated skilfully, as shown in Jerusalem at Mamilla, and in Los Angeles at the Skirball Center, where the imminent danger of mud slides was one of the considerable site constraints. Finally, this organisational strategy allows a strong variety of community spaces to be formed within building complexes – another aspect of buildings conceived as precincts. This is certainly the case

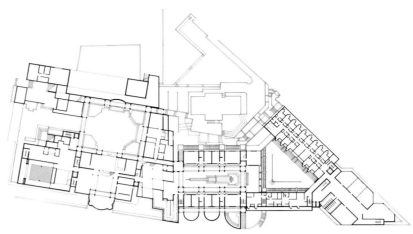

Hebrew Union College site plan

at both the Hebrew Union College, with its various academic and entry courtyards surrounded by classrooms, research centres and other facilities, and in the well-landscaped central open space of Ottawa City Hall.

At a technical level, the specific organisational devices most often used by Safdie are circulation spines – often of monumental proportions, as in the National Gallery of Canada and Ottawa City Hall – and the 'tartan grid'. The use of the tartan grid bears similarities to the work of members of Team 10, such as the original design for the Berlin Free University (1963), by Candilis, Josic and Woods.[3] The main difference is that in Safdie's projects, the buildings are more pronounced than the circulation. This is apparent in the Hebrew Union College, where the spatial modulation of a tartan grid is introduced through a system of passages, cloisters and arcades. In Canada's northern climate, glazed galleries are a common separating and organising device superimposed upon the building programme of the National Gallery and Montreal Museum of Fine Arts. In the Museum of Civilisation in Quebec City, Canada (1988), the spatial organisation delineated by the tartan grid is clearly evident throughout the major gallery spaces and is reinforced by the clustered placement of columns and zones of circulation and services. On the larger urban scale of Mamilla, a tartan grid underlies much of the housing, accentuated by the geometric returns in the housing unit plans to form partially-enclosed outdoor courts and patios.

In the light-filled processional halls, gradually ascending stairs, and linear walkways of Safdie's work, Modernist planning ideas of 'connectivity' emerge as a loose orthogonal gridwork of transportation and open space. These connectors are pronounced features of Modi'in, a new city plan under construction in central Israel. Again, variable terrain is integrated cohesively by this strategy. In turn, the city's underlying organisation promises to provide considerable legibility to the overall plan, not to mention 'imageability' in its eventual perceptual experience, to borrow terminology from another planner and theorist of the sixties and seventies, Kevin Lynch.[4] In particular, the idea of placing major roadways and expansive swaths of public open space within the valleys, while marking and accentuating the hilltops with dense construction, seems well gauged to meet the criterion of a more memorable and comprehensive place.

Traces: An Unsentimental Contextualism

Safdie's approach to the surrounding context is striking. Unlike some contemporary neo-traditional trends, Safdie's work shows no nostalgic or regressive preoccupations. Context is less a matter of history than one of certain fundamental characteristics about a region, or the invariant qualities and *genus loci* of a particular place. Neither does Safdie use the surrounding context simply to re-reflect prevalent

architectural styles, decorative motifs or building typologies. Instead, it becomes the basis for inventing something entirely new, and thus his work qualitatively advances one's understanding of its context.

Such an accomplishment is very evident in the expansive stepped public space that forms a central part of the Museum of Civilisation, and doubles as the roof for the museum space below. In the original scheme, the steps were to have arisen out of the St Lawrence River, recognising the palisades crowned with buildings that are so characteristic of central Quebec City. As built, the steps and rooftop park offer a sun-lit and unique outdoor public space of considerable quality, and introduce a route to the river through the long and massive seventeenth-century city block.

Safdie seems to respond to context in at least three specific ways. First, and perhaps most immediately obvious, is a general sensitivity to the region or part of the world where the project is located. The verticality and open glazing of many of the Canadian projects is clearly within the genre of architecture for a northern clime, whereas the horizontality and sunshading of the Israeli projects reside similarly well within the Mediterranean. In the end, Safdie's projects look somehow Canadian, Israeli or Californian, even given the difficulty of making such generalisations.

Working with a site – rather than against it – is another distinction which characterises this general acknowledgement of a locality. The Skirball Center certainly demonstrates this quality: its plan closely follows the topography and the amphitheatre cuts into the side of the hill to reduce the risk of mud slides. The Mamilla project also aligns with the site terrain and reinforces the building massing and topography along Ha'emek Street in Jerusalem, between King David Street and the Jaffa Gate. Further up the hill towards the old Christian Quarter, the placement of a large semi-underground car park between Ha'emek Street and Jaffa Street at once takes advantage of the vacant land and provides the city with an extraordinary landscape on top of the parking garage terraces. This built slope, in turn, recreates the escarpment leading up to the old city. In this respect, the Mamilla parking structure and its park are very similar to the rooftop steps and park in Quebec. Both have evolved from their context; they reassert within the architecture certain basic precepts of the larger urban condition.

Safdie's second response to the context of a place is to readily accept, and even revel in, the iconographical possibilities and responsibilities implicit in a site. The sharply rising tower-like forms of the National Gallery, together with the broad horizontal profile of the bulk of the building, clearly echo the nearby cathedral and Parliament buildings, which are intrinsic to Ottawa's Gothic skyline. The siting of the National Gallery, like an encrustation along the Ottawa River palisades, is almost identical to that of the Parliament buildings

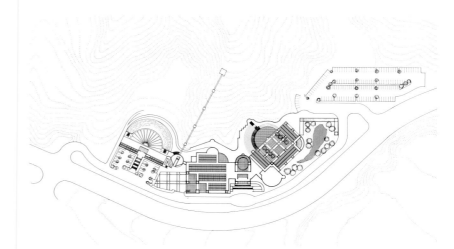

Skirball Museum and Cultural Center site plan

opposite. Similarly, the dormer roofs, tower profile and varied roofscape of the Museum of Civilisation reinterpret the old town of Quebec poised above the cliff that forms the museum's backdrop. In both cases, there is a sense of 'doubling' of what is already there. By contrast, the iconography of the Hebrew Union College in Jerusalem and the proposal for Mamilla is less literal in its overall scenographic qualities, yet clearly connected to the region. Indeed, the gradual growth of the Hebrew Union College – spanning some twenty years – has served the project well, for it seems to reside quite naturally within the irregular, almost timeless quality of much of Jerusalem's collection of urban buildings.

Finally, the third way in which Safdie responds to context is through the use of geographically particular building technologies, local palettes of materials, and recognised architectural practices. This is certainly why his buildings seem to belong so immediately and completely to their regions, and thus look, for instance, somehow 'Canadian' or 'Israeli'. But Safdie is far from a vernacular architect; even in utilising local materials, his buildings are contemporary and modern. The splendid monumental arcade along one side of the National Gallery is vertical and columnar like a church nave, but not simply neo-Gothic. Instead, it is a modern curtain-wall structure with regularly-spaced rectangular concrete columns. Thus, once the allusion is made, on closer inspection it is withdrawn. Even when confronting restoration projects, such as those built between 1972 and 1980 in the Jewish Quarter of Jerusalem, Safdie remains contemporary in his re-use of old materials and elements of domestic architecture. The quarter-dome swivelling glass doors in the Block 38 infill project are, for example, technically and spatially very modern; yet the overall effect is again undeniably of an older vernacular quarter of the city.

The localised, scenographic effect of many of Safdie's projects might also be seen as a strategic way of confronting contemporary problems posed by context, while maintaining a thoroughly modern and, therefore, reasonably singular approach to building technology, materials and programme. By making sufficient allusions scenographically to the place concerned, Safdie releases the architecture, at the level of the specific parts of the building, to deal more directly with functional and other technical exigencies. This capacity for an overall scenographic response to site is further enhanced by the inherent formal flexibility of Safdie's organisational strategies. Specific forms and building masses can be constructed and readily moved around, so to speak, to achieve contextual effects without adversely affecting the modern identity of the architecture itself.

Engagement with the surrounding landscape is yet another way Safdie seeks to place his projects purposefully in context. Moreover, this engagement often operates in both directions: as the building complexes literally project out into the landscape, simultaneously the

Ottawa City Hall

Quebec Museum of Civilisation

Yeshiva Porat Yosef

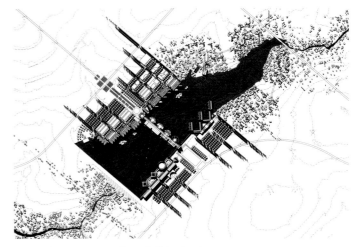

Superconducting Super Collider site plan

surrounding landscape is drawn into the buildings. The Skirball Center literally embraces the landscape of which it is part, formally incorporating overhead planters, trellises, and landscaped courtyards, and introducing views of the hills beyond into its interiors and courts. On top of the hill, a proposed pavilion extends the complex some distance into the landscape to offer panoramic views and to locate the project within the hills of Malibu Canyon as well as along the highway. The landscape of the site of the City Hall in Ottawa, where roads and trestle bridges intersect the island, is so well reflected in the orthogonal layout and structural motifs of the complex that the building itself appears to have generated the pattern of roads and bridges. This same quality of cooperation with its site is repeated in the constructed landscape of Mamilla.

Skirball Museum and Cultural Center

Tropes: A Geometric Formal Preference

A third striking aspect of Moshe Safdie's work is the consistent use of pure geometric figures. Both in plan and in section, three basic geometric figures and their three-dimensional variants emerge with a certain consistency. The square is a common planimetric form, and when rotated and extended into a cube, it is often used to mark the entry of an institution or the termination of a specific sequence of circulation. This use of the square can be seen clearly in the plan and section of the Skirball Center, in the Montreal Museum of Fine Arts (completed 1987), and the Hebrew Union College. Indeed, resonances are created within the body of work itself, as at the Skirball complex, for example, where the cubic tower punctuated with an open circle appears to refer to the Hebrew Union College complex.

Circles, semicircles, semicircular cylinders and spherical forms are also common, again in plan and section. In the Jewish Quarter Restoration of Block 38, for instance, a half dome is used to mediate between the interior of the apartment units and the outside balcony. Both at the Hebrew Union College and in the residential section of Mamilla, semi-cylindrical forms extend the fenestration, and also the view, beyond the horizontal wall line. On a grander scale, the same can be said for the external articulation of the office space facing the water at Ottawa City Hall, and along the bridgework over the cooling pond at the Super Collider site. This becomes a way of both relieving the monotony of a very long facade, and of projecting the volume of the building into largely unconstrained spatial areas of the site which have the potential for splendid views. The choice of a circle in plan, or a cylinder in section, obviously takes advantage of the equi-directional form of such figures, especially at moments when no assignment of priority to an internal space is required. In fact, there is a strong consistency in the use of these cylindrical and spherical devices throughout Safdie's work. They are used to 'round off' the apparent thrust of an internal programmatic element, like the long

Ottawa City Hall

Block 38 Restoration

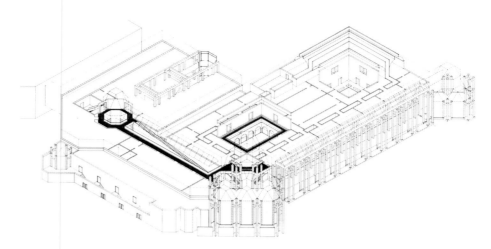

National Gallery of Canada axonometric

classrooms at the Hebrew Union College, but only when the area beyond the external facade is relatively unencumbered and spacious.

Triangles, pyramids and prismatic shapes – a third family of geometric figures – are often used to 'crown' prominent public spaces and grand halls. Usually, the effect of these forms is to centralise the space beneath, and to lend an air of monumentality to the projects. In all respects, this is clearly the intention in the National Gallery of Canada and Ottawa City Hall. Given the extensive circulation in these places, the serene and static quality of entry and gathering spaces crowned in this pyramidal manner also helps to reorient and create a pause in one's trip through the complex. The perceptual upward lift of galleries and arcades also often terminates in a pyramidal cross-section, again with the same centring effect.

While powerful spatially, in Safdie's work regular figures are largely nonrepresentational *per se*. It is a use of geometry that doesn't have to be justified in any historically representational sense. These forms can, therefore, populate a complex formal aggregate of building components to convey a particular spatial or scenographic aura that is referential to a context, without being directly figurative. In turn, Safdie can remain thoroughly modern in his approach, and yet avoid the unnecessary universality and cultural enmity of orthodox Modernism. Safdie's proclivities for modern plans, pure geometries and the incorporation of local building practices work together harmoniously, and allow him effectively and distinctively to tackle broad, complex programmes in many parts of the world – without the anonymity of a vernacular chameleon or the raucousness of a stylistic peacock.

National Gallery of Canada

Notes

1 Alison Smithson, *Team 10 Primer*, Studio Vista (London), 1968

2 Josep Mantaner and Jordi Oliveras, *The Museums of the Last Generation*, Academy Editions (London), 1986

3 Jürgen Joedicke and Shadrach Woods, *Candilis, Josic and Woods: Building for People*, Praeger (New York), 1968

4 Kevin Lynch, *The Image of the City*, The MIT Press (Cambridge, Mass), 1960

National Gallery of Canada

NORTHERN LIGHTS

WITOLD RYBCZYNSKI

In the short span of twelve years, Moshe Safdie has been commissioned to design major civic buildings in Canada's three largest cities: the Ballet Opera House (unbuilt) for Toronto, a significant expansion to Montreal's Museum of Fine Arts, and Library Square in Vancouver, which incorporates a public library with a Federal Government headquarters. Safdie-designed civic buildings have also appeared in Quebec City and Ottawa – from sea to shining sea, indeed. But that is not all. Safdie has built the most memorable monument in Canada's capital since the Parliament Buildings were inaugurated in 1867: the National Gallery of Canada.

It is rare that an architect is given the opportunity to build on a national scale. One thinks of Daniel Burnham, who designed important buildings in Chicago, New York City and Washington, DC, and whose ideas of urban planning influenced cities across the continent, or the firm of McKim Mead and White, which dominated the American architectural scene for several decades. That peripatetic genius Frank Lloyd Wright built in no less than thirty-seven of the states, although most of his work was for private not public clients. During the eighties, Philip Johnson built commercial skyscrapers in a great many American cities, but the most prestigious public commissions eluded him too. In that regard, he was bested by IM Pei, who is the premier American architect, at least in the public's eye, and the designer of the acclaimed East Wing of the National Gallery in Washington, DC and the Kennedy Presidential Library in Boston.

Still, it is difficult for an individual to dominate the built landscape of a country as large as the United States. In Canada, Arthur Erickson comes close to matching Safdie's prodigious output of buildings (Erickson has built prominent civic buildings in British Columbia and Ontario, but not in the province of Quebec). But perhaps the best modern example is the Modernist master, Alvar Aalto, who, in the first half of the twentieth century, put his indelible stamp on the public architecture of his native Finland.

Although Aalto designed buildings in several countries, there was no question that the man, like his buildings, was anything but Finnish. Safdie, on the other hand, has his feet planted firmly on two continents. Born in Israel and educated in Canada, he holds citizenship of both countries. In Israel, where he spends part of the year, he is well known for his extensive contribution to the reconstruction of Jerusalem. At the same time, Safdie's main architectural office – and his current home – is in the United States, where he has recently completed several important public buildings, including two additions to the Harvard Business School and the Skirball Museum and Cultural Center in Los Angeles, and where he is currently working on the Wichita Science Center and Children's Museum.

Like so many globe-trotting architects today, Safdie takes his clients where he finds them. I think it was Burnham who is alleged to

have said, 'In architecture, there is only one job and that is getting the client.' Just so. 'Getting the client' can mean having the right social contacts, being part of the establishment that builds, or simply being lucky. Luck has certainly played a part in Safdie's career – how else to explain that a young and inexperienced architect could snare a project as prestigious as Habitat '67? But, like Aalto, who also started young, Safdie has won his share of architectural competitions. One could say that his success has been likewise a case of talent and ability being recognised.

But Safdie's recognition in Canada was belated – or at least, interrupted. After completing Habitat to international accolades, he received no Canadian commissions at all for the next dozen years. During that period he designed projects for Puerto Rico, Jerusalem, New York City and San Francisco. In 1978 he moved his office to the Boston area, accepting a post as Director of the Urban Design programme at Harvard and expanded his practice in Israel. Then, beginning in 1981 with the Museum of Civilisation in Quebec City, Safdie set out on an extraordinary architectural trajectory across the Canadian nation. This culminated in Vancouver's Library Square, which opened its doors in 1995. This last commission, like the Museum of Civilisation, the Toronto Ballet Opera House and Ottawa City Hall, was the result of a competition. Remarkably, Safdie's library design was the first choice not only of the competition jury, but also of a large part of the Vancouver public which voted its approval for the design in an informal ballot.

What is the basis for Safdie's appeal? To answer this question it is necessary to appreciate his rather complicated position in the multifarious field of contemporary architecture. Since the late sixties, when the International Modernist approach that had held sway for fifty years began to lose its ascendancy, a number of different tendencies have developed. Most prominent among them are Post-Modernism and Deconstructivism. Post-Modern architects repudiated the Modernist aesthetic and incorporated more traditional architectural elements in their buildings. Instead of the so-called 'International' Style, regional and local motifs showed up in buildings such as Charles Moore's Sea Ranch and Michael Graves' San Juan Capistrano Library. The sweep of Post-Modernism has been broad, and it includes such buildings as Graves' neo-Classical office building for the Disney Company in Los Angeles, Thomas Beeby's neo-Richardsonian Harold Washington Library in Chicago, and many of the works of Robert Venturi, although in the latter case, they are more often used with an ironic or humorous inflection. Architects like Allan Greenberg and John Blatteau work with the Classical language in a more straightforward fashion.

Deconstructivism is also a repudiation of Modernism, but if Post-Modern buildings are intended to create a particular sense of place, to make us feel more at home and linked to the past, the aim of

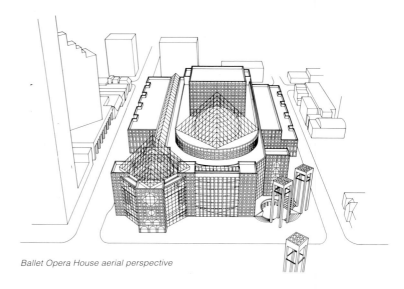

Ballet Opera House aerial perspective

Deconstructivism is different. Self-professedly avant-garde and elitist, if not downright nihilist, it aims to challenge and shock the public. The designs, brittle and often collage-like, incorporate rough industrial materials and unusual forms: walls tilted at precarious angles, fragments assembled in apparently haphazard fashion, warped surfaces. Deconstructivism is disjointed, trendy and sunnily oblivious to tradition and the past.

Moshe Safdie has been publicly critical of both Post-Modernism and Deconstructivism. In 'Private Jokes in Public Places', an article published in *The Atlantic Monthly*, he deplored the tendency of Post-Modern architects such as Moore and Graves to build public buildings that incorporated obscure stylistic and historical references.[1] Elsewhere he wrote of Deconstructivism: 'The emphasis is on novelty and how to be different, how to be shocking, how to scandalize'.[2] In many ways, Safdie has remained a stalwart Modernist, and his Canadian success could be seen as part of Modernism's resurgence. Irving Kristol has written that 'an orthodoxy has far greater staying power than a counter culture', and this certainly has been true in the field of architecture. Although orthodox Modernism lost its supremacy, it has hardly disappeared. In fact, many of the most prominent buildings of recent years have been designed as precisely Modernist: IM Pei's addition to the Louvre; Norman Foster's Hongkong and Shanghai Bank and Stanstead Airport; Richard Rogers' Lloyd's Building; Renzo Piano's De Menil Collection and Kansai International Airport; and Richard Meier's Getty Museum.

Like Piano, Safdie is concerned with technology, and his details combine technical sophistication and simplicity. Like Foster, he is an inventor: in the National Gallery of Canada he pioneered the use of light-reflecting shafts to bring daylight into lower-level galleries. Like Pei, he has often incorporated dramatic glass roofs, such as the glazed lobby of Montreal Museum of Fine Arts or the crystalline Great Hall of the National Gallery of Canada. But Safdie differs from his Modernist colleagues in several respects. He demonstrates none of the obsessive technological theatricality that characterises the work of Rogers, for example. Unlike Meier, he has not developed a stylistic signature: Safdie's designs change character according to their location. And in contrast to both Meier and Pei, he rarely treats his buildings as abstract sculptures; instead, Safdie's buildings invariably respond to local conditions.

During the period when he built nothing in Canada, it was in Jerusalem that Safdie was given the opportunity to build. After the unification of the city in 1967, he was responsible for restoring and rebuilding a number of residential structures in the destroyed Jewish Quarter. In 1972 he began work on Mamilla, a large urban design project that is still underway; two years later he was commissioned to prepare a master plan for the Western Wall precinct. In addition, he

realised several larger institutional buildings, including Yeshiva Porat Yosef, Yeshiva Aish Hatorah and the Hebrew Union College. This experience of fitting buildings into a rich and complex historical setting is crucial in understanding Safdie's first Canadian projects. Safdie's Quebec Museum of Civilisation, beside the brooding St Lawrence River, skilfully blends into its surroundings, its dormers and tower forming a sympathetic part of the roofscape when seen from the terrace of the Chateau Frontenac above. Similarly, the Great Hall of the National Gallery of Canada mimics the pinnacles of the neo-Gothic chapterhouse *cum* library of the nearby Parliament Buildings. At the same time, this landmark building, which sits on a dramatic outcrop overlooking the Ottawa River, is carefully adjusted to respond to the neighbouring Notre Dame Basilica and the War Museum. Additionally, the extension to the Montreal Museum of Fine Arts offers a monumental facade of marble to Sherbrooke Street, but on the two side streets the facades are finished in granite and brick.

The next two buildings – Ottawa City Hall and Toronto's Ballet Opera – represent a different direction in Safdie's work. While these buildings continue to demonstrate his concern for fitting in, they are also buildings that assertively stand out. They incorporate large, simple volumes: pyramids, cones and drums. Although the buildings do respond to their surroundings (natural, in the case of City Hall; urban in the Ballet Opera), the forms themselves are abstract and appear to have a life of their own. They represent a return to Safdie's obsession with geometry that is so evident in his early work. There is also the unmistakable influence of the late work of Louis Kahn, for whom Safdie worked in the sixties. The results, to my mind, are far less compelling than the magisterial National Gallery. The Ballet Opera remains unbuilt, but Ottawa City Hall is a curious amalgam of impenetrable, obscure shapes, culminating in a particularly intrusive over-sized observation tower. Only on the north side, where the curved bays gracefully flank the Rideau River, does this busy building achieve a sense of repose.

One explanation for the architectural assertiveness of a building like the Ballet Opera House is its context: downtown Toronto is hardly old Jerusalem. Unlike the museums in Ottawa, Quebec City and Montreal, which were located in historic architectural settings, the Ballet Opera is surrounded by contemporary buildings of indifferent quality. This was the same situation that Safdie faced in Vancouver, a city that has grown quickly in the last few decades and, like most west Canadian cities, is a *mélange* of architectural styles from the seventies, eighties and nineties. How can a civic building create a dignified presence in such polyglot surroundings? The Vancouver library succeeds by establishing a sense of place with an architectural approach that is neither simplistic nor overbearing.

Vancouver's Library Square consists of a twenty-one-storey Federal Government office tower as well as a seven-storey central public library. The library is really two buildings, not one. There is the library proper, a practical place where people read and work, with book stacks, computers, study tables and reference counters. It can be a hive of activity, crowded with people, young and old. Wrapped around the rectangular library block is an elliptical colonnaded wall containing more intimate reading and study areas. The architectural concept is undoubtedly influenced by Kahn's library at Phillips Exeter Academy in Exeter, New Hampshire. Where Kahn wrapped a brick ring of study carrels around a concrete structure holding the stacks, Safdie has expanded the idea, and added a third type of space: the elliptical wall also encloses a glazed concourse. This brings the public street right into the building and serves as the entry foyer to the library. With its cafe tables and storefronts, the tall space recalls Milan's famous Galleria Vittorio Emanuele and in Vancouver's rainy climate it is destined to be intensively used.

What is most striking is the change that takes place in the architecture of the enclosing elliptical building. Unlike the rectangular library block that resembles an unremarkable office building, it is built of sandstone-coloured precast concrete, set with stone panels forming a pattern of marquetry. It also has a different character to that of the functional library – a sort of Mediterranean half-ruin, partly Piranesi and partly English garden folly. Classical elements even appear: colonnades, arches and columns topped by simplified capitals. Some have likened the library to the ancient Coliseum in Rome; the comparison is far-fetched, but the references to the classical past are unmistakable.

The Vancouver Public Library, surely Safdie's most ambitious design to date, is a curiously Canadian building, a pragmatic response to the realities of the here-and-now as well as a reflection of the desire to transcend the humdrum and the ordinary to create a place of poetry and beauty. In some ways, Safdie seems to fulfil the functional needs of a modern post-industrial society, but also meet the desire for fantasy that remains a part of the human condition. Architecturally, this puts him somewhere between the full-blown technological optimism of the purist Modernists and the wistful backward looking historicism of the Post-Modernists. Is this, too, a part of his success? This equable position probably appeals to Canadians, a sensible and conservative northern people who prefer compromise to radical rhetoric. Safdie, like Aalto, is best understood as a humanist. His buildings – like the man – are a blend of the romantic and the rational, of the Mediterranean past and the North American present.

Notes

1 Moshe Safdie, 'Private Jokes in Public Places', *The Atlantic Monthly*, December 1981

2 Moshe Safdie, *The Language and Medium of Architecture*, The MIT Press (Cambridge, Massachusetts), 1989, p7

Ballet Opera House

Montreal Museum of Fine Arts

Vancouver Library Square

MOSHE SAFDIE IN CONVERSATION

WITH WENDY KOHN

Wendy Kohn: Your life has focused intensely on several different countries. You were born in Haifa, moved to Montreal when you were fifteen, and as an adult you've lived both in Israel and Canada, as well as eighteen years in the United States. How has this background influenced you?

Moshe Safdie: Because my cultural foundations come from extremes, I integrate the cultures of the Mediterranean, of Arabs and Jews, of North America, of Quebec, and they're totally within me. I love the tune of the *nai*, the wooden flute of Iran, as much as I love Bach's French Suites.

WK: How do you relate East and West?

MS: It's the differences that I'm aware of. I think I've spent much of my life as a kind of detective. When I was working in Senegal and the Ivory Coast, I found myself trying to understand – through the music, through the architecture, through the dress, through the cuisine, through the literature when possible – what made the essence of the place. It's not that you ever become a profound expert, but you're there with your antennae out, trying to absorb it.

At the same time, when I was working for Louis Kahn, he was designing the Indian Institute of Management in Ahmedabad. He was into burning the brick in kilns, very much echoing Gandhi's philosophy of self-sufficiency and finding what is culturally appropriate to India.

I was working on the project, and I would write in my notebook that Kahn is a 'romantic', celebrating hand labour; he should be bringing industrialisation to India; he should be finding new modes of expression. I was very critical. I did not mean that he should ignore India, but I just felt this sense of a greater world.

WK: In emulating pre-industrial building techniques in the 1960s, his respect for the culture seemed sentimental to you?

MS: Yes. In the same way, when I reviewed Hassan Fathy's book *Architecture for the Poor* in the *New York Review of Books*, I praised him for reviving the vernacular and giving it new meaning.

But when he wrote about the water well and what a wonderful social experience this was for the women – to come to the well and get the water and chit-chat as they marched up the hill towards the village – I said to myself, 'the women would love a pump, and give up all this nostalgia for the convenience of not having to carry water'. It's all very easy to say, 'what a nice social institution', but it's slavery to have to carry water which could easily be pumped.

You see, that statement proves that I'm a Westerner. Yet, people go through the National Gallery of Canada and talk about the Mediterra-

nean courtyard; they talk about Egypt; they talk about Syria; they talk about Persia. The National Gallery, in my mind, was an intense attempt to find the appropriate expression for a Canadian national institution, yet people walk through and see all these things that have to do with the East.

WK: Some have said your architecture seems chameleon-like: changeable in a way that defies categorisation.

MS: You know, I think that goes back to reading a place intensely. Basically, I feel my real strength as an architect has to do with the fact that I can study a site, or discover a site for that matter, and get the most that one can extract out of it.

If you take the Quebec Museum of Civilisation design, all the generative ideas relate to the experience of a visitor to that particular place. Towers rise out of a building, roofs become accessible as parks . . . these are all to do with my reading of the site. Somebody else would come to that site and read it completely differently.

Very often, great, inventive architecture has to do with someone reading the secrets of the place in a profound way. In Michelangelo's Campidoglio, there is an understanding of the hill and the city, of the space of the piazza, of how to make a window to the city. But it's all to do with that particular hill in Rome.

At Fallingwater, it's a natural site. It's Frank Lloyd Wright taking the land and celebrating it in architecture. Any number of different buildings could have been built on the Kaufmann property, none seizing on the idea that water is flowing across it.

In the case of the Temple Mount in Jerusalem, another example again, there was a little temple on a hill. The city was growing, and what did Herod do? He created a platform, which became a seat for the new city not yet built.

Sometimes what you read into a site has to do with its future, not with what is already there.

WK: You've spoken about your experience of returning to live and work in Jerusalem in the 1970s as profound. What did you learn in Jerusalem and from Jerusalem?

MS: I think what is important about the work in Jerusalem is that I was forced to design in a context for which I had a great deal of affection and awe. Therefore I was interested in the issue of harmony. I was interested in the issue of continuity, the issue of belonging.

Before I went to Jerusalem, the thrust of my projects – Habitat in Montreal or Puerto Rico or New York – focused on creating urban structure. So the questions of what is street, what is public space, what is private space, were considered in terms of a new invention. Not only

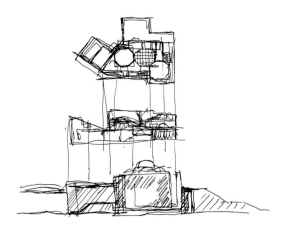

Study sketches, 1971,
Yeshiva Porat Yosef

assuming a clean slate, but assuming everything could be reinvented.

The fundamental difference when I came to Jerusalem was that my projects themselves were within an existing, rich and awesome urban fabric. Building into this existing fabric meant one needed to understand contemporary buildings in terms of their relationship to historic archetypes. This was a revelation.

WK: Do you think your work might have taken a different direction had you not built in Jerusalem at that particular moment in your development?

MS: I suspect it is possible that if I had been commissioned early on to do a series of public buildings in the Old City of Quebec or downtown Ottawa, as later I did, perhaps I would still have addressed these issues, but I would have been less awed. I would have allowed myself to stay more in the spirit of the 60s, or the early 70s.

The experience in Jerusalem led me to try and reinterpret building and urban forms in a contemporary way, yet with a sense of belonging and connection to the past. And that was enriching for me. When I came later to Ottawa and Quebec City, I returned having learnt the lessons of Jerusalem.

WK: Did Jerusalem humble you?

MS: When one feels such awe towards a place – its heritage, its beauty, its completeness – one treads so carefully. And that's humbling. When Bruno Zevi, in the Jerusalem Committee meeting, said 'we must build with concrete and glass, not stone. We can create modern expression for a modern culture and not be intimidated', he was not acting humbly.

I was really finding myself in Jerusalem to be conservative, and humbled, and attentive. The very notion of wanting to belong is in itself a conservative position to be in.

WK: Did it surprise you to find yourself in that position?

MS: No. It was natural.

WK: After Library Square opened in Vancouver, you were asked about its relationship to the Roman Coliseum and its appropriateness to that city. Your answers seem contradictory.

You said that after intensive study, the 'Roman' expression of the concrete shell seemed to you the *only* appropriate solution to the design as it evolved. Elsewhere, you argued that one needed to 'get past' the Coliseum as a metaphor. Can you explain your thinking on that project?

MS: When I began working on Vancouver, the idea came forward to centralise the stacks – the bulky, massive, non-transparent element in the building – and create a reading gallery around them, towards the street and the city. We ended up with a rectangular block, surrounded by an ellipse. As the office building cried out to be subordinated to the library, it became an extension of that elliptical wall system.

At this point, we recognised the similarity to the Coliseum, both dimensional and proportional. And we actually were amused, as it had appeared completely unconsciously.

When we won the competition, the question in my mind was, do we make an attempt to edit out those elements of the design in favour of detailing that would be iconographically abstract? We developed a number of schemes: one replaced the double columns with a series of free-standing columns that made it like a forest of columns rising eight storeys high – like a bunch of west coast redwoods; a second scheme had a very flat, taut facade of metal and glass; a third was all glass.

WK: You developed a glass pavilion? That's almost an antithesis of the competition design.

MS: Yes, and you could see all the books through the glass. But the test was when we started making models and tried to imagine placing reading tables and people in that free-standing wall. The glass schemes made you feel like you were up there on exhibit; they created no *place* at all. The metal and glass schemes could create solidity, but at the same time they lacked any scale that could make you feel comfortable.

It became absolutely obvious that the solidity of the original scheme made a place to be inside of, to read, to look out to the city, that was more compelling than any of the other schemes. It was a real lesson in classicism as a scale-making, humanising device in space.

WK: And the design process convinced you that the proportions and solidity of the design were appropriate for a library in that city?

MS: Vancouver is a city of glass and metal towers: no sense of solidity, no sense of rootedness, tentative. To really become a place in that city, I felt the building needed mass, needed to act as a counterpoint. I felt the city needed a building to anchor the downtown.

WK: You saw the design for your building and the needs of the city as mutually dependent. Is this always the case in your urban projects?

MS: From the beginning of my career as an architect, the design problem of a city and a building seemed inseparable. In other words,

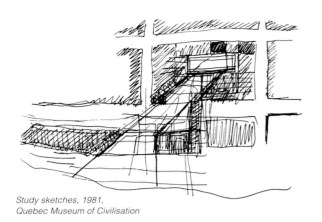

Study sketches, 1981,
Quebec Museum of Civilisation

it always seemed to me that if you were thinking of housing, or if you were thinking of a community, or if you were thinking of a way of life, that you couldn't deal with these things only at the scale of a building.

I think I saw myself as a revisionist to those people who in the 1920s and 1930s and, to a lesser extent, the 1940s, were speculating about the city. Le Corbusier built *Unité d'Habitation* as a piece of the city as a whole. I saw myself as re-examining the possibilities in the context of the questions which those architects had asked. I might not have been inclined to think urbanistically, had I not reacted to the framing of architecture at that time.

WK: Since you began designing, you've rarely been without your sketchbook. Can you talk about what happens in the sketchbook?

MS: In some ways, it is a response to the conditions of my life. Since I am often away from the office, without a drafting table, without the model shop, without the tools that normally I use to draft and to design, my sketchbook evolved as a discipline to make it possible to work continuously, unaffected by where I am.

Because it is the place of continuous work, the sketchbook becomes a diary. It has anything from the first diagram of thoughts on a project to trying to work out glazing details for a building under construction. At the same time, I'm commenting to myself as to what seems worth developing further and what seems worth abandoning. It has kind of a cryptic running commentary. It becomes sort of a conversation.

I have even gone back in the sketchbook after a building is completely finished and said 'if I were doing it all over, I would do it that way.' I will go back to something, built or unbuilt, and work on it as a sort of theoretical exercise.

WK: I was surprised to find phone numbers, meeting notes, drafts of letters or information from a consultant on the same pages in your sketchbooks as colour perspectives and renderings of projects.

MS: I don't treat the sketchbook as a precious thing, as a place for the art of drawing architecture, but as a place for the development of ideas. Ideas are drawings *and* words for me.

Technical concepts, abstract concepts, formal concepts are all intertwined, and with them the happenings around the making of architecture. The sketchbook is simply an expression of the way I think and the way I act.

WK: You've talked about Columbus Center as a big disappointment in your career. As you think about the process in retrospect, what do you feel went wrong?

MS: I think that when all has been said and done, the real event that led to the fall of Columbus Center was the collapse of Wall Street and the following decline in the economy. With the collapse of the real estate market, who was going to invest hundreds of millions of dollars in New York in luxury apartments when they weren't selling? I don't think anything I could have done would have changed that.

I think if Wall Street hadn't collapsed, no matter what objection was going on, the project would have been built. It might have been made slightly smaller in the process, but it would have been built. The timing was inevitably against it.

WK: Why was there so much conflict over the project?

MS: I would say that 80 per cent of the opposition had to do with shadow, height, massing, zoning. It was a legitimate debate. But I had no latitude. I was designing to the maximum the zoning allowed, instructed by the City of New York and by my developer.

But I don't want to underplay the fact that people did not like the design: 20 or 30 per cent of the opposition was to the design *per se*.

WK: Do you think the design was misunderstood?

MS: I think it was not appreciated because it was out of tune with the prevailing fashion. The dogma of 'this building must mimic a pair of West Side Art Deco towers' has by now discredited itself.

The discussion at the time did not focus on the issues of how this building deals with the public domain and the street; how it creates continuities between inside and outside; how it relates the various activities within it; how it responds to the civic stature of the site, or maintains sight lines and view corridors.

The reason that it was so tragic for me personally was not only the disappointment of not realising it – the steel and the fabricated stone had all been ordered – but that we will never know what impact it might have had on the way people think about high-rises in cities. This design was the coming together and expression of many thoughts and ideas about high-rise buildings in a city, which had evolved over many years.

WK: How does your view of architecture as an inherently public art relate to the dimension of architecture as self-expression, which you've called 'capricious'?

MS: I've often tried to understand what it is about my attitude towards the making of architecture that doesn't permit me to enjoy Manneristic gestures; to use architecture as an outlet for humour; to free myself from a whole set of constant constraints that I impose upon myself.

Study sketch, 1983,
National Gallery of Canada

I like to say that my problem is not the expansiveness of my imagination, but the skill to edit it. There's a very big difference between one who is into expanding one's imagination, and one who is into editing.

WK: What are the 'constant constraints' you impose on your design process?

MS: The first constraint is that I can't free myself from the problematic imperatives of the building, from asking what is the building for? In other words, I can't free myself from the question: is this building, in every gesture it makes, wondrous for those who are going to experience it once I'm out of the picture?

WK: Couldn't a space that came purely out of your head, not in response to the 'problematic imperatives', be wondrous?

MS: That's fine, wondrous coming out of my head as an artist, so long as it's wondrous for those experiencing it in their daily lives. I can't disassociate from that.

In that sense, I've fundamentally changed. I think that in early works, such as the San Francisco State College, or the early Habitats, there was an obsession with geometry which transcended place and even programme.

It was only later that I began to feel a strong sense that you cannot totally ignore place. We must have an attitude towards those who are part of the place and for whom we are building. Designing a school, I have to be the teacher for a moment. I have to be the student for a moment. That has to do with a certain sense that you are building for others.

It goes back to what I understand the role of an architect to be. The role of an architect is to build for others, not for oneself.

WK: So building is an act of generosity?

MS: It's a selfish act as well. It's getting great satisfaction and great excitement out of being able to conceive and realise your ideas, through the labour of others, through craftsmen and builders and workers. You orchestrate it, but it's a collective effort. You're the composer. You're partially the conductor. Sometimes you're the soloist, but usually not. You are doing this *in* society, not extra to society.

Therefore, when I think about architecture, if I can't communicate to society, my communications are meaningless. I think of those I'm building for. If it's not meaningful to them, I'm not prepared to speak about architecture.

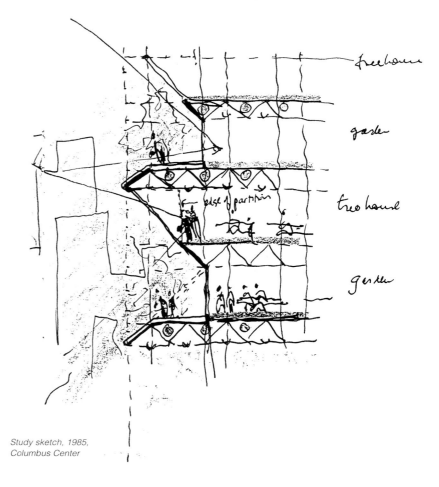

Study sketch, 1985,
Columbus Center

EARLY WORK

HABITAT '67
MONTREAL, QUEBEC   1964-67

■ Habitat was the major theme exhibition of the 1967 Montreal World Exposition. As a demonstration, the project pioneered the design and construction of prefabricated housing. As an urban building type, Habitat sought to mix residential, commercial and institutional uses to create a more vital neighbourhood, and to provide the amenities of the single-family home in a form adaptable to high densities and constrained budgets.

Each dwelling in Habitat is, therefore, a separate house, recognisable in space, whether on the second or the 12th floor. Houses at all levels are accessed by outdoor pedestrian streets that widen into play areas for children at numerous places throughout the building. Covered parking for all tenants, outdoor parking for visitors, and several stores is provided on the ground level. A geometric fountain doubles as a cooling pond for central air-conditioning.

The residences range in size from one-bedroom dwellings of 57 square metres to 160-square-metre, four-bedroom houses. With views in three directions, each of the 15 different house types opens out to at least one large garden with irrigated planters on the roof of the box below. The duplication of walls, ceilings and floors in adjacent dwellings provides acoustical privacy.

Habitat is a three-dimensional space structure in which all the parts of the building, including the units, the pedestrian streets, and the three elevator cores participate as load-bearing members. To create 158 residences, 354 pre-finished factory units are connected by post-tensioning, high-tension rods, cables and welding to form a continuous suspension system. The interior components were produced, assembled and installed into each box unit in the factory, with single-unit bathrooms of gel-coated fibreglass, kitchens manufactured by Frigidaire, and window frames made of Geon plastic.

McGill University thesis sketch, 1961

THE ORIGINAL HABITAT PROPOSAL, 1964

The original Habitat proposal was conceived as a sector of the city in which residential, commercial and institutional facilities are integrated within a single complex – a critique and radical revision of widespread existing urban conditions. Large inclined surfaces, like grand, hollow hillsides, form the residential component, oriented towards unobstructed views and sunlight. On the ground below, partially sheltered, are parking and transportation facilities, shops, schools, office space and an extensive network of parks that connect with the surrounding city.

The housing is constructed as a series of rhomboidal membranes facing south-east or south-west, and resting on large A-frame supports that enclose inclined elevators and fire stairs. Every three floors, a horizontal pedestrian street creates an outdoor corridor and accommodates mechanical services. The membrane of dwellings is composed of prefabricated concrete boxes that step back in spiral formation to form roof gardens for each unit.

Large gaps between the A-frames allow sunlight and air to reach the public areas below; light and air also pass through voids between the spiral housing clusters.

Each component acts as part of the whole structure: the modular concrete boxes carry vertical loads to the ground; the horizontal street girders resist horizontal wind and earthquake forces, and the A-frames function as monumental arch structures spanning the public facilities at ground level. The original proposal consisted of one 12-storey section and one 22-storey section, with a total of 1,200 housing units, a 350-room hotel, two schools and a neighbourhood shopping area.

The proposal was presented to the Cabinet of the Government of Canada for approval as the primary theme exhibit of Expo '67. The Government decided to build only a small part of the proposal – 158 housing units within a 12-storey section – which was subsequently redesigned as Habitat '67.

Above: *McGill University thesis sketch, 1961*
Centre: *Axonometric of housing unit cluster, with section through pedestrian street*
Below: *Site section*

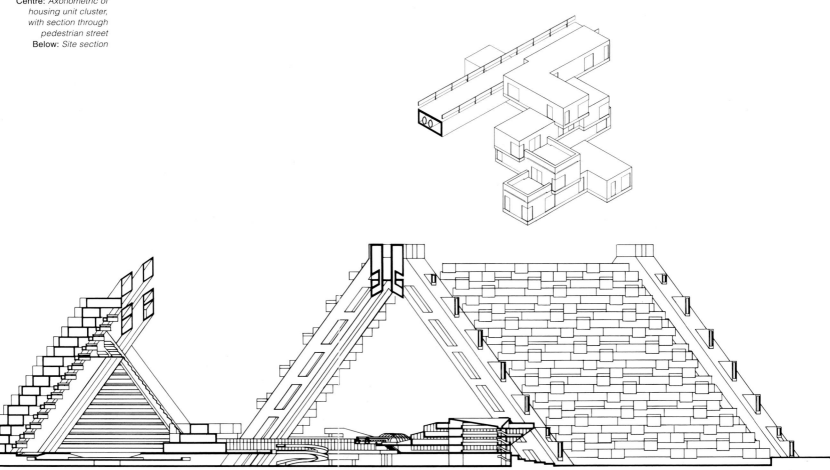

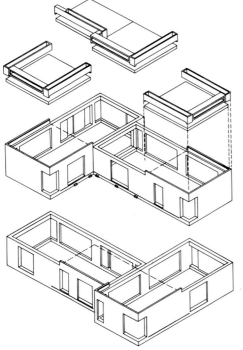

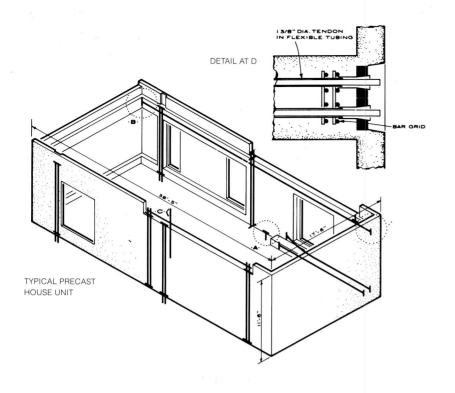

DETAIL AT D

1 3/8" DIA. TENDON
IN FLEXIBLE TUBING

BAR GRID

TYPICAL PRECAST
HOUSE UNIT

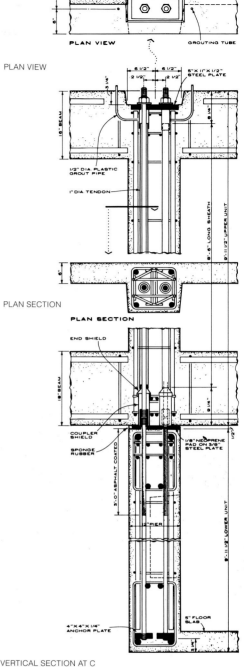

PLAN VIEW

GROUTING TUBE

PLAN VIEW

5"X 11"X 1/2"
STEEL PLATE

18 BEAM

1/2" DIA PLASTIC
GROUT PIPE

1" DIA TENDON

PLAN SECTION

PLAN SECTION

END SHIELD

18 BEAM

COUPLER
SHIELD

SPONGE
RUBBER

1/8" NEOPRENE
PAD ON 3/8"
STEEL PLATE

4"X 4"X 1/4"
ANCHOR PLATE

5" FLOOR
SLAB

VERTICAL SECTION AT C
(TENDON DETAIL)

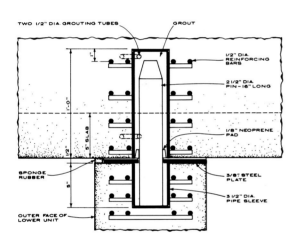

TWO 1/2" DIA. GROUTING TUBES

GROUT

1/2" DIA.
REINFORCING
BARS

2 1/2" DIA
PIN - 16" LONG

1/8" NEOPRENE
PAD

3/8" STEEL
PLATE

3 1/2" DIA.
PIPE SLEEVE

SPONGE
RUBBER

OUTER FACE OF
LOWER UNIT

DOWEL DETAIL AT A

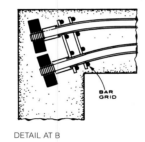

DETAIL AT B

BAR
GRID

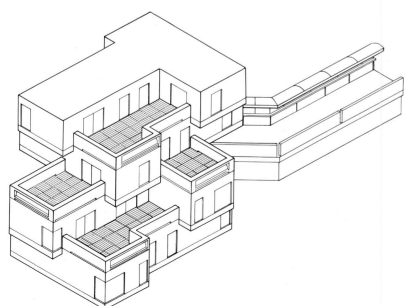

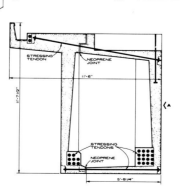

STRESSING
TENDON

NEOPRENE
JOINT

STRESSING
TENDONS

NEOPRENE
JOINT

SECTION THRU GIRDER

(CORNER OF HOUSE)

STRESSING TENDONS

(CORNER OF HOUSE)

NEOPRENE JOINT

NEOPRENE PAD

ELEVATION OF GIRDER LEG (AT A)

Opposite, Above and Below Right:
Habitat '67 under construction, 1966
Opposite, Below Left: *Precast
concrete component diagram*
Above: *Construction details of box
connections*
Below Left: *Axonometric of unit
cluster, with pedestrian street*
Below Right: *Post-tensioning details
of pedestrian street girders*

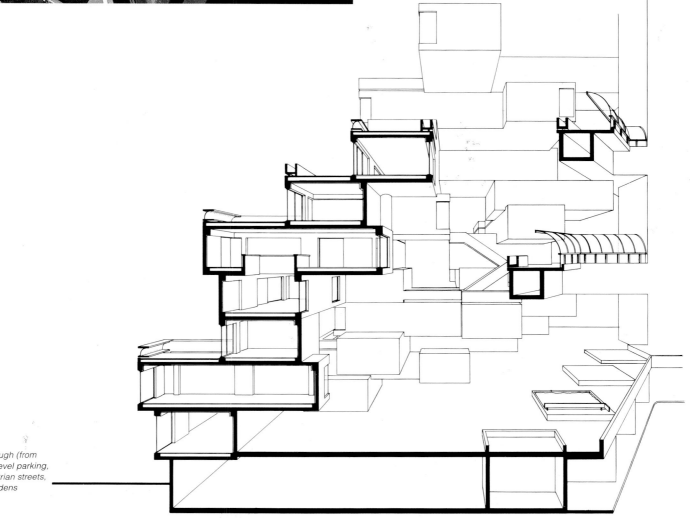

Perspective section through (from base upwards) ground level parking, pedestrian deck, pedestrian streets, residences and roof gardens

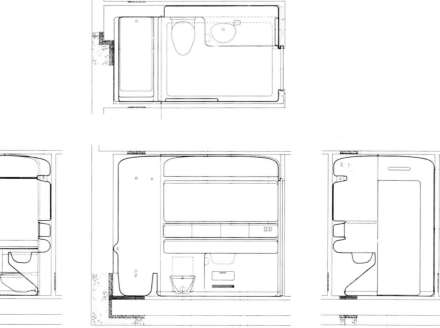

Below: *Prefabricated fibreglass bathroom plan and sections*
Opposite, Above Right: *Two-box unit upper level plan; lower level plan*
Opposite, Below Right: *Three-box unit upper level plan; lower level plan; section*

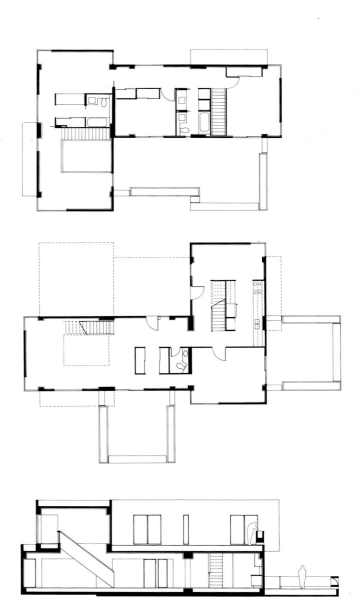

HABITAT PUERTO RICO
SAN JUAN, PUERTO RICO   1968-71

■ Habitat Puerto Rico, sited on 20 acres of a steep hill in the San Patricio area of San Juan, was designed to provide the amenities of Habitat '67 within the budget constraints of the Title 236 moderate-income housing programme.

Achieving a relatively high density community, as well as light and views by utilising the natural slope of the site, the design was a prototype for developing similar unused portions of land on the island. At the crest of the hill are shops, cafes, community rooms and offices, 14-storey high-rise towers and an outdoor amphitheatre surveying the panoramic views. Pedestrians and cars travel entirely separate paths of circulation, with parking cut into the slope beneath each house. Substantial areas of the hill are left untouched to preserve the natural vegetation.

800 prefabricated, prefinished concrete housing units of 40 square metres were to be delivered by truck or barge to the site. Cost was reduced by minimising the need for interior stairs, eliminating

structural complexity and consolidating plumbing. With all components installed in the factory – including bathrooms, kitchens, windows, mechanical and electrical systems – modules would be combined to form one- to four-bedroom units in a variety of layouts. Each unit has complete visual and acoustical privacy and a private terrace shaded by cantilevered units overhead. The upper portions of the windows are louvred and shaded; the lower halves are clear glass.

A prefabrication plant was built and the project commenced construction. Due to the government's withdrawal of financial support, the developer abandoned the project with only 30 modules produced and in place.

Opposite, Above Left:
Axonometric of
unit cluster
Opposite, Above Right:
Site section
Below Left: Typical two-
bedroom unit plan
Below Right: Exploded
axonometric of
precast module

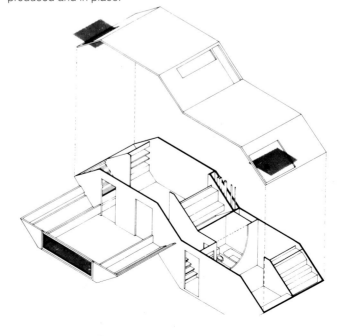

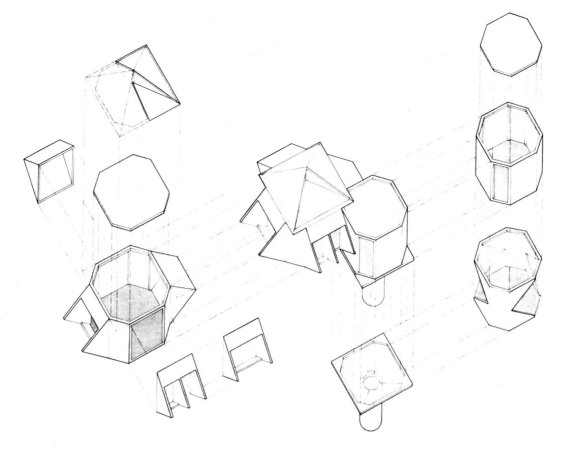

TROPACO RESORT
ST THOMAS, US VIRGIN ISLANDS   1968-69

■ A spectacular rocky peninsula on the north coast of St Thomas provided the 48,500-square-metre site for this proposed development of 180 condominium units, a hotel and a discotheque.

Inspired by the magnificent natural growth of the area, the design was developed to disturb the site minimally. Octagonal modules containing bathrooms, kitchens and services stack vertically to become support columns based on the ground rock. Larger modules containing living spaces are suspended from the core columns, their windows shaded and ventilated with moveable overhanging shutters. At the base of each column, water is collected from the roof.

The client desired a resort that would function equally well as clustered private family dwellings and a guest hotel, so that homeowners would be able to rent their units for part of the year. Thus, a building system was designed in which a group of four units with a central glazed courtyard could form either a three-bedroom house or four separate guest rooms around a central public courtyard.

The modules were designed to be prefabricated in 8-centimetre-thick, precast lightweight concrete at a plant in Puerto Rico, shipped by barge, then erected on site by helicopter or mobile crane.

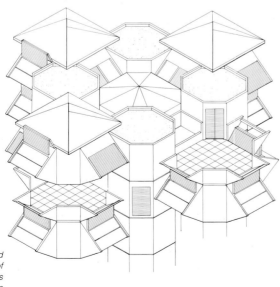

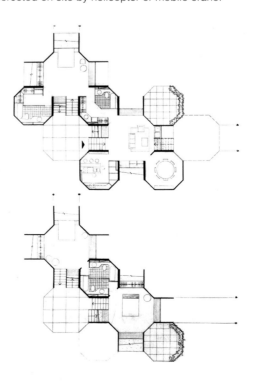

Above: *Exploded axonometric of precast components*
Below Left: *Axonometric of unit cluster*
Below Right: *Typical unit plans*

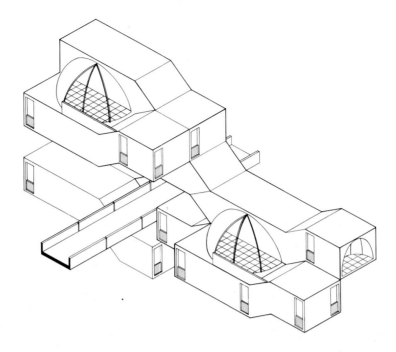

HABITAT ISRAEL

JERUSALEM 1969-70

■ Habitat Israel was designed as an industrialised housing system for the Israeli Government's Ministry of Housing. Tremendous climatic variation across the country required a design with great versatility in fenestration, heating, cooling, insulation, topographical adaptability and density.

The basic factory-produced module, therefore, constitutes both a building and an environmental system. Units can combine easily into either two- and three-storey carpet housing, hillside terracing or high-rise clusters. Semi-circular convertible domes over the terrace gardens rotate to adapt the basic module design for varying climates. In the desert, an inner dome-shaped shutter screens strong sunlight; in colder mountain regions, a clear glass dome window creates a warm, light-filled interior.

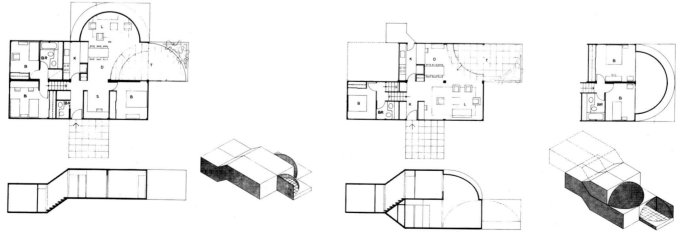

Above: Axonometric of unit cluster
Below: Typical subdividable three-bedroom unit plans and sections

HABITAT NEW YORK I
NEW YORK CITY   1967-68

■ Habitat New York I was designed as luxury housing for a site on the East River, just north of the Mayor's residence, Gracie Mansion. With shopping facilities, a marina and on-site parking, the project adapted the amenities of Habitat '67 to the major density constraints of Manhattan.

The vertical loads of a high-rise tower demanded different structural strategies from Habitat '67. The original concept, with varying wall thicknesses and strengths of the structural connections, limited the system to moderate heights. Therefore, for the New York project, fireproofed structural steel frames cast into lightweight concrete membranes form prefabricated units that were designed to bear loads by virtue of their own geometry. When joined, the octahedral units act as a continuous, vertically-inclined space-frame capable of rising 40 storeys,

spanning the East River Drive, and supporting exterior pedestrian streets carrying mechanical services. Great structural efficiency derives from the geometry of the system, allowing the structural steel members to be only 22 centimetres thick at ground level.

Each octahedral structural frame contains a cube: a skylit duplex dwelling open to an outdoor roof garden between the exterior and interior geometries. The units are 9.75 by 9.75 metres, and in clusters of two, they form spacious, luxurious apartments commanding views across both the East River and the Manhattan skyline. Mechanical services occupy crawl space between the floor and bottom apex of each individual octahedron. Shopping and other conveniences form a bridge to 96th Street across the East River Drive.

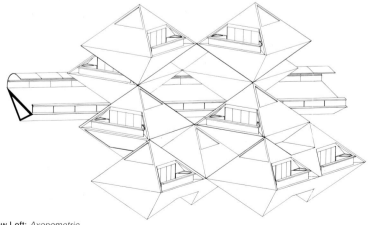

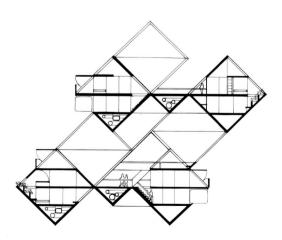

Below Left: *Axonometric of unit cluster*
Below Right: *Section through units and pedestrian streets*

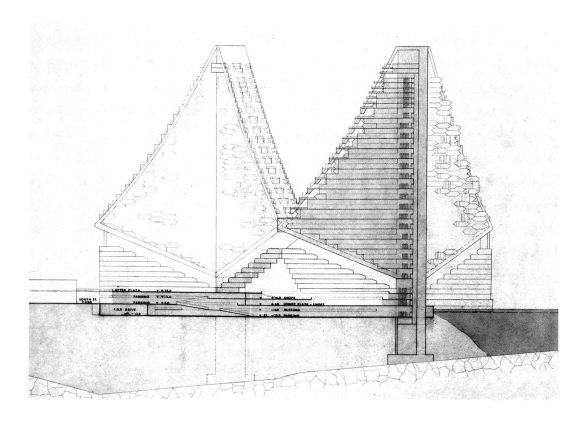

HABITAT NEW YORK II
NEW YORK CITY   1967-68

■ During the design of Habitat New York I, the site for the project was moved several miles down the East River, from the Upper East Side of Manhattan to a district of unused piers south of the Brooklyn Bridge and adjacent to the Fulton Fish Market.

With the change of site came the new challenges of developing a tower-scale Habitat. New density requirements of 300 people per acre surpassed any previous Habitat project, while the city required that the building maintain both access and views to the river. Rethinking the structural logic of the project led to the design of an ultra-light unit suspended entirely from catenary cables like those in a suspension bridge. The concrete-encased cables are anchored at the top to three towers containing the elevator cores and mechanical services, and at the bottom to a compression beam and multi-level structure

holding 92,900 square metres of office and commercial space. Together, the towers, cables and compression beam act structurally like the mast and boom of a sailboat.

Two modules, each octagonal in plan but different in shape and size, provide a variety of dwelling units with one, two or split levels. The modules are suspended on either side of a pedestrian walkway that leads from each core tower. An additional fire stair descends through each catenary cable to the ground. Plumbing and electrical services are stacked vertically through the octagonal modules, collected at the bottom, and sloped back to the core. The open ground plane between the building and the river provides public outdoor spaces, small-scale community services and continuous access from the street to the waterfront.

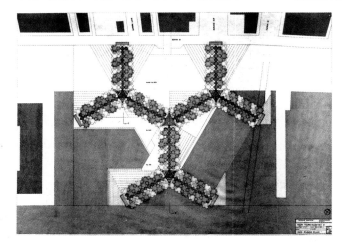

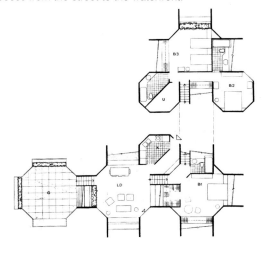

Above: *Site section*
Below Left: *Site plan*
Below Right: *Typical unit plans*

SAN FRANCISCO STATE COLLEGE STUDENT UNION

SAN FRANCISCO, CALIFORNIA   1967-68

■ The San Francisco State College Student Union contains offices and study areas, student stores, dining halls, classrooms and meeting rooms for the 20,000 student population. Located at the hub of campus pedestrian movement, the building is designed to incorporate this activity and create a meeting place that is integral to the busy central campus green.

A hard edge of existing buildings bordering the site contrasts with the more organic, informal Union, a building of 'glass and grass' that emerges from the green as a three-dimensional park. A continuous network of stairs, landings and entrances constitutes

the building's exterior, and with additional interior stairs and elevators, this extensive circulation allows thousands of students to access the many facilities throughout the day and night.

The structure is composed of several distinct precast concrete modules that can be mass-produced and easily assembled on-site. Modules combine to form spaces of various sizes and qualities of light without sacrificing fast and cost-efficient construction.

Initiated and approved by the students, the design's rejection by the College Board of Trustees in 1968 incited campus riots.

Below Left: *Site plan*
Below Right:
Building section

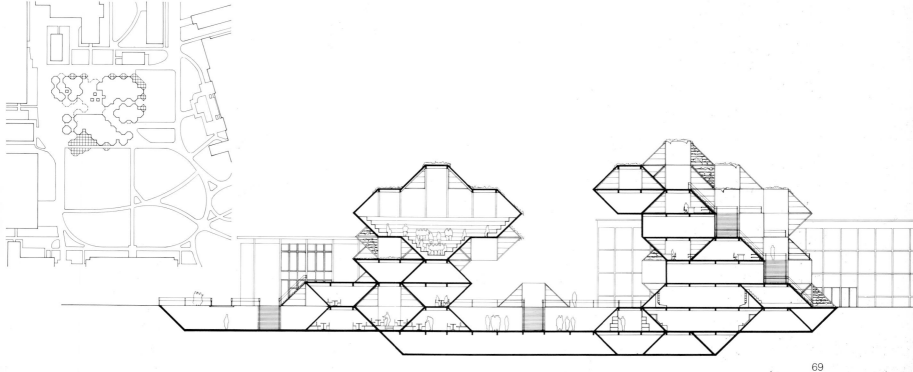

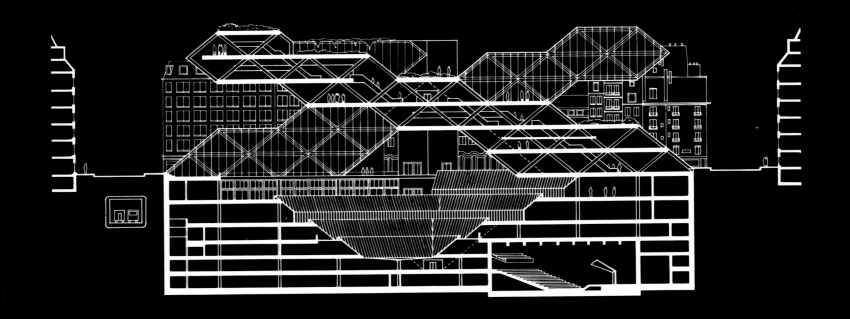

POMPIDOU CENTER
PARIS 1971

■ The competition entry for the design of a major cultural centre for the Place Beaubourg in Paris was produced in conjunction with a design studio and 14 students at the Yale School of Art and Architecture. The programme included a national library, museums of art and industrial design, theatres, restaurants and cafes, as well as an RER station for high-speed trains connecting to the metropolitan region.

The centre was conceived as two inclined planes cantilevered from the sidewalk across the centre of the block. From one corner, the pedestrian sees only terraces of glass and greenery – a public park – that can be ascended from street level. On the opposite corner, the whole sheltered superspace is visible,

with the facades of the surrounding Paris *hôtels* forming the enclosing walls of the complex. Glass walls and roofs allow sunlight directly into the lower levels, and invite public views to and from the surrounding streets.

One cantilevered wing holds the library; the other, the art museum. Stepping down six levels below the street are daylit art galleries, the industrial design museum, museum administration, theatres and a restaurant. Circulation through the cultural centre is based on the concept of a Ferris wheel, with continuously rotating cabs stopping periodically at each level from subway to rooftop restaurant.

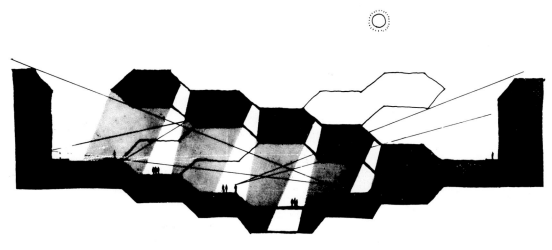

Opposite, Above:
Site section
Below: *Daylighting and sightlines section diagram*

BUILDING IN JERUSALEM

YESHIVA PORAT YOSEF

1970–

■ Constructed on the site of a *yeshiva* (rabbinical college) destroyed in the 1948 Arab-Israeli war, Yeshiva Porat Yosef sits on the rock escarpment that rises from the Western Wall plaza offering spectacular views of the Temple Mount and El Aqsa mosque, the Old City walls, the Mount of Olives, and an Arab village.

The 13,650-square-metre college engages the cliff and rises ten storeys across the site from east to west. A multi-level arcaded passage divides the site in two. Above it, residences for 400 students stretch along the ridge of the hill and arch over a large main dining hall. Below the circulation arcade, the academic facilities include classrooms, study halls, a library, an auditorium and a public synagogue.

The building juxtaposes and combines traditional forms and materials with modern construction. Jerusalem by-laws require that all exterior building surfaces, both wall and roof, be built of stone. Thus, stone walls 3 metres thick enclose the site and define the major zones of the building. They also support all the passages, staircases, light shafts and mechanical services. Within these heavy walls, a contemporary structural system of modular concrete arches cast *in situ*, each 3 metres high and 3 metres across, combine to form rooms of various heights and sizes.

On the exterior, concrete arches emerge above the warm stone walls, arcades, ramped passages and apertures to echo the domes of the city's shrines. Made with an aggregate of Jerusalem stone, the sandblasted arches match the colour of the masonry walls.

The synagogue rises six storeys, pierced with arches and protected within thick walls. Skylights created by the intersection of the interior and exterior structures, and translucent fibre-glass domes, filter light throughout the chamber. To fulfil the clients' desire for bright colours in the sanctuary, 4.5-metre prisms are positioned to break the entering daylight into the full visible spectrum. Patterns of colour cast on the chamber wall vary with the position of the sun, and white light fills the space on cloudy days.

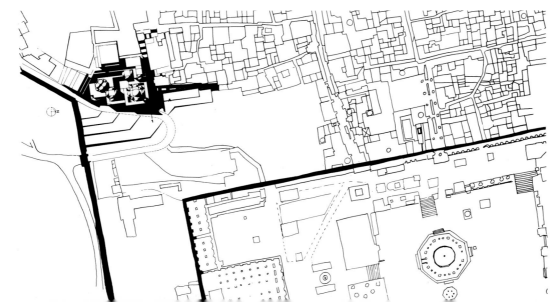

Site plan

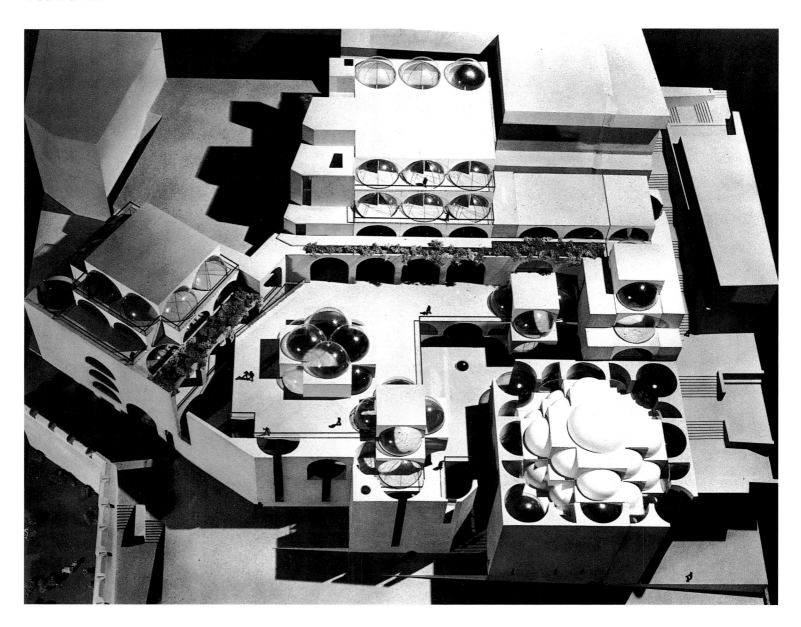

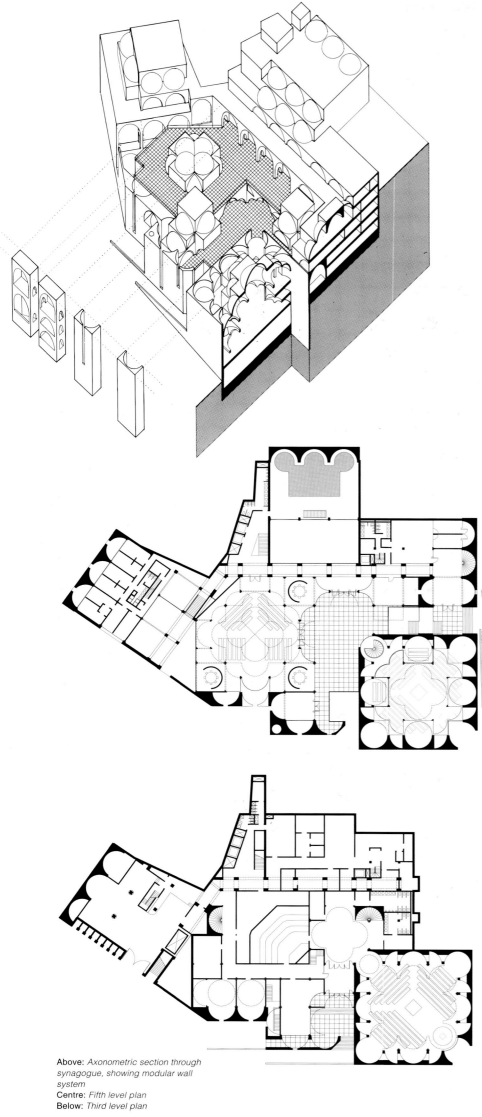

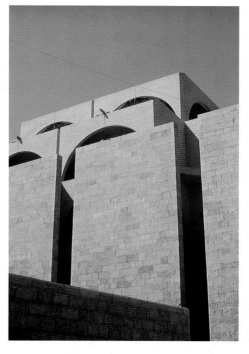

Above: *Axonometric section through synagogue, showing modular wall system*
Centre: *Fifth level plan*
Below: *Third level plan*

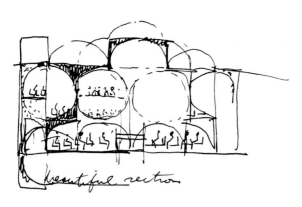

beautiful section

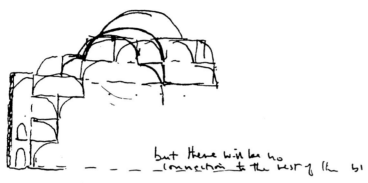

but there will be no connection to the rest of the b1

a design revolving around prism

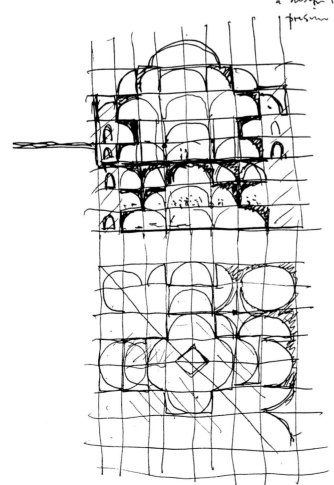

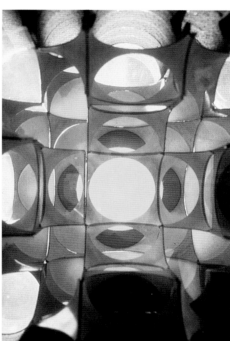

Left: *Early studies of prism daylighting, building geometries*

WESTERN WALL PRECINCT

1972–

■ Since AD70, when Titus invaded Jerusalem and destroyed Herod's Second Temple, the Western Wall has been the holiest place for Jews. Until 1967, a dense and dilapidated 14th-century residential district crowded so close to the massive wall surface that a narrow corridor, 5 metres by 30 metres, constituted the entire space for congregation. An open space in front of the Wall, randomly shaped and larger than the Piazza San Marco, was created after the Arab-Israeli war to accommodate the many pilgrims who pray and celebrate there daily.

The proposed plan will transform this cleared plaza and integrate it with a series of public spaces, existing archaeological gardens, and public institutions planned to border and define the precinct. The space must provide intimacy for individuals to pray and meditate by the Wall, yet accommodate the hundreds of thousands who gather for religious festivals and national celebrations. It must also integrate the precinct with the surrounding fabric of the old and new cities, improve access to the adjacent Temple Mount and incorporate a rich underground topography of newly discovered archaeological remains.

Pedestrian traffic in the precinct falls into two

groups: those coming to the Wall for worship and celebration, and those traversing the district from Dung Gate to the Old City markets. The plan proposes to separate the sacred traffic from the secular. An arcaded street running parallel to the Wall would connect Dung Gate to the markets, with excavated sections of the ancient Roman *cardo maximus* forming its floor. Perpendicular to this path, a new series of grand stairs would descend from the Jewish Quarter into the entire Wall precinct.

The praying area would be excavated down to its original Herodian street level, 9 metres below the present terrain. There, segments of the original stone – its paving and drainage still intact below 2,000 years' rubble – would become the surface for the praying area immediately beside the Wall. A series of public squares would terrace nine storeys up towards the Jewish Quarter from this area, following the bedrock.

Urban design guidelines proposed for the site would impose a geometrically transforming grid to accomplish a gradual transition from the grand scale of the Wall to the intimate scale of the Jewish Quarter. Stepping upward, this terraced geometry would also integrate several layers of archaeology.

Opposite: *Aerial photomontage looking north-east towards Western Wall and Temple Mount*
Below Left: *Excavation at base of Western Wall revealing ancient stones that extend 9 metres below ground level*
Below Right: *Existing base of Western Wall, looking east across archaeological gardens*

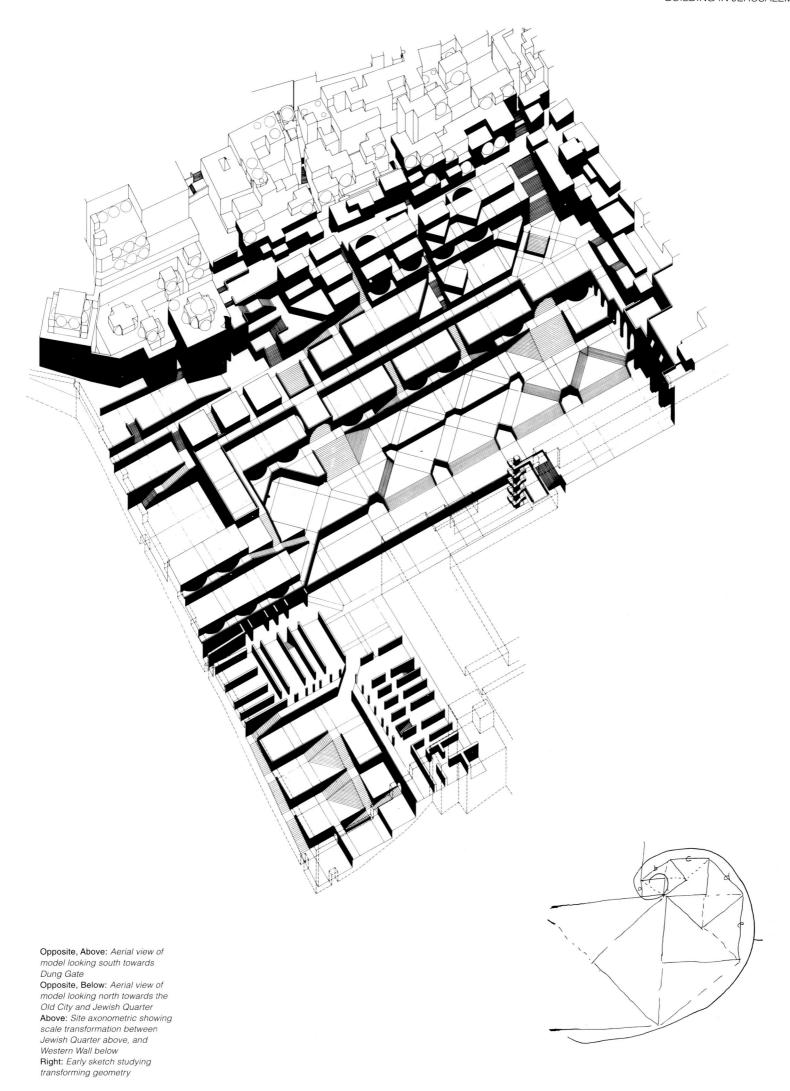

Opposite, Above: *Aerial view of model looking south towards Dung Gate*
Opposite, Below: *Aerial view of model looking north towards the Old City and Jewish Quarter*
Above: *Site axonometric showing scale transformation between Jewish Quarter above, and Western Wall below*
Right: *Early sketch studying transforming geometry*

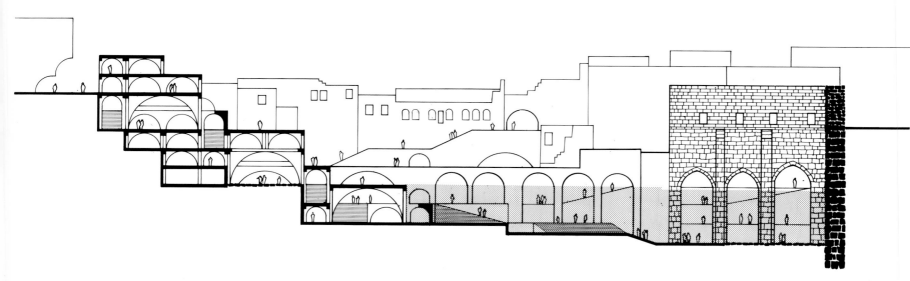

Above: *Detail of model looking north towards Old City, showing restored Herodian street as praying area*
Below: *Site section descending from the edge of the Jewish Quarter down to original Herodian street level adjacent to Western Wall, indicating proposed area of excavation*

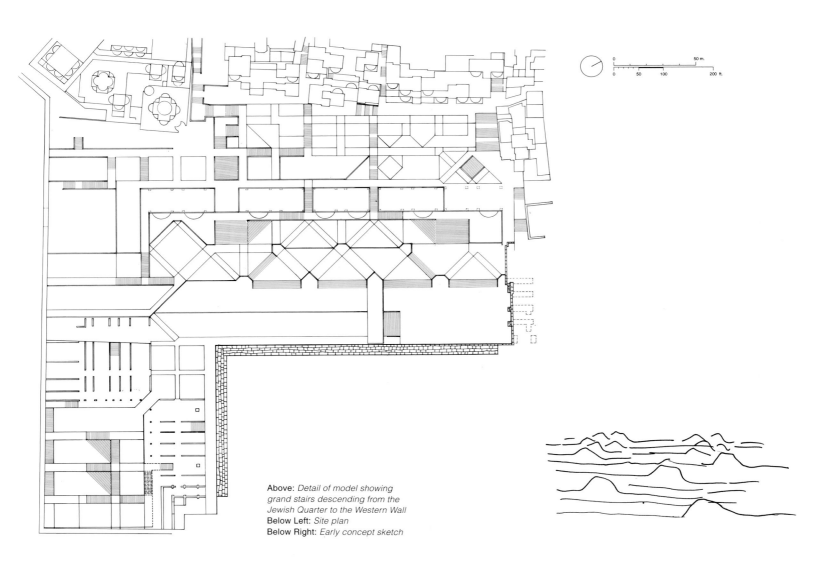

Above: *Detail of model showing grand stairs descending from the Jewish Quarter to the Western Wall*
Below Left: *Site plan*
Below Right: *Early concept sketch*

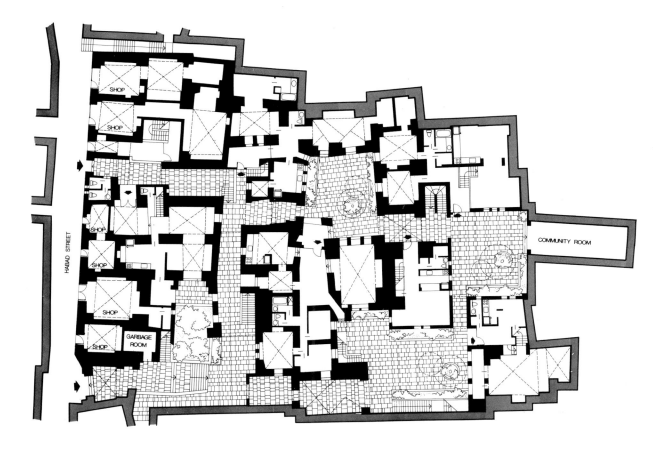

RESTORATION OF THE JEWISH QUARTER

1971-94

■ In 1967, following the unification of Jerusalem, the Government of Israel established the Corporation for the Reconstruction of the Jewish Quarter. The rebuilding of this mostly destroyed sector involved several components: Block 38 to the east, the Hosh District to the west, two private residences and several institutions, including the Yeshiva Aish Hatorah under a separate contract.

The reconstruction work entailed stabilising and restoring ancient masonry buildings, devising innovative techniques for waterproofing, and installing modern sanitary and mechanical systems. New construction techniques were designed using local stone to integrate each project harmoniously into the historic quarter.

Opposite: *Aerial view of Jerusalem, with Jewish Quarter in foreground*
Above: *Ground level plan of restored Hosh District*
Below: *Site before restoration*

HOSH DISTRICT
1976-78

■ The Hosh District represents a section of ancient buildings at the edge of the Jewish Quarter, adjacent to the Armenian Quarter. Ranging in age from one hundred to several hundred years old, the structures of the ancient complex include a synagogue that was used through the early part of the 20th century.

After the 1948 Israeli War of Independence, the complex deteriorated and 20 years later, the city decided to restore the area and convert it into dwellings. 17 apartments of various sizes have been created in a structure of renovated existing buildings and new infill construction. Private gardens, roof terraces, and a series of courts linked by passages form private outdoor spaces for the residences, woven through the new and old building fabric.

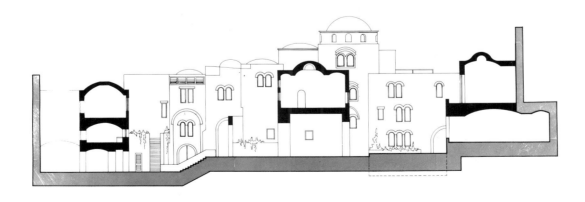

Site section

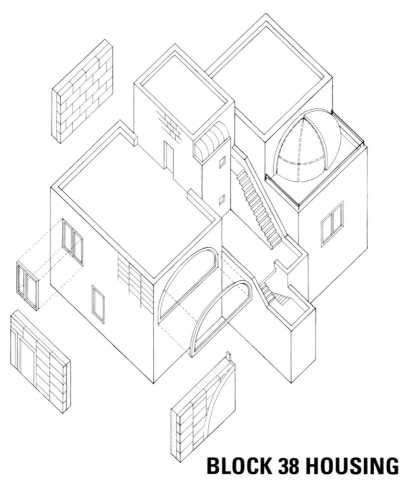

BLOCK 38 HOUSING

1971-77

■ Block 38 is one of several areas of the destroyed Jewish Quarter reconstructed between 1967 and 1982. The project, overlooking the Western Wall and Temple Mount, includes both restored and newly constructed buildings.

The new buildings are organised into service cores flanked by 6 by 6 metre bays. The cores contain entrances, access stairs, bathrooms, kitchens and other services, while the bays hold living rooms and bedrooms. Units are terraced to create roof gardens covered by half-opaque convertible domes. Open, the domes form roofless terraces; closed, they form greenhouse solariums.

Traditional load-bearing walls of Jerusalem limestone form the cores, while the flanking bays are constructed of reinforced concrete sandblasted with a limestone aggregate, with openings framed with precast concrete. Concrete walls are faced in Jerusalem limestone to form continuous surfaces. Terraces and roofs are paved with stone.

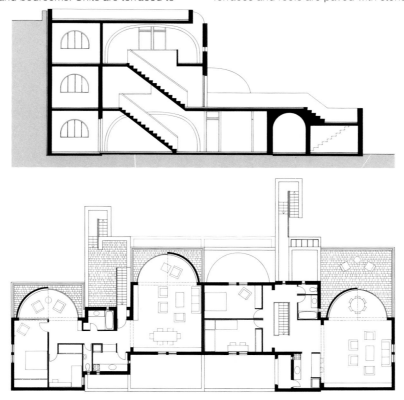

Above: Exploded axonometric of construction elements
Centre: Typical plan of two units
Below: Section

YESHIVA AISH HATORAH
1985-94

■ The Yeshiva Aish Hatorah consists of three adjoining 200-year-old buildings from the Ottoman period, which are poised on the escarpment overlooking the Western Wall and the Temple Mount. Converting the structures into a modern *yeshiva* with a large *beit midrash* (study hall), dining room, classrooms and offices involved a combination of restoration, demolition and new construction.

Thick rubble walls in the existing buildings were faced with dressed stone on the exterior and plaster on the interior, their roofs vaulted or domed to create classrooms and offices. The demolition of the middle structure created a light, airy space as a centre for

the four-storey complex. Within the void, a three-storey steel structure was built to enclose the *beit midrash*. The boundaries of the hall are formed by the original exterior stone walls of the adjacent buildings, while steel columns and corbelled steel arches rise up to form domes and half-domes lit by clerestories above. A large circular window frames a view of the Western Wall and the Temple Mount, and provides a setting for the ark.

One level below the *beit midrash*, a dining hall extends east, its roof forming a terrace to meet the entry stair rising from the Western Wall precinct.

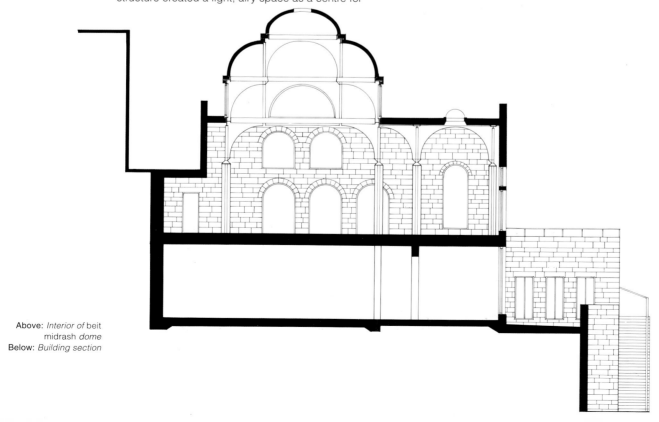

Above: *Interior of* beit midrash *dome*
Below: *Building section*

PRIVATE RESIDENCE
1972-73

■ This residence sits on the escarpment of the Old City of Jerusalem, within the city walls, with a 270-degree panorama of the Holy Sepulchre, the Temple Mount and mosques, the Western Wall and the Jordanian Hills of Moab by the Dead Sea.

The entire structure was composed over time: its lowest level during the Crusader period, its second level in the Ottoman period, and its upper level newly constructed as a living area and kitchen to capture light and views.

An original 200-year-old Ottoman courtyard and three domed rooms at the second level – one creating a bridge over the alley below – form the entry floor of the house. As the structure threatened to collapse during restoration, arched buttresses were constructed against adjacent structures to support the building. The domed rooms were restored and the courtyard roofed in glass. On the new upper level, the terrace is enclosed by a convertible glass dome that opens to the city in warm weather and creates a greenhouse in winter.

The additions are constructed traditionally of load-bearing stone with the ancient base of the building housing electric transformers and other infrastructure.

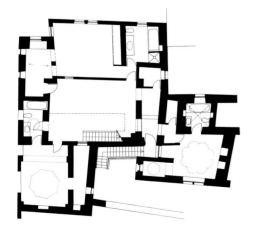
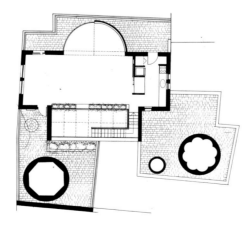
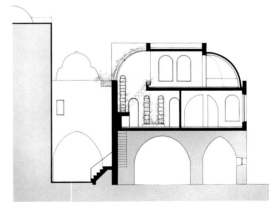

Left: *Entry level plan*
Centre: *Upper level plan*
Right: *Section*

MAMILLA CENTER
1972-99

■ Just outside the Old City walls, the area of cisterns and pools that supplied Jerusalem with water for hundreds of years became known as Mamilla, Arabic for 'Water of the Gods'. The area was first developed at the turn of the century, as urbanisation moved beyond the walls into the historic Valley of Hinom. From 1948 to 1967 the border separating the Jordanian and Israeli sectors ran through the eastern half of the site, while the western half, within the Israeli city, deteriorated into a slum. The master plan seeks to establish the 113,300-square-metre site as a synthetic part of the new city, connecting the Arabic and Jewish sectors; the Jerusalem central business district to the west and the Old City to the east.

The restoration of the topography of the Valley of Hinom – obliterated by landfill and buildings from the past hundred years – cues the entire urban design. The valley will stretch north from the National Park to Independence Park in downtown Jerusalem as a major park, and new buildings will terrace up the valley sides towards the Old City and the modern central business district once the project is complete.

On the northern bank, Old Mamilla Street will be restored to connect Jaffa Gate and the Old City with downtown. Several historic structures on the north side of the street have been preserved and incorporated. On the opposite side, new structures gradually will rise to seven storeys in height as they meet the downtown area. The pedestrian street is lined with 120 apartments, a 300-room hotel, a cinema complex, major shopping and service facilities. An underground garage and bus terminal, completed in 1995, form a series of landscaped terraces descending from the Gate. The south bank, completed in 1996, holds 200 terraced apartments and a 350-room hotel that faces King David Street.

Continuous vehicular and pedestrian paths crisscross the district. A boulevard runs through the valley towards Jaffa Gate, connecting the Russian compound and City Hall to the south with Yemin Moshe, the Hebrew Union College, and the King David Hotel district to the north. Pedestrians flow through the now continuous park system with its network of walkways, watercourses and arcades. A series of descending and ascending staircases also cuts through the project from north to south.

Above: *Aerial view of site under construction looking north-west*
Below Left: *19th-century artist's rendering of site, with water cisterns that gave Mamilla its name*
Below Right: *Location plan*

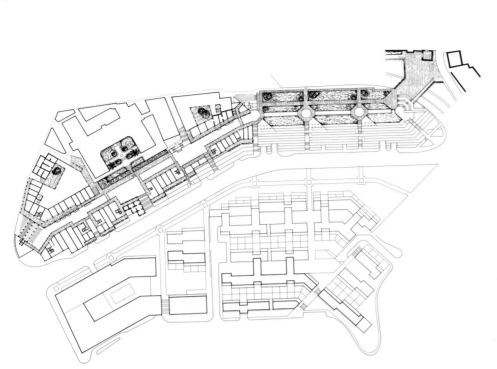

Above Left: *Upper level site plan*
Above Right: *View of Mamilla Street (c1975), looking towards Jaffa Gate*
Centre Left: *Mamilla Street level site plan*
Below: *Elevation along Mamilla Street looking north*

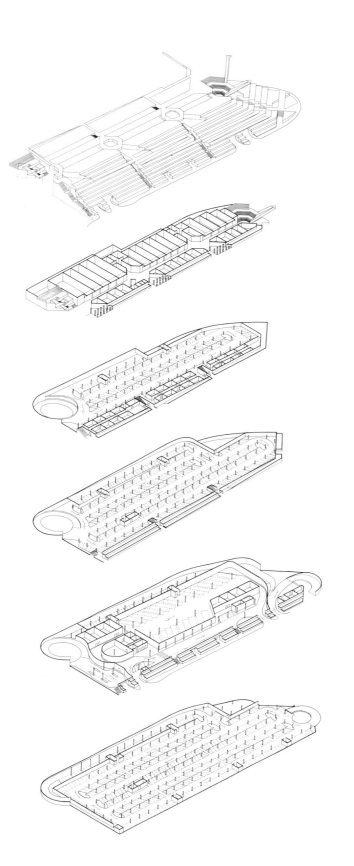

Left: *Exploded axonometric plans of Jaffa Gate Parking*
Above Right: *Interior of Jaffa Gate Bus Terminal and Parking*
Centre Right: *Early sketch of terraced Jaffa Gate Parking*

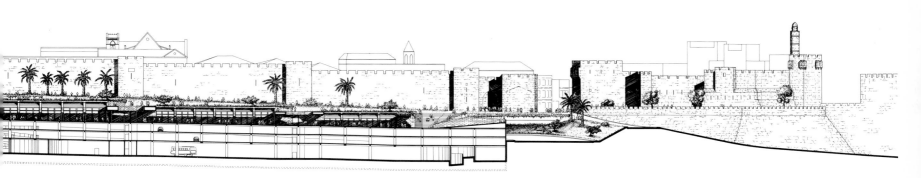

A connecting element

HEBREW UNION COLLEGE

1976–

■ The campus of the Hebrew Union College is adjacent to the Mamilla district of Jerusalem, just outside the Old City walls. The complex includes a variety of educational buildings with classroom facilities for 300 students, a major library, an archaeological museum and research department, and a youth centre and hostel. A reception centre with an auditorium and exhibition area will be located at the entrance of the complex, along King David Street. A Great Hall is currently in progress at the east corner of the site.

The buildings focus around three major internal courtyards defined by arcaded pedestrian paths and upper level skywalks. From King David Street, the public enters the campus and climbs to the upper level of the arcade, proceeding from the reception centre through the campus. Turning past views of courtyards and gardens, these walkways culminate at the panoramic entrance to the Great Hall, overlooking the Old City. Students also enter from King David Street, passing through the courtyards and lower-level arcades.

External walls of rough, golden stone create a series of screens, garden walls and arcades that define the boundary of the campus. Within the walls, concrete frames and precast concrete beams hold aluminium infill panels, reflecting the yellow stone of the perimeter walkways and the competing colours of lush plant life.

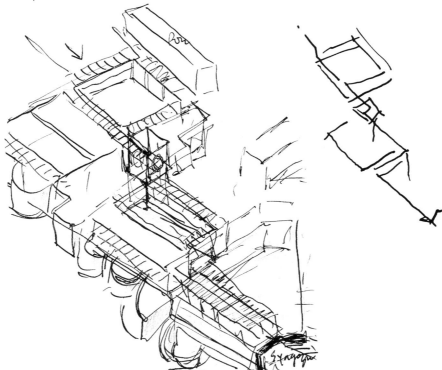

Early study sketch of 'skywalks'

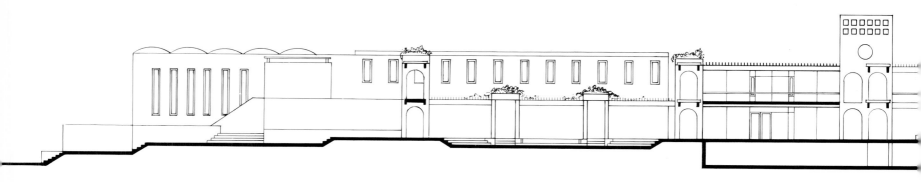

*Site section through entrance court,
ceremonial court, academic court,
youth hostel and future Great Hall*

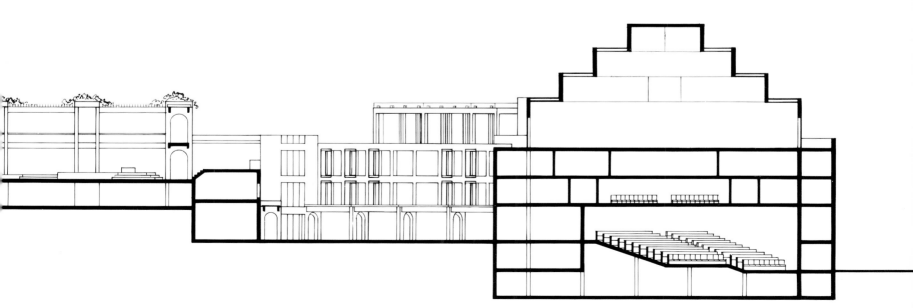

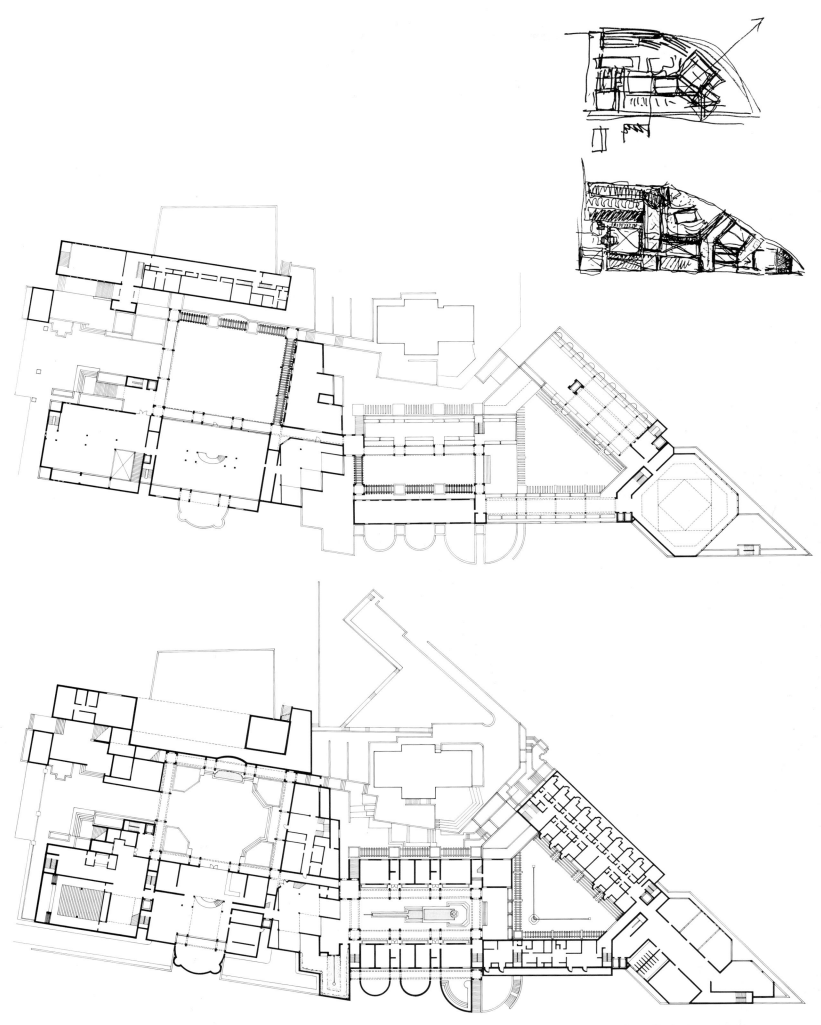

Above: *Site development sketches*
Centre: *'Skywalk' level plan*
Below: *Ground level plan*

111

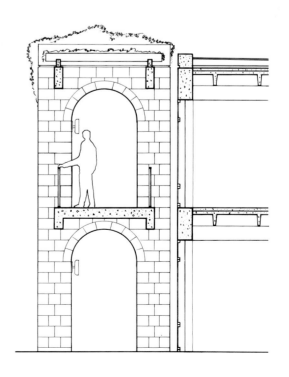

Section through trellised courtyard arcade

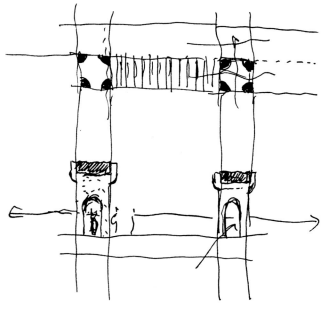

Early sketch plan and elevation of trellised courtyard walkways

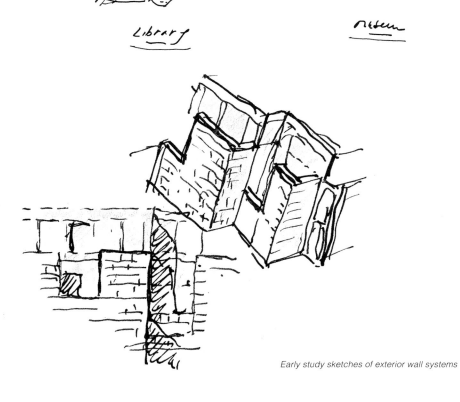

Library

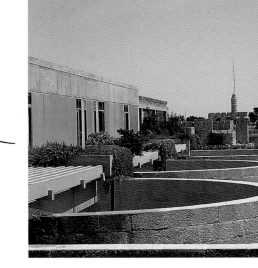

Early study sketches of exterior wall systems

Opposite Above and Opposite
Below Right: *Campus library*
Above: *Skirball Museum*

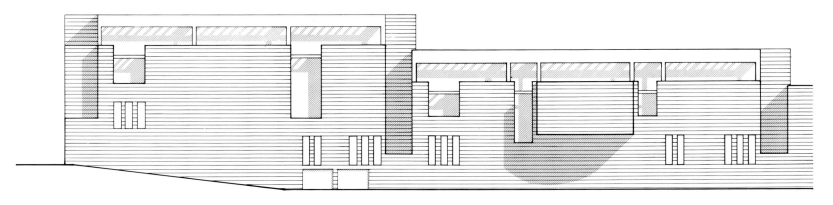

Partial exterior elevation of administration building

YAD VASHEM CHILDREN'S HOLOCAUST MEMORIAL
1976-87

■ In 1976, the Yad Vashem Holocaust Museum sought to build a memorial on a hillside site to the 1.5 million children who perished in the Holocaust.

Entered through a natural arch formed by a rock outcropping overhead, the memorial is underground. Descending a ramp carved into bedrock, one reaches a chamber buried within the hill. Inside, the octagonal room is pitch dark, but for the flame of a candle. An echoing chant quietly fills the space. Semi-reflective panels and mirrors multiply the single candle into an infinite halo.

One exits towards a widening view of the forested hills of Jerusalem. Marking the ground above the memorial's interior, an octagonal outdoor amphitheatre echoes the shape of the space beneath. Seven sides of the octagon are defined by double rows of cypress trees, and on the remaining north side stands a series of monolithic stone pillars. The tallest pillars reach the height of an adult; others are randomly broken, jagged against the sky, symbolising the abrupt endings of the many young lives taken by the Holocaust.

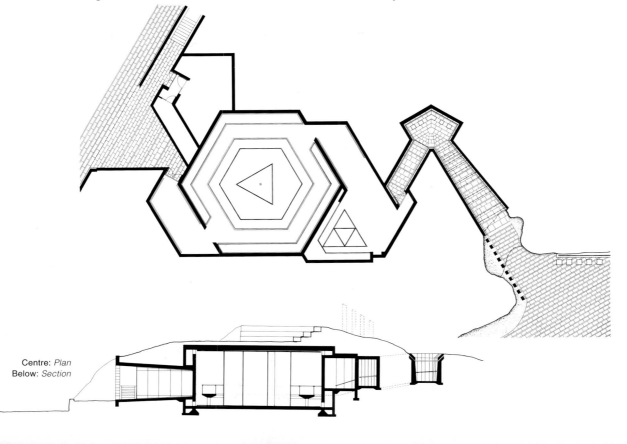

Centre: *Plan*
Below: *Section*

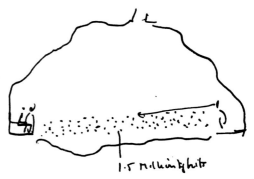

1.5 million white

burned in earth

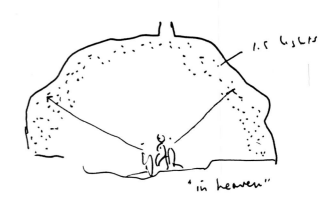

1.5 lights

"in heaven"

Millions reflected stars
of lives not born
reflections into infin

1,500,000 Candles

800 / Meter m². say 1000 →

£ 300 / 1,500,000 Meters.

so that it could not be in one
layer - 5-6 layers.

Preceding Pages: *Interior
of chamber*
Above Left: *Entry*
Above Right: *Concept
development sketches*
Below: *Expanded section*

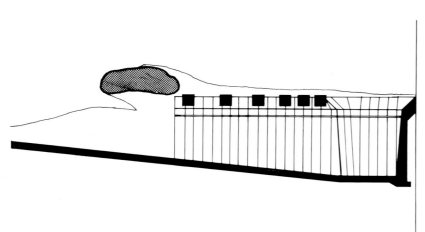
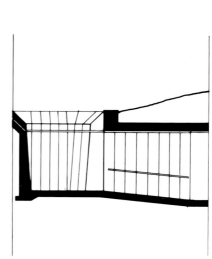

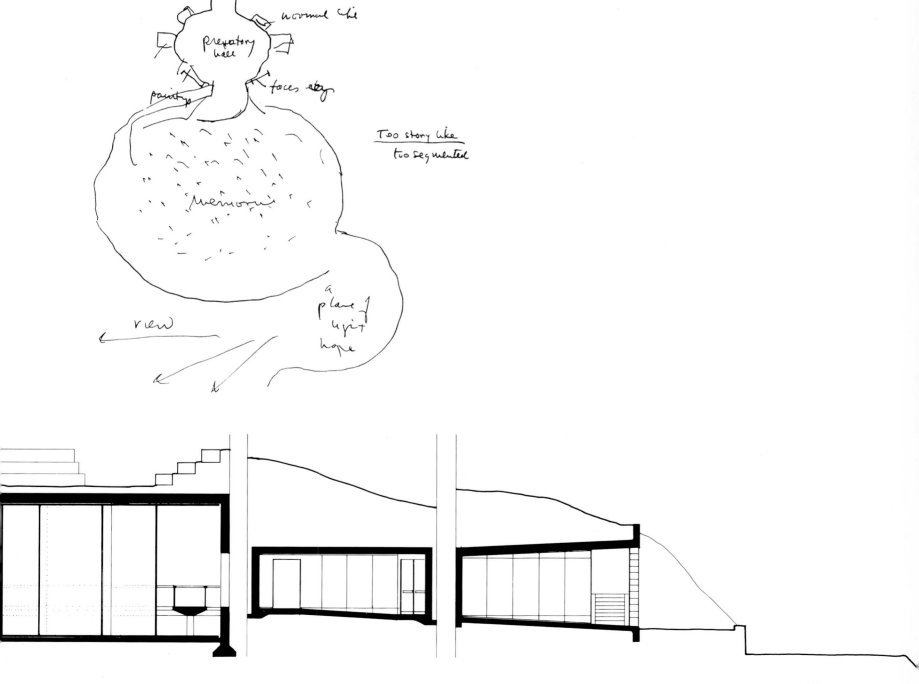

SUPREME COURT OF ISRAEL
1986

■ Poised on the highest hill in the city and on axis with the Knesset Parliament building, the competition design for the Supreme Court of Israel seeks to respond to the Israeli tradition of justice expressed in Psalm 85: 'Truth rises from the earth, and justice reflects from heaven.'

Cut 5 metres into the ground and shielded from cold winter winds, a square compound is divided into a triangular forecourt to the south and a court building to the north. At 12-metre intervals across the protected public court, golden limestone pillars reach 16 metres into the air, inscribed with legal teachings from scriptures, holy books and the annals of world justice. This forest of pillars creates a shaded grove of entry, a place for contemplation.

Visitors enter the court building through a public hall in which the solid pillars of the forecourt become hollow clusters of concrete columns that support pairs of beams. With trellises overhead, an interior pattern of light, shade and living plants evokes the Jewish *sukkah*, a place of public gathering.

Delicately balanced like the rule of law, the grand court in the building acts in plan as a corner fulcrum for two wings of secondary courtrooms. Changing light conditions colour the two intersecting glass roofs over the courtrooms and shift their apparent relationships. With partial sunlight, the outer shell dominates, reflecting glints of the sun, cloud movements and the sky. In early morning and late afternoon the two roofs appear collaged. At night, light from within the court illuminates the inner shell. Rising over the evening skyline, the lit courtrooms join the light of justice with the lamps of government and religion, embodied in the lighted Knesset, mosques, churches and synagogues.

Above: *Courtroom roofs, night view of model*
Below: *Elevation sketch*

Above: *Site elevation sketches with
Knesset, day and night*
Centre: *Site plan*
Below: *Site elevation*

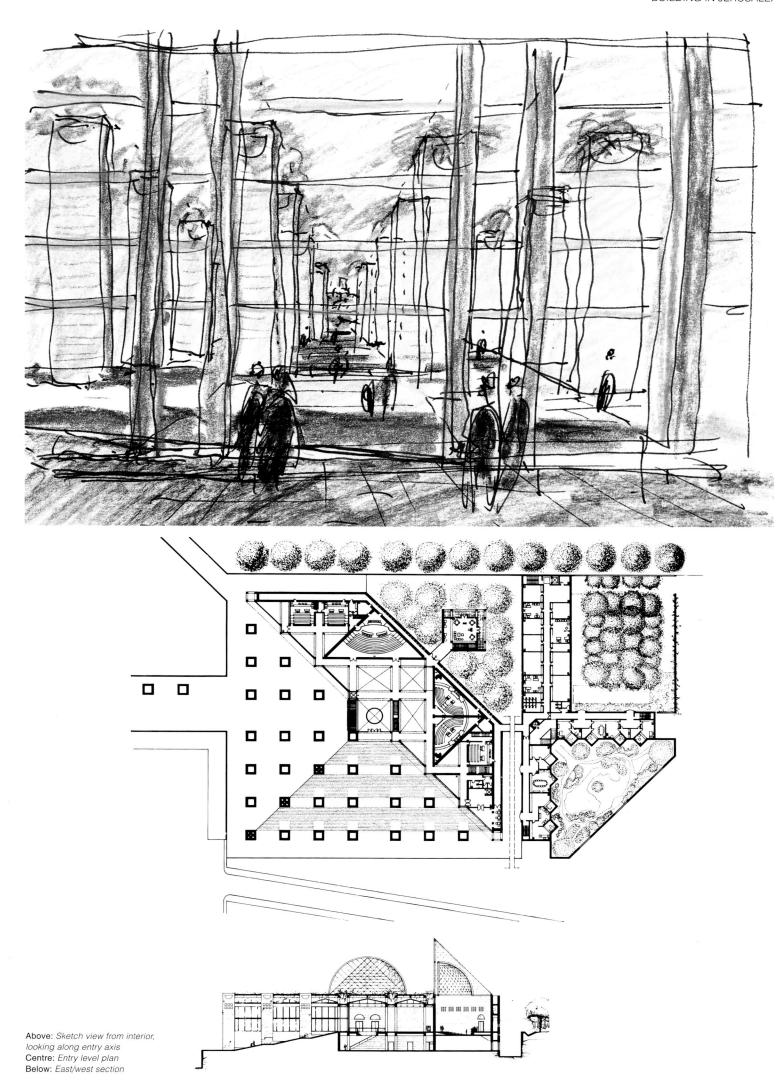

Above: *Sketch view from interior, looking along entry axis*
Centre: *Entry level plan*
Below: *East/west section*

"OVER 100 PEOPLE WERE PACKED INTO OUR CATTLE CAR... IT IS IMPOSSIBLE TO DESCRIBE THE TRAGIC SITUATION IN OUR AIRLESS, CLOSED CAR. EVERYONE TRIED TO PUSH HIS WAY TO A SMALL AIR OPENING. I FOUND A CRACK IN ONE OF THE FLOORBOARDS INTO WHICH I PUSHED MY NOSE TO GET A LITTLE AIR. THE STENCH IN THE CATTLE CAR WAS UNBEARABLE. PEOPLE WERE DEFECATING IN ALL FOUR CORNERS OF THE CAR... AFTER SOME TIME, THE TRAIN SUDDENLY STOPPED. A GUARD ENTERED THE CAR. HE HAD COME TO ROB US. HE TOOK EVERYTHING THAT HAD NOT BEEN WELL HIDDEN: MONEY, WATCHES, VALUABLES... WATER! WE PLEADED WITH THE RAILROAD WORKERS. WE WOULD PAY THEM WELL. I PAID 500 ZLOTYS AND RECEIVED A CUP OF WATER - ABOUT HALF A LITER. AS I BEGAN TO DRINK, A WOMAN, WHOSE CHILD HAD FAINTED, ATTACKED ME. SHE WAS DETERMINED TO MAKE ME LEAVE HER A LITTLE WATER. I DID LEAVE A BIT OF WATER AT THE BOTTOM OF THE CUP, AND WATCHED THE CHILD DRINK. THE SITUATION IN THE CATTLE CAR WAS DETERIORATING. THE CAR WAS SWELTERING IN THE SUN. THE MEN LAY HALF NAKED. SOME OF THE WOMEN LAY IN THEIR UNDERGARMENTS. PEOPLE STRUGGLED TO GET SOME AIR, AND SOME NO LONGER MOVED... THE TRAIN REACHED THE CAMP. MANY LAY INERT ON THE CATTLE CAR FLOOR. SOME WERE NO LONGER ALIVE."

IN A CATTLE CAR TO THE DEATH CAMP - TESTIMONY OF A SURVIVOR

134

YAD VASHEM HOLOCAUST TRANSPORT MEMORIAL
1991-94

■ The Yad Vashem Holocaust Transport Memorial is dedicated to victims of the Holocaust who were transported by railway car to the death camps. A railway car given to Yad Vashem by the Government of Germany is positioned on a hillside retained by a massive concrete wall. The car, which was used during the Holocaust, stands at the tip of a destroyed replica railway bridge, reaching towards the Wadi Valley from the hillside and partially supported

by the wall. Its steel beams twisted, the cantilevered bridge stands above the valley – a journey into an abyss.

A small platform echoes the memory of a railway station. Visitors descend from the road to the base of the retaining wall carved with the testimony of a victim of the Transport. From here, the natural landscape falls away, down to the bottom of the valley.

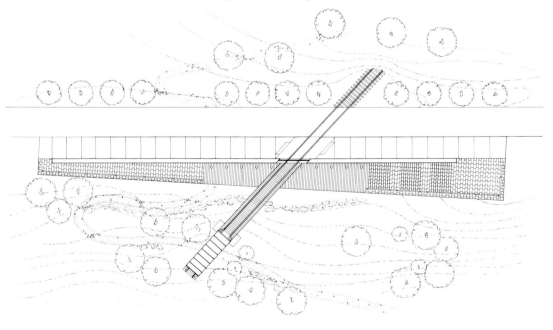

Opposite, Below:
Inscribed witness testimony
Centre: *Site plan*
Below: *Site section*

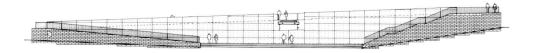

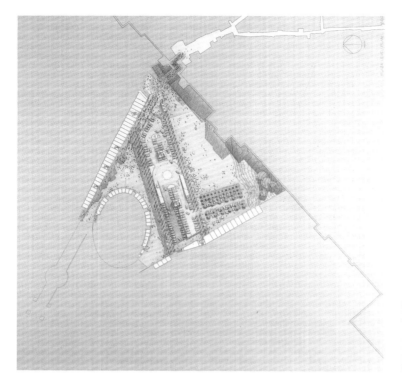

DAMASCUS GATE PRECINCT PEACE SQUARE

1994–

■ This triangular precinct is bounded by the Arab business district to the east, the Jewish sector to the west, and the Old City wall with Damascus Gate to the south. A continuous valley originally sloped from north to south through the Gate, the focal point of the district. Once prominent in the landscape, Damascus Gate now appears partially sunken as the ground level has gradually risen. The area was inaccessible from 1948 to 1967 and has been occupied only temporarily since then.

A road (Hatzanchanim Street) currently divides the triangular precinct into two segments, north and south. The recently constructed Highway 1 runs along the edge of the precinct and, with its acoustic baffle walls, has been criticised for separating the eastern and western parts of the city almost as brutally as the old barbed wire of the Jordanian-Israeli border. The design, therefore, proposes to reconnect the city. Through excavation, the district's topography will be reshaped to create a continuous series of public spaces with numerous points of access to join the individual precincts, East and West, Arab and Israeli.

The area north and south of Hatzanchanim Street will be lowered and an arcaded structure supporting the street will accommodate a taxi terminal and three levels of underground parking. To the south will be an active, market-like, paved piazza contiguous with Damascus Gate. The area north of the road will follow the topography of the old valley towards the Gate, descending gradually southward. The Street of the Prophets will become a pedestrian promenade to the east, its historical buildings restored as shops and cafes. Carved into the street's retaining wall, stalls for vendors will open onto the piazza. At its current level, a large elliptical park in the centre of the triangle will be filled with pine trees: a tranquil space that overlooks the Old City wall and Damascus Gate, with more stalls embedded in its piazza-level base.

At the precinct's northern apex, a new peace gate is proposed as a celebration of the 1993 Israeli-Palestinian peace accord. At this point, travellers from the north first view the Old City, the golden Dome of the Rock and Temple Mount. The precinct will be called Peace Square.

Opposite, Above Left: *Lower level plan*
Opposite, Above Right: *Upper level plan*
Opposite, Below: *Aerial view of model looking west over Damascus Gate*
Above: *Aerial view of existing site looking towards Damascus Gate*
Below Left: *Perspective looking south into excavated piazza*
Below Right: *Perspective looking north towards elliptical park and Peace Gate*

HOUSING

ARDMORE HABITAT

SINGAPORE   1980-85

■ The Ardmore Habitat condominiums are situated in the heart of downtown Singapore, adjacent to a major boulevard. The project consists of two 17-storey towers of vertically stacked units with terraces. Developed by Robin Loh Enterprises, shipbuilders and developers, the design sought to provide amenities similar to Habitat '67 on a constricted downtown site zoned for vertical massing. Both towers consist of alternating flats and two-storey apartments opening on to a large outdoor garden with a swimming pool and squash courts. The maisonettes are organised around a double-height central space that extends to an outdoor terraced garden – an external counterpart to the interior living area.

Centre: *Typical plans of south tower*
Below: *Site plan*

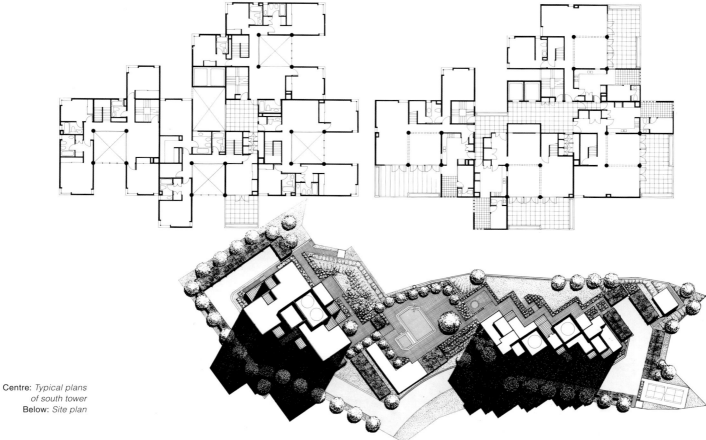

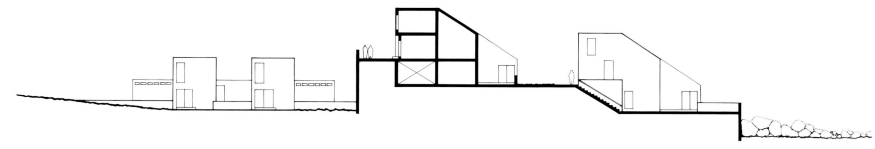

KIBBUTZ IDMIT

IDMIT, ISRAEL   1980-82

■ Founded by young immigrants in 1970, the Idmit Kibbutz is located on a hilltop in Galilee, overlooking the Mediterranean to the west and the Lake of Galilee to the east, adjacent to the Lebanese border. Walkways and passages connect dwellings across the sloping site, and public gathering spaces focus social events amid the individual residential clusters.

Kibbutz members were deeply involved in all stages of the design process. Each dwelling consists of a living space, bedroom, kitchen and bathroom, forming a total area of 49 square metres. Maisonette and single-level units are grouped to form communal courtyards. Single adults and couples occupy these new units, many with private patios that set a precedent in kibbutz housing. The children of the kibbutz live together in children's housing.

The construction is concrete cast *in situ*, with 20-centimetre-thick exterior walls to conform to the security standards of border construction.

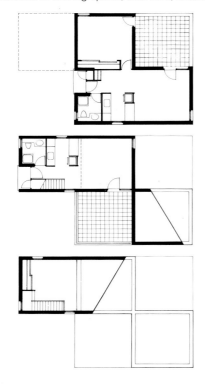

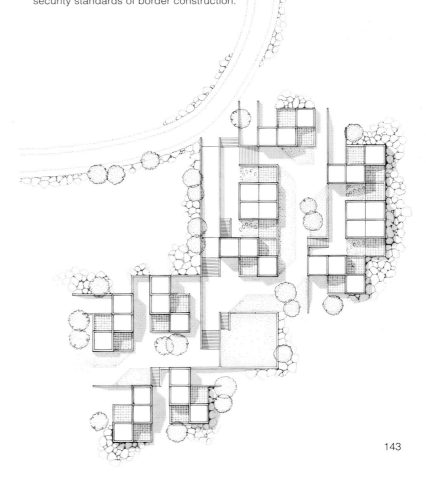

Opposite, Below:
Site section
Below Left: *Typical first, second, and third level unit plans*
Below Right: *Site plan*

CALLAHAN RESIDENCE
BIRMINGHAM, ALABAMA   1978-81

■ In its geometry and relationship to the site, this house responds to the client's fantasy of living in the control tower of Dulles International Airport. The result is a house that climbs up through the woods to survey the city of Birmingham.

The timber-frame structure consists of three principal levels connected centrally by a stair. The lowest level, embedded in the hill, contains the bedrooms and a fully glazed garden room facing north towards the city. On the second level are the entry and living areas: the kitchen, dining room and library. The upper level, occupied entirely by a large living room, is cantilevered towards the city skyline.

The continuously inclined roof, facing south, turns large skylights towards the sun for warmth during winter; in the summer months, a white canvas screen unfurls to shade the interior.

Site plan

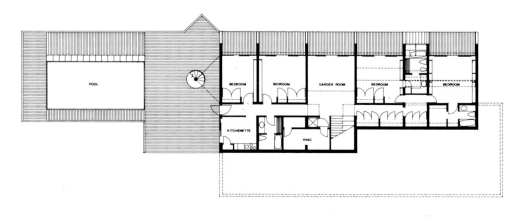

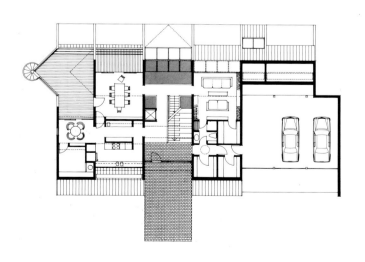

Below Left: *Lower level plan*
Below Right: *Entry level plan*

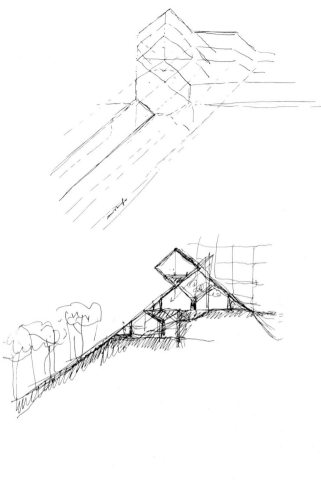

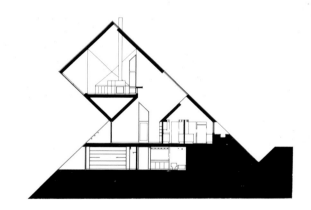

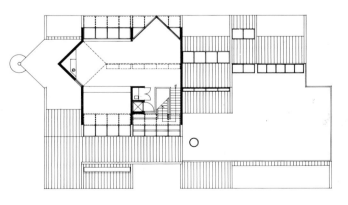

Above: *Development sketches*
Centre: *Section*
Below: *Upper level plan*

ESPLANADE APARTMENTS

CAMBRIDGE, MASSACHUSETTS 1986-89

■ The Esplanade is a 206-unit luxury condominium development along the Charles River. Conforming to strict urban design guidelines that limit height, require brick construction and a continuous street edge, the two terraced blocks maximise water views and provide many apartments with outdoor spaces.

By orienting the units diversely with respect to views, layouts and circulation, 35 different unit types offer residents a wide spectrum of choice. Apartments range from one-bedroom units of 75 square metres to three- and four-bedroom units of 240 square metres.

The vertical brick street facade, punctuated with bay windows, contrasts with the building's southern elevation: a terraced 'hillside' facing the water. Constructed of white precast concrete panels, layered roof terraces descend towards the river's edge with southern exposures and panoramic views of Beacon Hill and downtown Boston. Above-ground parking, necessitated by a high water table, is completely concealed by screens along the street and by apartments along the water, its roof serving as a community garden facing the Charles.

Typical apartment level plan

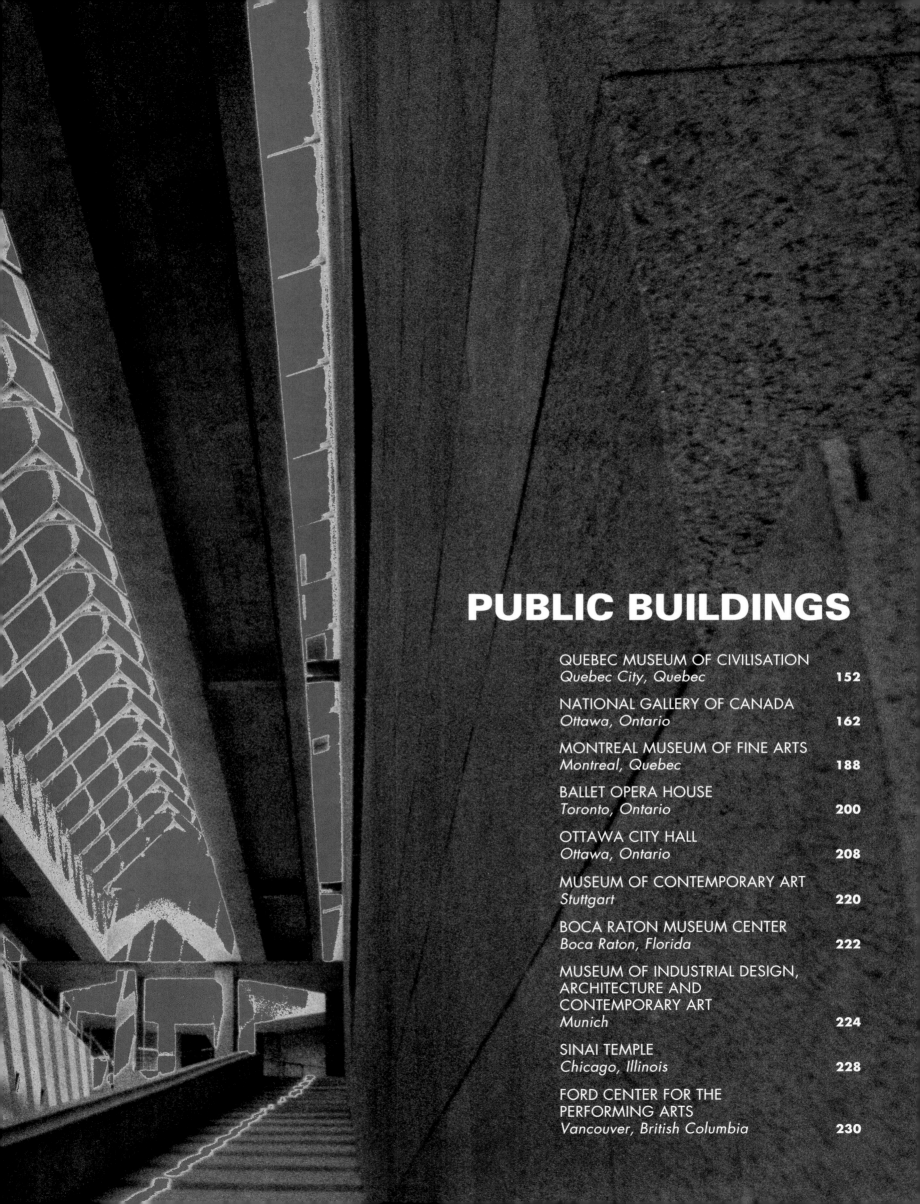

PUBLIC BUILDINGS

QUEBEC MUSEUM OF CIVILISATION
QUEBEC CITY, QUEBEC   1981-87

■ The Museum of Civilisation is located in the lower Old City of Quebec, within the Place Royale historic district along the St Lawrence River. Planned in two phases, the museum's first phase accommodates both a permanent anthropological collection and temporary exhibition galleries. The second phase, not built, would connect the main wing of the museum across a waterfront street to the river.

The museum developed in strong response to the site: as a platform to observe neighbouring urban landmarks and the sweep of the St Lawrence, and as a strong built piece of the historic urban district sloping towards the city's edge. Preserving continuity with the surrounding street edges and integrating two historic buildings on the site, the museum provides views from its roof walks and gardens up the escarpment to the monumental structures of a seminary and the Château Frontenac Hotel, across the dormers and peaks of the Old City, and out across the harbour.

Entrances from both the river side and the city side of the building connect upper and lower city in the museum's main foyer. This central meeting place incorporates an original court formed by the stone wall of the preserved and restored Maison d'Estebe, and is flanked by upper and lower level galleries connected by a bridge. The original river's edge, uncovered during construction, is now restored within the heart of the building, inscribing a memory of the city's past within this museum devoted to cultural preservation. The roof of the concourse forms a grand public stairway leading to a rooftop park; from here, a publicly accessible glass tower surveys the site and city.

The galleries are ordered on a tartan grid, with mechanical services running through a 3-metre module, and exhibition bays structured by a 9-metre module. Museum storage and workshops, as well as an auditorium, cafeteria and cloakrooms, occupy a full basement. The historic houses hold administrative offices.

Light entering through the multi-faceted clear glass skylights is diffused and evenly distributed in the galleries by polycarbonate panels framed with aluminium tubes. The exterior walls of the building are clad with local grey limestone; the roof structure, framed in steel, is sheathed with copper.

Above: *Perspective rendering of Phases I and II*
Below: *Conceptual site sketch*

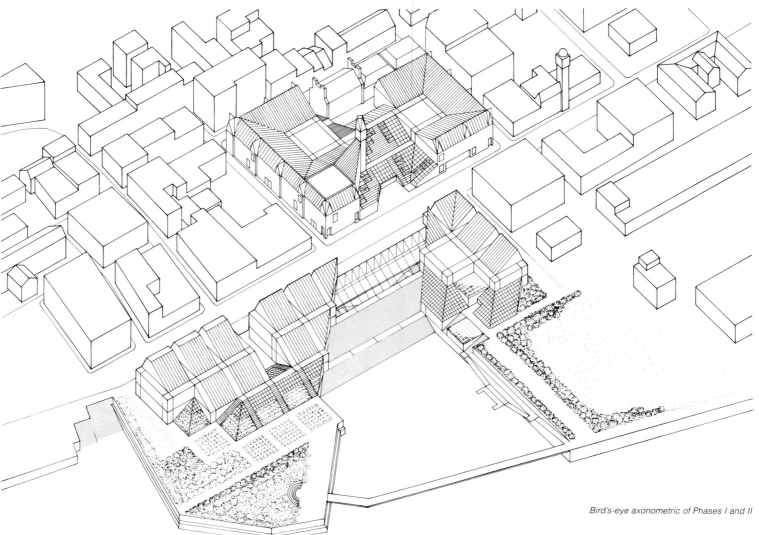

Bird's-eye axonometric of Phases I and II

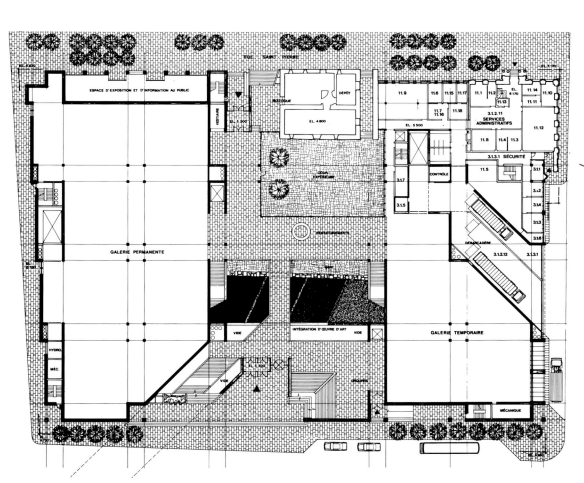

Below Left: *Ground level plan*
Below Right: *Study sketch*

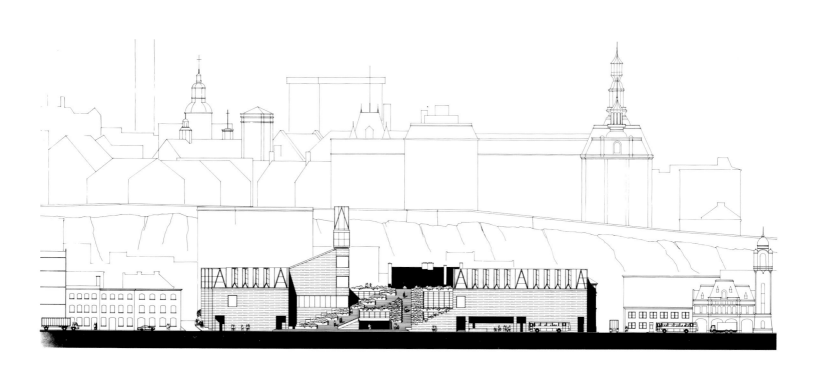

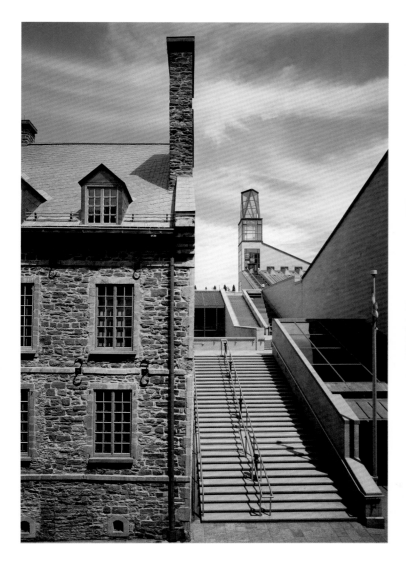

Opposite, Below: *Main entry elevation*
Centre: *Section through museum from river to roof garden*
Below: *Section through museum and Maison d'Estebe*

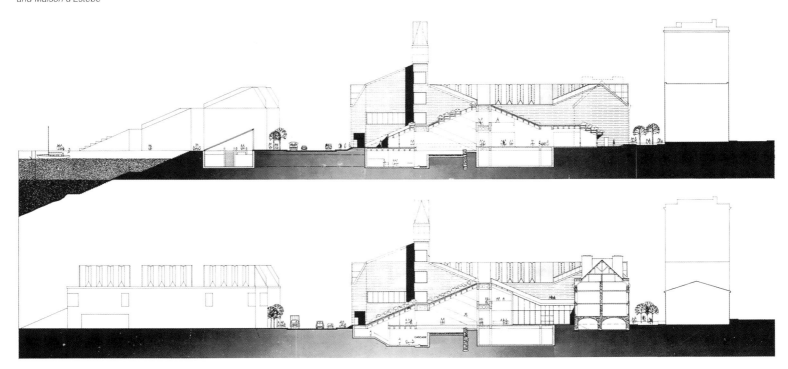

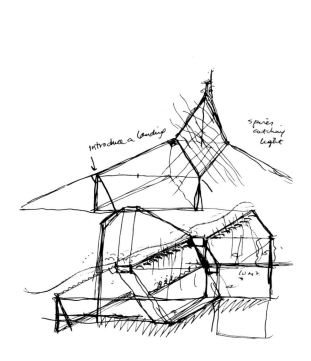

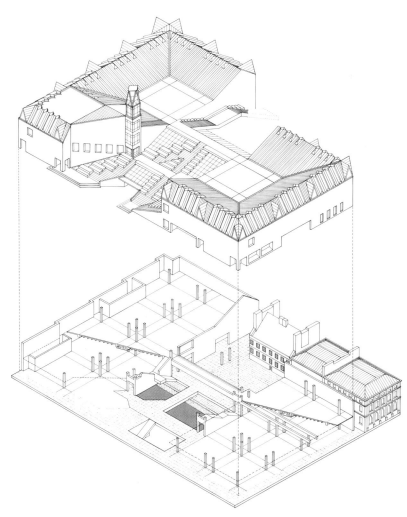

Below Left: *Development sketches
of tower and ascent to upper city*
Below Right: *Exploded axonometric
showing museum interior and roof
topography, with original* quai *and
restored Maison d'Estebe*

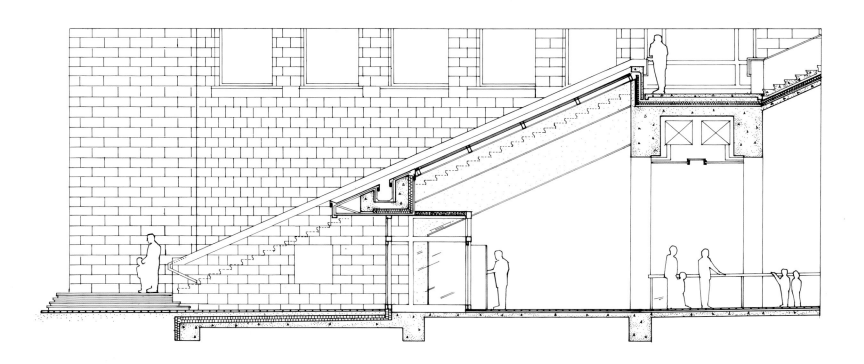

Detail section through main entry and stepped roof

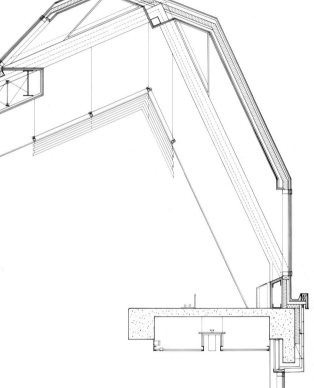

Detail section through gallery roof and skylight

NATIONAL GALLERY OF CANADA
OTTAWA, ONTARIO   1983-88

■ The National Gallery is sited on the crest of a spectacular, rocky promontory overlooking the Ottawa River and Parliament Hill. Built to display and store the country's finest collection of art, the building contains over 12,300 square metres of exhibition space on two levels, seminar rooms, a reference library, an auditorium, two restaurants, a bookstore, and a major curatorial and conservation wing.

The museum is conceived as a rich experiential sequence juxtaposing 'extroverted' public spaces with 'introverted' gallery and contemplation spaces. From the main entrance pavilion, visitors ascend a ramped, glazed colonnade to the Great Hall, where a continuous view of Parliament Hill and the Ottawa River forms an urban panorama before the meditative experience of the galleries.

The design reflects an intense focus on the interaction between space and light. Galleries on both the upper and lower levels receive natural daylighting. The upper level is lit by traditional skylights, while the lower levels are illuminated by a system of shafts lined with reflective mylar, which bounces natural light deep into the museum. Light from each of three different courtyards is filtered into adjacent galleries, and through the glass bottom of the Water Court's reflecting pool to the large group entrance below. In the Great Hall, nylon 'sails' shade intense sunlight from overhead, operated by a system of counterweights that is stabilised by suspended rings supporting artificial lighting. For concerts or special events these 'sails' can be exchanged and adjusted to control acoustics or create colourful patterns overhead.

The building's exterior and parts of the interior are clad with pink-grey Tadoussac granite. Glazed promenades and crystalline pavilions enclose public circulation and assembly spaces. Their transparency visually joins the museum with the city; their forms relate the building to the natural site and surrounding architecture of Ottawa.

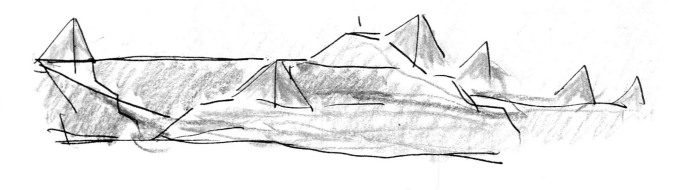

Initial sketch in response to site

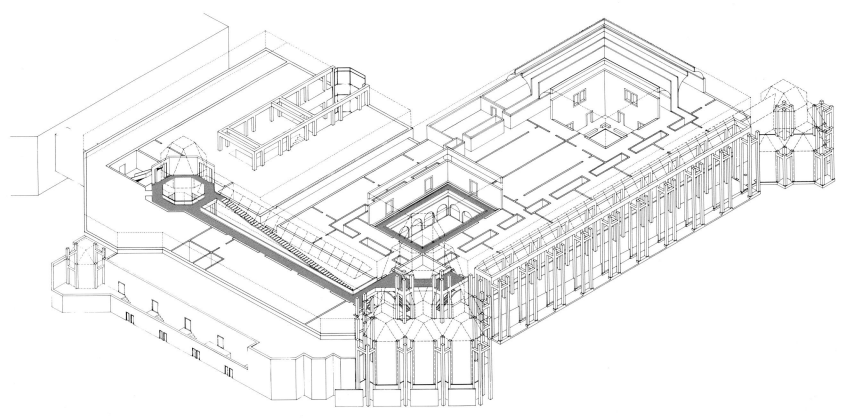

Axonometric with Great Hall in foreground

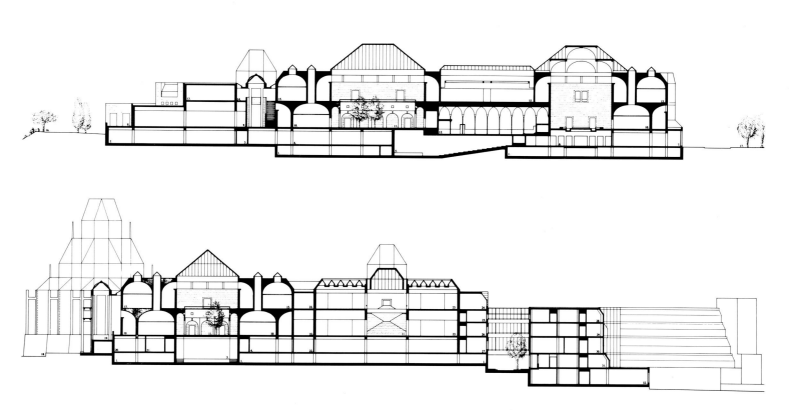

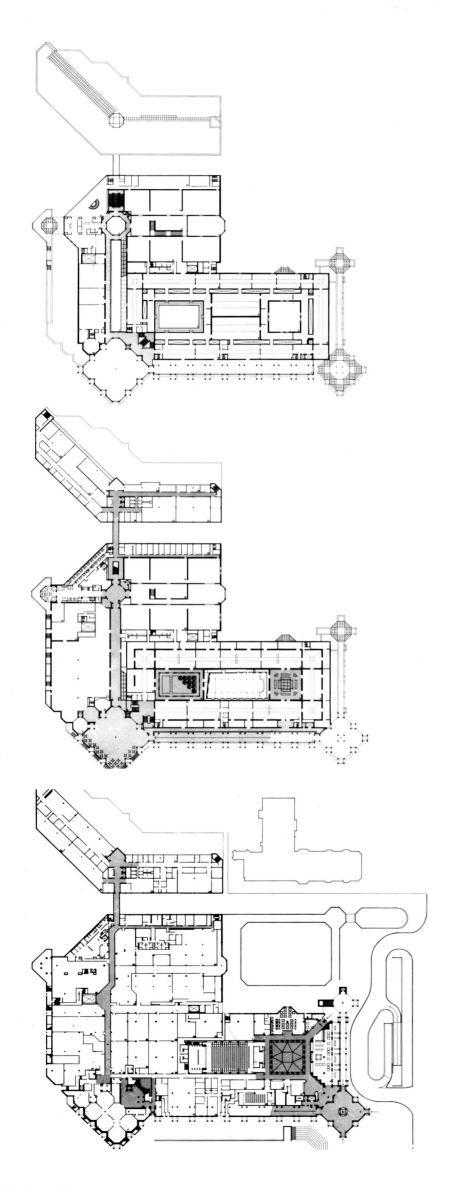

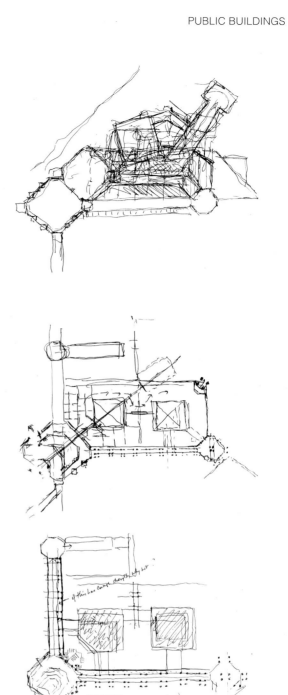

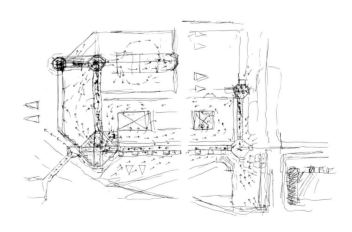

Opposite, Centre: *Longitudinal building section*
Opposite, Below: *Building cross section from ramped colonnade to curatorial wing*
Above Left: *Upper level plan*
Centre Left: *Main level plan*
Below Left: *Entry level plan*
Right: *Plan development sketches*

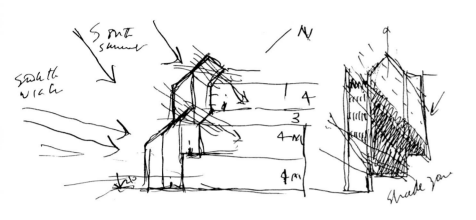

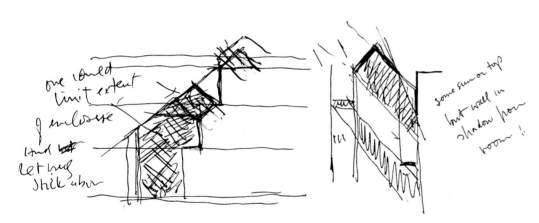

Lighting and section study sketches

Above Left and Above Right: *Early elevation and perspective sketches of 'introvert' scheme*
Below Left and Below Right: *Early elevation and perspective sketches of 'extrovert' scheme*

Above: *Conceptual sketch*
Below: *Perspective sketch of colonnade elevation*

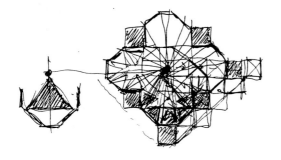
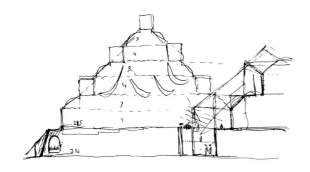
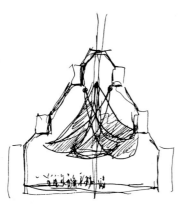

Above Left: *Development sketches of Great Hall acoustical and sunshading treatment*
Below Left: *Detail axonometric section of Great Hall framing and sunshading 'sails'*

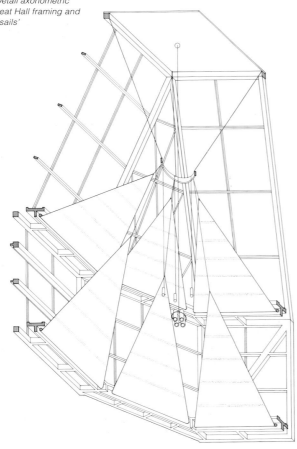

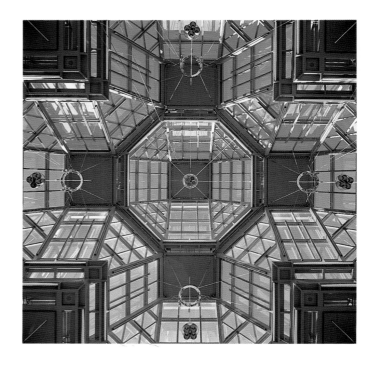

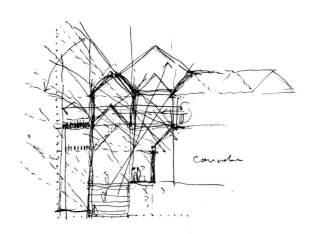

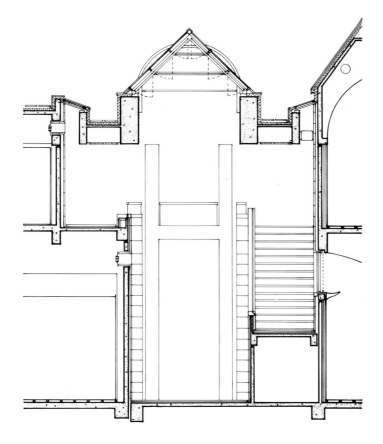

Above Left: *Lighting study sketch of ramped colonnade*
Centre Left: *Detail cross section through concourse*
Below: *Longitudinal section through concourse*

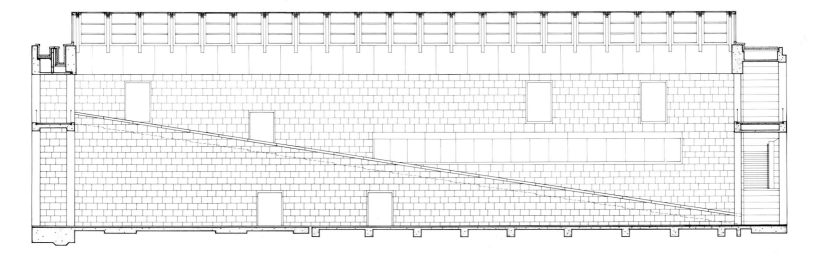

Above: *Canadian Art gallery,
lower level*
Below Left: *Gallery lighting
study sketches*
Below Right: *Sketch and model
section studies of upper and lower
gallery lighting with mylar shafts*
Opposite, Above: *European and
American Art gallery, upper level*
Opposite, Below: *European and
American Art gallery, upper level*

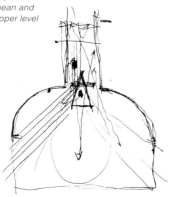
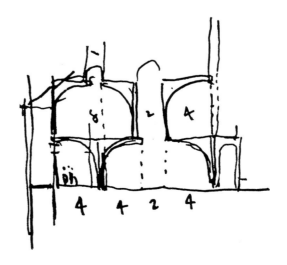

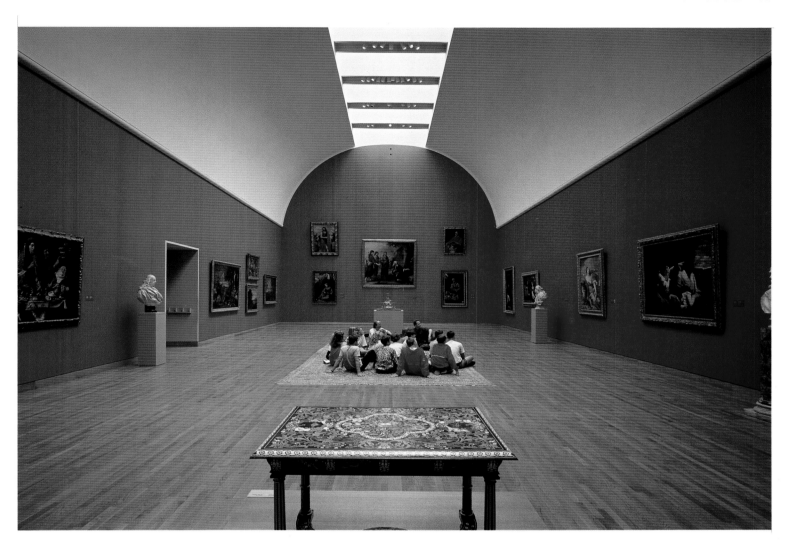

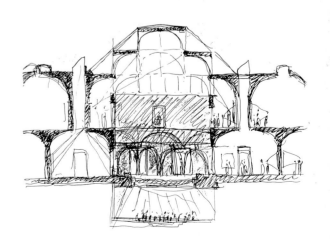

Section sketch of water court and
refracted light below

185

Above: *Contemporary Art wing court*
Below Left: *Contemporary Art gallery*

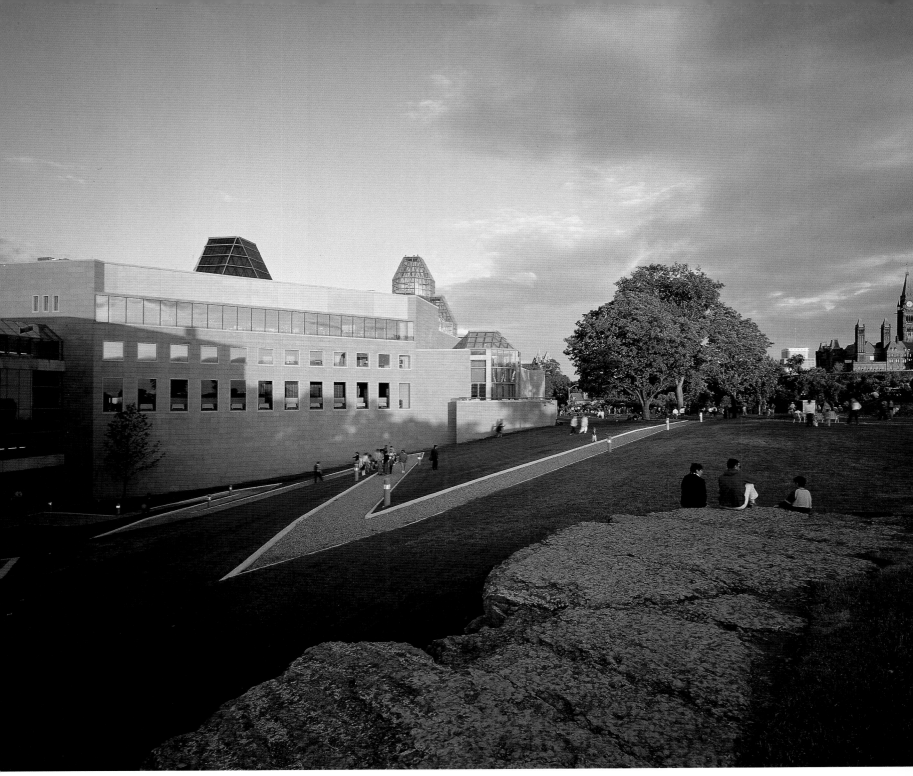

MONTREAL MUSEUM OF FINE ARTS

MONTREAL, QUEBEC   1985-91

■ The addition to the Musée des Beaux-Arts de Montréal doubles the museum's exhibition and educational spaces, linking underground galleries beneath a main downtown shopping street to the original 1912 Classical Revival museum building.

Two schemes for the project were developed: one occupied the entire site but preserved the mid-block alleys as required by the city's urban design guidelines; the other, which was finally selected by public decision, also preserved the facade of an existing 1902 Italianate apartment building.

Visitors enter the new building through a ceremonial gateway into a light-filled public foyer. From here, a scissor-like ramp stair rises to four levels of galleries oriented diversely with respect to the city. In this northern climate, the inclined glass facade allows light to fill the central room despite shadows cast by tall buildings across busy Sherbrooke Street. Between the lobby and the galleries at street level, an existing urban alley becomes a glass-enclosed public *passage culturelle* lined with shops.

Gallery spaces are designed to respond to a richly varied museum collection. Forming the tunnel passageway to the original museum, flat-vaulted galleries display objects from the Ancient, Asian and African collections, and minimalist galleries display contemporary art. Above, vaulted spaces with adjustable skylights house changing exhibitions. A variety of skylit galleries at the top level exhibit the permanent European collection. Facing east, a glass-enclosed *verrière* sculpture court and garden overlooks the neighbourhood's Victorian rooftops, with views across the city towards the river beyond.

The entrance facade on Sherbrooke Street is clad with white Vermont marble, the material of the original museum. Smaller-scale rhythms and varied colours integrate both side elevations with neighbouring storefronts and houses. On its east elevation, the building wall is articulated into a series of tower-like slabs faced with rough-textured black, green, red and grey granite, while the west elevation is brick with precast concrete bands.

Night elevation sketch

Above Right: *Night study sketch of alternate proposal, without preserved facade*
Centre Right: *Model of alternate proposal, Sherbrooke Street elevation*
Below: *Exploded axonometric of new museum and linking galleries to original building*

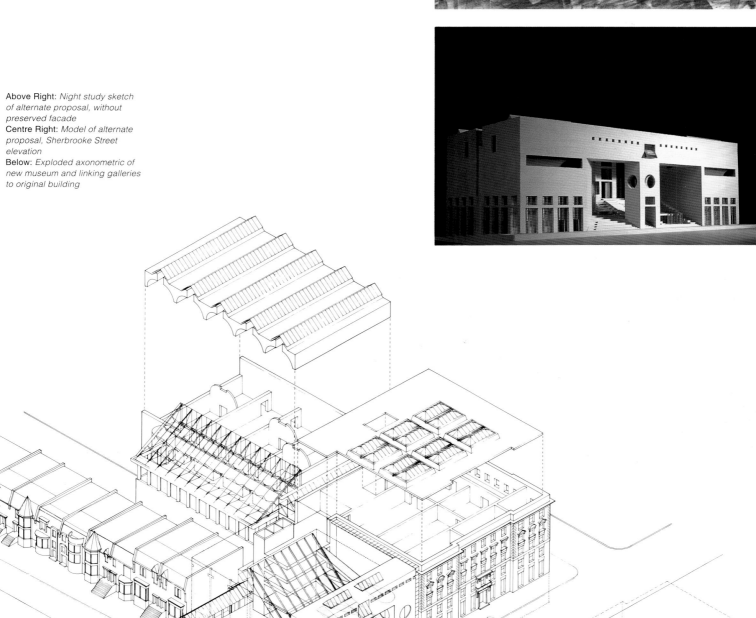

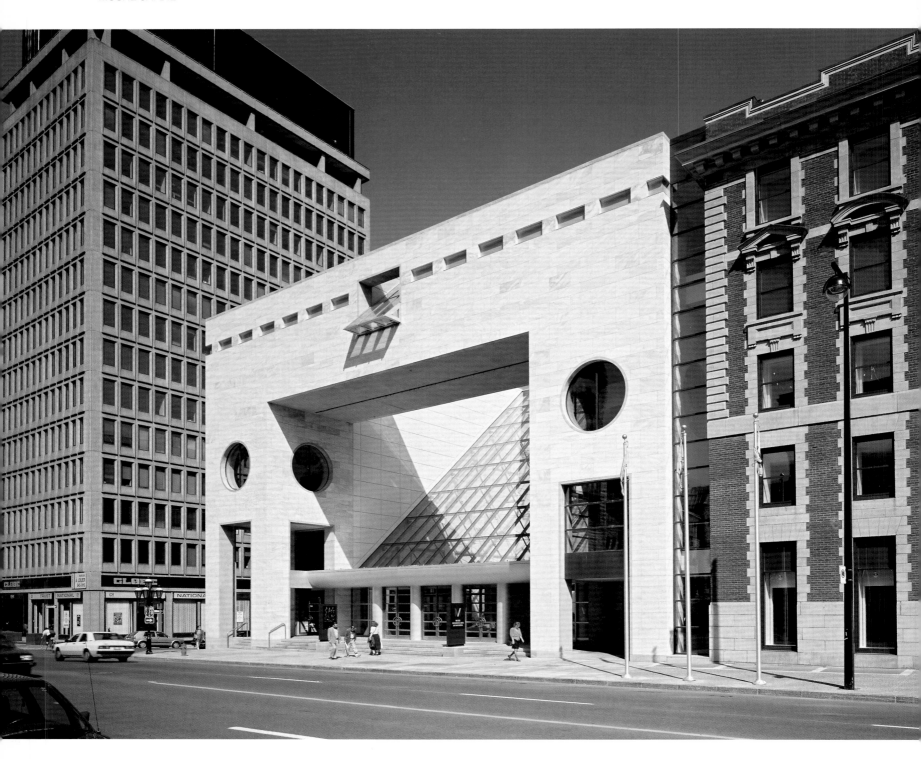

Opposite, Below: *Sherbrooke Street elevation*
Below Left: *Study sketch of museum lobby and stair*

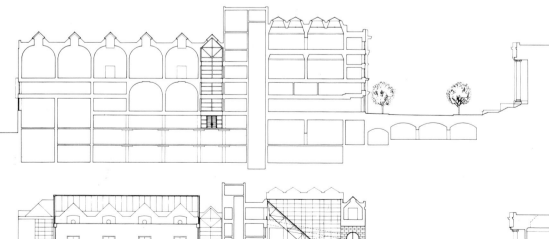

Centre: *Section through Sherbrooke Street*
Below: *Section through verrière room, lobby and original building*
Opposite: *Verrière room*

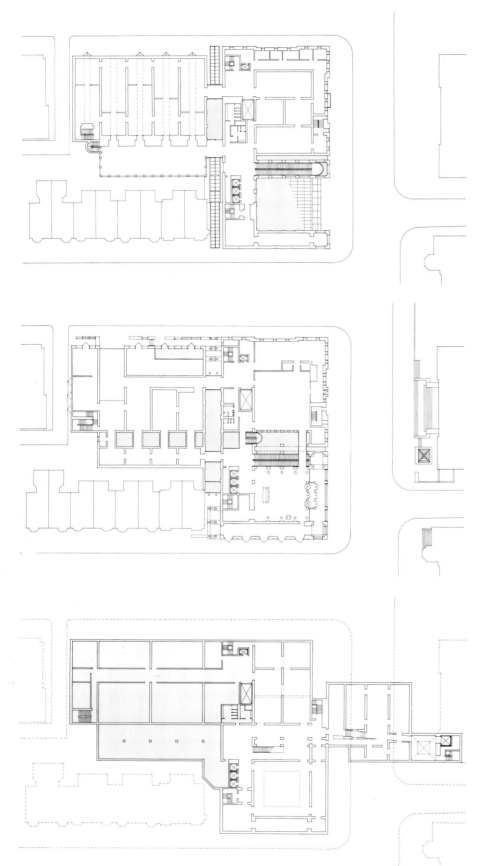

Above Left: *Upper level plan*
Centre Left: *Ground level plan*
Below Left: *Lower level plan*
Opposite, Below Left: *Section through stair and entry facade*
Opposite, Below Right: *Early study sketch of stair*

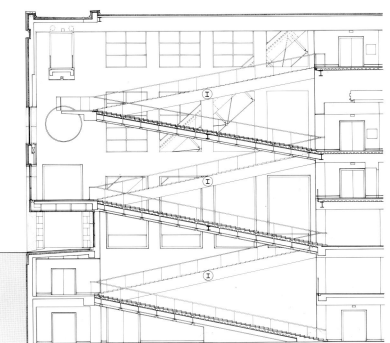

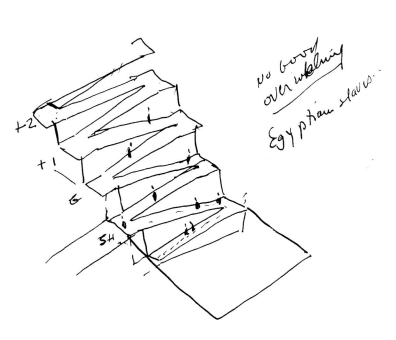

No good
over walking
Egyptian stairs.

+2
+1
G
SH

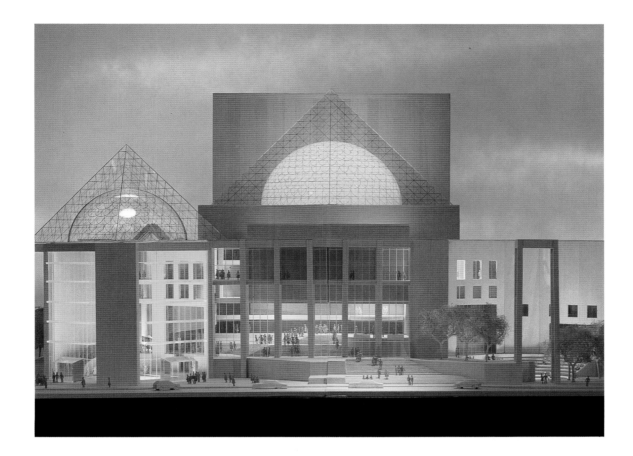

BALLET OPERA HOUSE

TORONTO, ONTARIO   1987-90

■ A new performance centre and home for the National Ballet of Canada and the Canadian Opera Company, the commission to design the Ballet Opera House included 42,270 square metres of performance spaces, rehearsal rooms and administrative offices for a city block in downtown Toronto.

At the heart of the project is a 2,000-seat auditorium and a foursquare arrangement of the main stage and three support stages. An acoustically isolated fifth stage accommodates full rehearsals. The main auditorium is traditionally planned after the great horseshoe opera houses of Europe, seeking an intimacy atypical of many modern performance halls, while providing direct sightlines and state-of-the-art acoustics.

A glassy, five-storey rotunda forms the corner entry and connects directly with the surrounding city: an interior urban piazza animated by the daily rhythms of pedestrians, shoppers, rehearsing

performers, theatre administrators and night-time crowds. The orchestra level of the rotunda gives access to a 'Gallery of the Artists', a linear spine organising the myriad operational rooms of the complex. Views into this space from the rotunda further conjoin the life of the city with the life of a major performing arts complex. Virtually every office, workshop and rehearsal room receives daylight.

Precast concrete panels inlaid with marble and granite marquetry enrich the basic exterior surface cladding of the building. An outdoor amphitheatre encourages informal performances and seeks to establish the Ballet Opera House as a destination for urban recreation. At night, domes above the public halls glow in the urban skyline.

The project was suspended by the newly elected provincial government in the spring of 1990, one month before construction was scheduled to begin.

Opposite and Above: *Competition model, night view* **Below:** *Conceptual sketches*

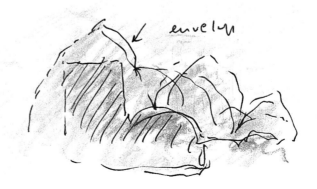

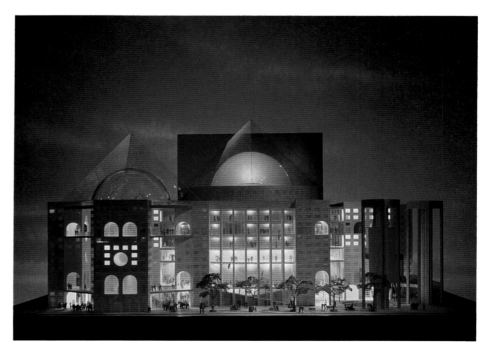

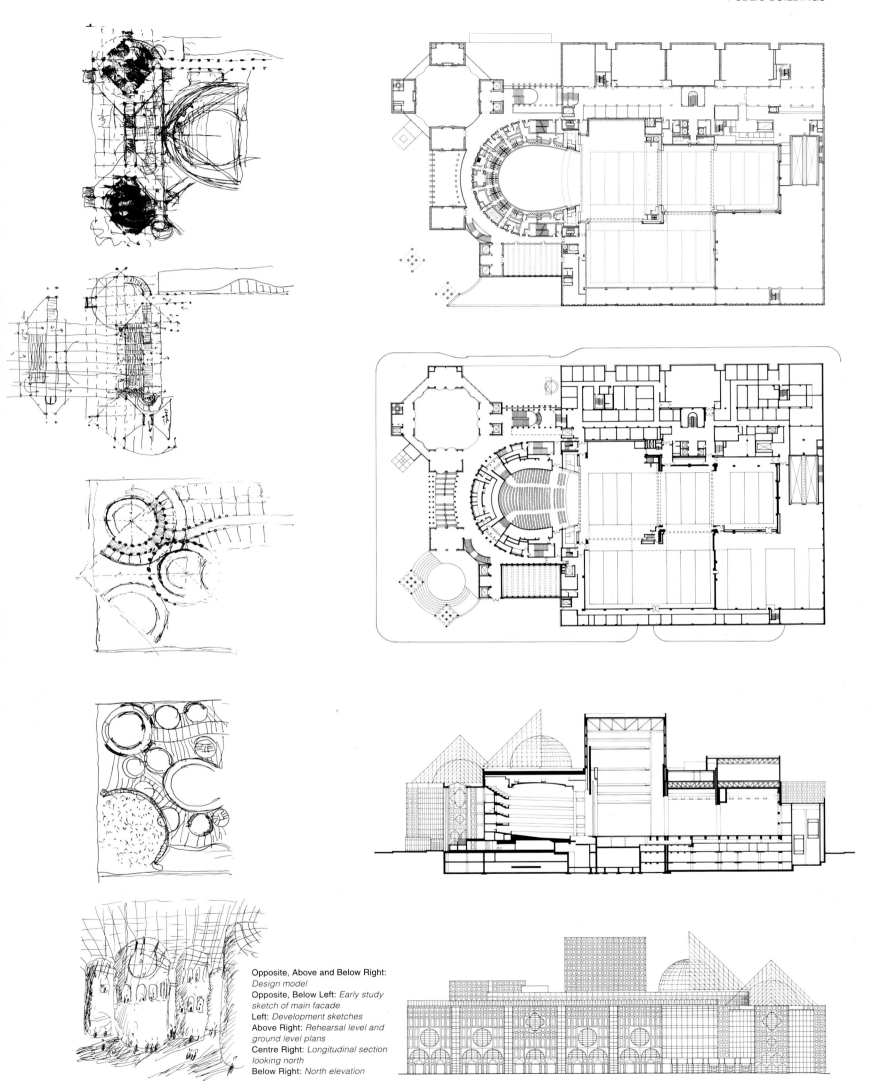

Opposite, Above and Below Right:
Design model
Opposite, Below Left: *Early study sketch of main facade*
Left: *Development sketches*
Above Right: *Rehearsal level and ground level plans*
Centre Right: *Longitudinal section looking north*
Below Right: *North elevation*

Above: *Perspective renderings of ballet, orchestra and choir rehearsal rooms*
Below Right: *Early section sketch*

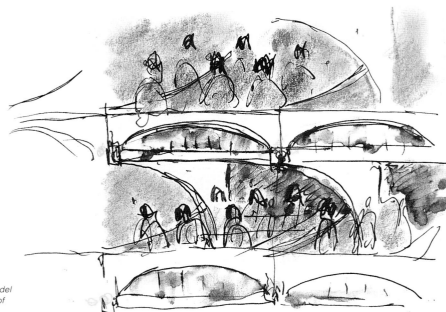

Above: *Main auditorium model*
Below Right: *Study sketch of balconies*

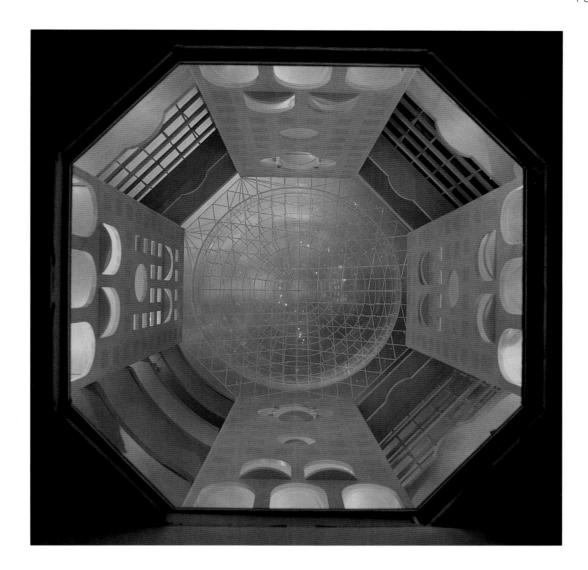

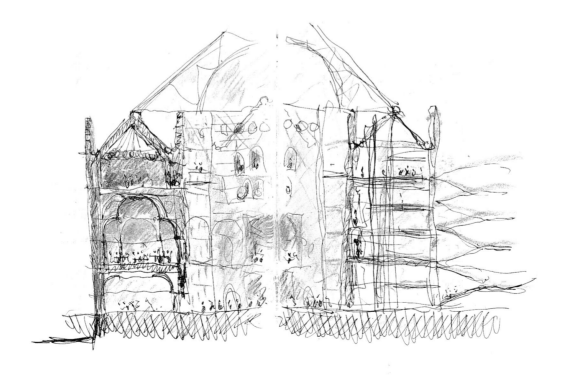

Above: *Detail of rotunda dome*
Below: *Section study sketch of rotunda*

OTTAWA CITY HALL
OTTAWA, ONTARIO   1988-94

■ The Ottawa City Hall complex includes over 37,000 square metres of new construction and renovation of the existing 1958 City Hall, to triple the size of the institution. As a complement to the original Modernist slab building, a series of indoor and outdoor spaces seeks to create a community of public functions on the grassy island site in the Rideau River.

The entrance to the complex opens directly on to the city's ceremonial route from Parliament Hill to the Governor General's residence. From this pavilion, a slightly curving, 140-metre, three-storey colonnade forms the open, public edge of the institution. This spine connects the old City Hall building and the new entrance with the most public functions of the complex: the community hall and cafeteria, the busiest municipal offices, the mayor's office pavilion and the council chamber. Bridging the central court, secondary passages lead from the spine to those

functions requiring only moderate public access, a series of city departments curved out to the river.

Transparent and metallic forms punctuate the roof line of the complex, creating dramatic light-filled rooms within and marking important public spaces on the exterior. Inscribed stainless steel and glass, these roofs rise from a base of solid masonry walls. Precast concrete columns and beams frame the public thoroughfares and, on the south-facing colonnade, support stainless steel brise-soleils.

A formal, stepped garden court bisects the complex and extends east. From the old City Hall, its succession of terraces form an outdoor porch, a flower garden and a pond that cascades into the Rideau River. An observation tower anchors the complex, giving the City Hall presence from downtown Ottawa.

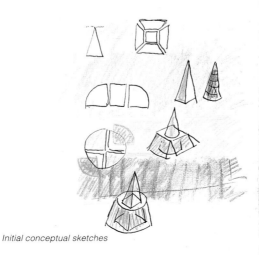

Initial conceptual sketches

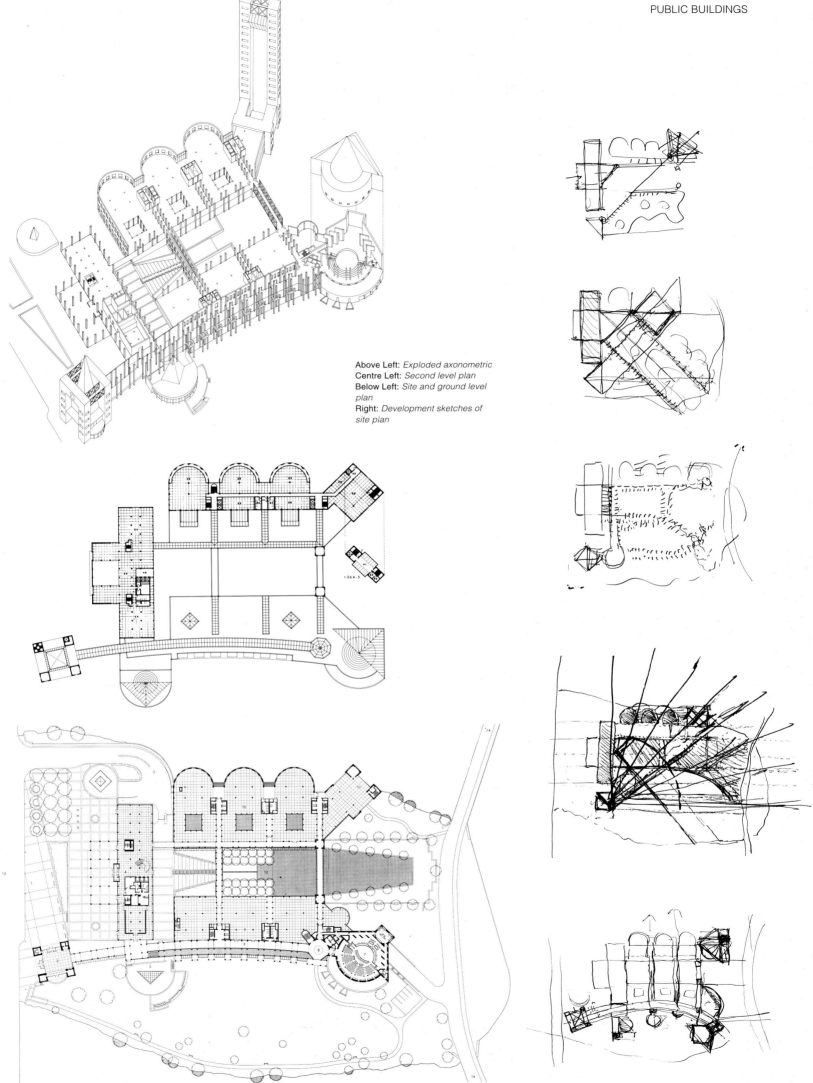

Above Left: *Exploded axonometric*
Centre Left: *Second level plan*
Below Left: *Site and ground level plan*
Right: *Development sketches of site plan*

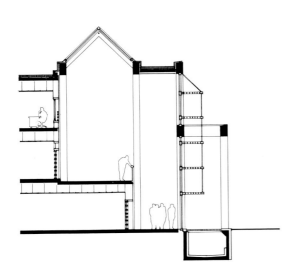

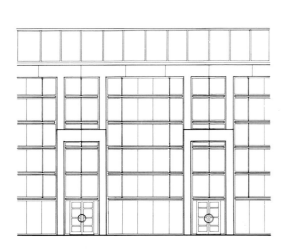

Above Left: *Detail section through colonnade*
Below Left: *Partial elevation of colonnade*

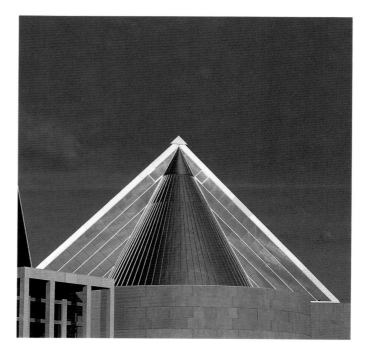

Detail section through council room

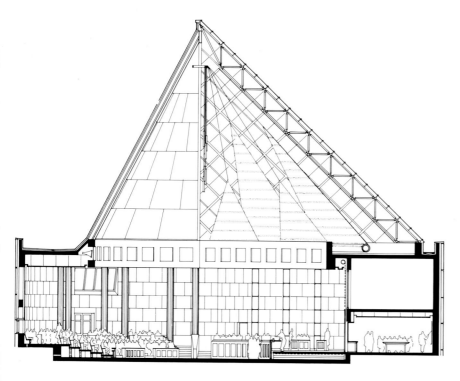

MUSEUM OF CONTEMPORARY ART
STUTTGART 1990

■ Many contemporary artists work outside the traditional forms of painting and sculpture, yet the spaces in which their work is shown often prevent the full realisation of complete installations, perform-ance art and large-scale constructions: artists rarely have the opportunity to create a total environment.

The proposed design for the new Museum of Contemporary Art in Stuttgart affords artists such an opportunity. In addition to a series of permanent galleries whose character, geometry and lighting can be changed as desired, the scheme is de-signed to accommodate galleries created specifi-cally to meet the requirements of temporary exhibitions.

Initially, proposed temporary gallery spaces include large rooms with pyramidal skylights, narrow rooms with sawtooth daylighting, black boxes, and an egg-shaped gallery with translucent walls. Served by a giant crane, these galleries can be replaced with new gallery forms and moved to off-

site storage. The crane, which becomes a spire when not in use, is anchored to a tower housing part of the permanent collection in a vertical sequence of galleries. In operation, the crane pivots to install new works or to exchange contemporary galleries.

Adjacent to downtown Stuttgart, the site forms a gateway to the city's cultural and civic core. Permanent galleries, organised as a linear sequence of 'houses', constitute the building's spine and relate the museum to the Alte Staatsgalerie, historic buildings across Konrad Adenauer/Neckarstrasse, and neighbouring residences rising on the hill towards the east.

Approached from the opposite direction, the museum is experienced in the context of a park bordered by a series of cultural institutions: the planetarium, the opera, and the theatre. The changing galleries, against the backdrop of the fixed museum spine, become an active part of the visitor's experience of the park.

Opposite, Above: *Site plan*
Opposite, below: *Competition model, view from park*
Above: *Competition model, east elevation*
Below Left: *Study model, gallery lighting and building section*
Below Right: *Competition model, showing installation of new temporary gallery*

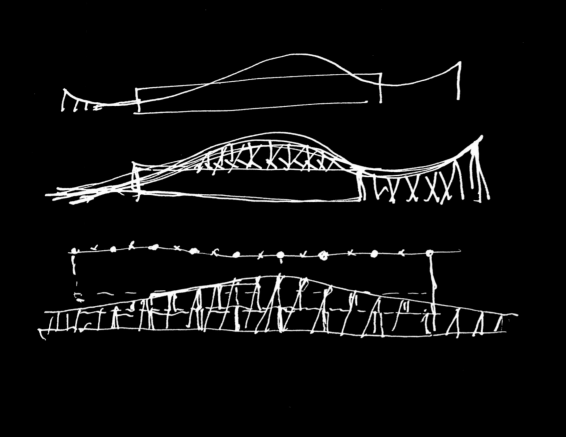

BOCA RATON MUSEUM CENTER
BOCA RATON, FLORIDA   1992-95

■ Boca Raton Museum Center, a conversion of a former IBM light industrial building, was designed to include exhibition space, an automobile museum, a large gallery for special exhibitions and large events, a 700-seat theatre, an art school, administration areas, support spaces, a restaurant, rental space, a library and a museum store.

Approximately two-thirds of the total 16,700 square metres in the existing single-storey building consists of 12-metre by 12-metre bays with 6-metre ceiling heights. The remaining space is organised in 6-metre by 12-metre bays, 3.5 metres high. A mezzanine level running north/south through the building accommodates mechanical equipment.

A large container for many diverse activities, the museum functions as a village of buildings within a building. The galleries, library and other spaces exist as roofless pavilions beneath a vast overhead framework of steel trusses. Throughout the project, daylight and artificial light are integrated as complementary systems, with a major skylight over the centre of the automobile museum.

A glazed pedestrian street cuts through the space, connecting entrances at each end and organising the diverse activities over the large floor space. On one side lies a large gallery and art museum; on the other, three small courtyards, the library, auto museum and theatre. In plan and section, the steel framing of this axis undulates, its skeletal structure glinting towards nearby Interstate 95.

Opposite, Above:
Conceptual sketches
Opposite, Below: *Design model, night view*
Above: *Interior perspective looking towards courtyard*
Below Left: *Study sketch of exhibition pavilions*
Below Right: *Early plan sketch*

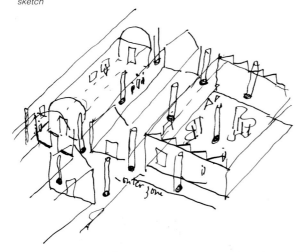

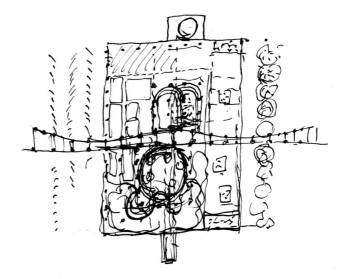

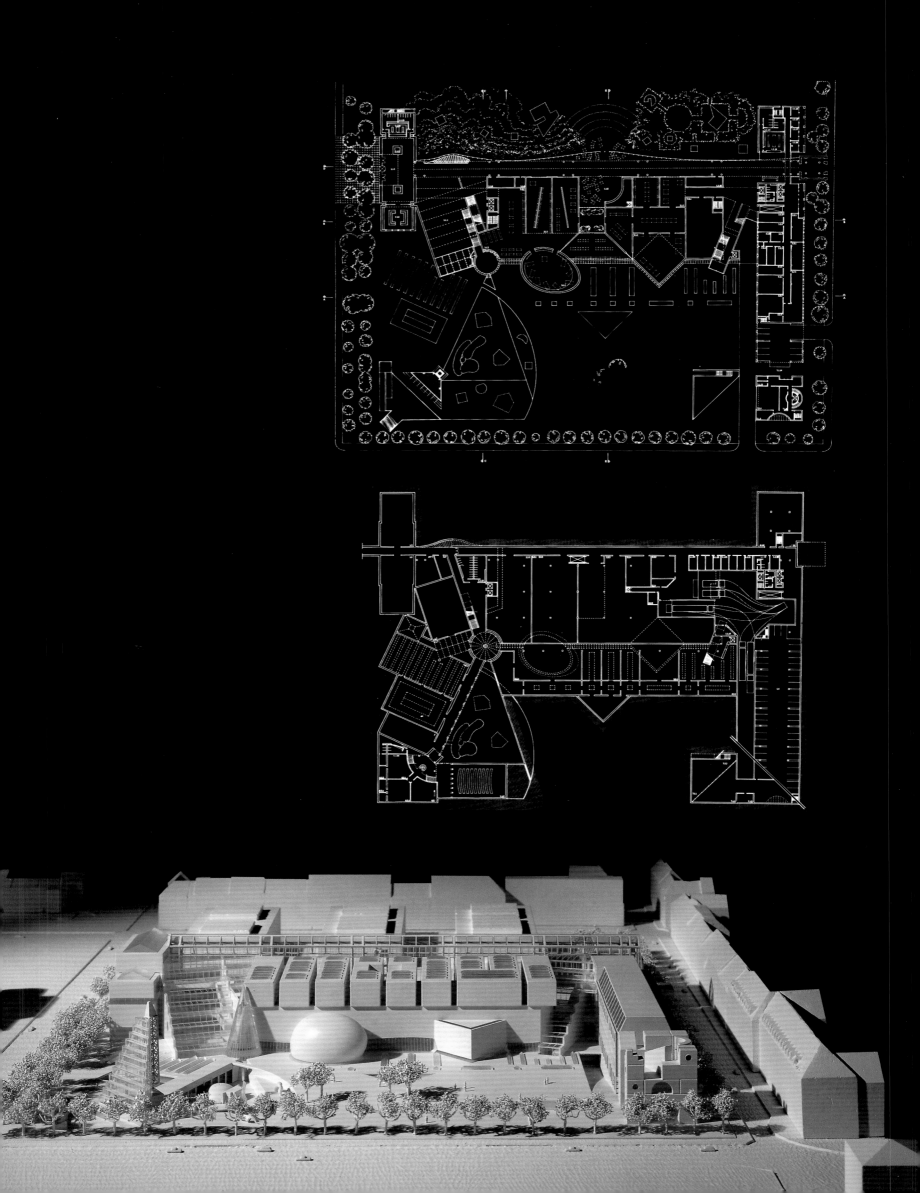

MUSEUM OF INDUSTRIAL DESIGN, ARCHITECTURE AND CONTEMPORARY ART
MUNICH 1992

Opposite, Above: *Site plan*
Opposite, Centre: *Lower level plan*
Opposite, Below: *Competition model*
Above: *Competition model, night view looking north*
Centre: *Museum cross section looking east*
Below: *Longitudinal building section looking north*

■ The competition design for the Munich Museum echoes the urban strategy of the adjacent Leo von Klenze Alte Pinakothek, centred upon a landscaped site. The two museums, set together in a grand park and surrounded by active, well defined streets, help to create a major museum precinct joining residential neighbourhoods with downtown cultural institutions. The museum is ordered by a glazed pedestrian 'street' that extends from the Alte Pinakothek across the street, with entrances at each end.

The diversity of the museum's departments and collections suggested the design of galleries that vary in shape, form, views and relationship to the exterior. The client's emphasis on daylighting led to the development of a number of natural lighting systems. Four gallery levels – one at street level, two above street level, and one below park level – each introduce daylight through different sources: skylights, clerestories and reflective light shafts. Skylights have also been integrated into the landscaping to illuminate the lower exhibition spaces designated for architecture, graphics and changing exhibits. Glass and porcelain collections are displayed against backlit walls. A translucent room – the egg – is intended for large three-dimensional objects.

The corner pavilion is a crane structure, 24 metres in height, which can convey large-scale work from delivery trucks along the street to the outdoor exhibition area. With its capacity to accommodate the unknown, the pavilion-crane matches the dynamism of the work displayed within its walls.

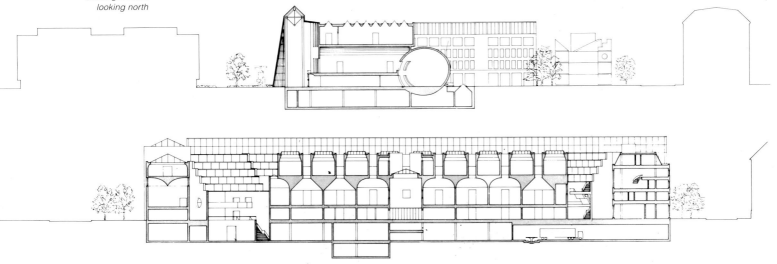

Opposite: *Initial concept studies*
Above: *Competition model, north elevation*
Centre: *Study sketches of south elevation, night and day*
Below: *Perspective sketches of south elevation, looking towards Alte Pinakothek*

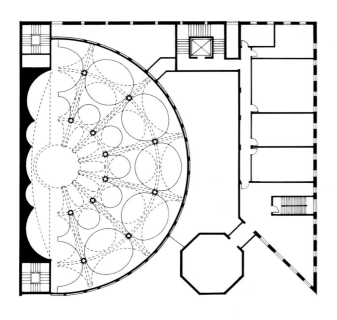

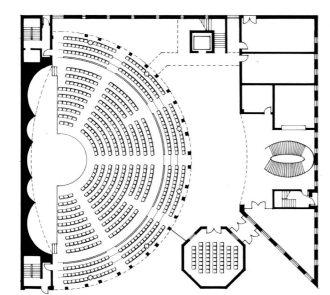

the sanctuary on the street
the school within

memory of
Borromini...

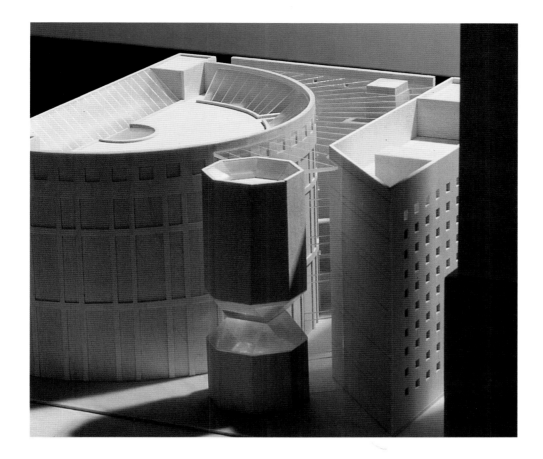

SINAI TEMPLE

CHICAGO, ILLINOIS 1994

■ During its long history, Sinai Temple has had several locations in various parts of Chicago, including a building designed by Louis Sullivan. The site for the new temple is within the Loop, flanked by a high-rise apartment building on one side and a five-storey, 19th-century structure on the other.

The competition design houses the sanctuary and a religious school with administrative offices in two independent volumes on either side of a light-filled, glazed court, which opens up to the street. Along the street edge, an octagonal tower marks the entrance, enclosing a day-lit chapel below and a library above.

The sanctuary is focused towards an undulating wall that contains the ark at its centre. Semi-circular arches step upwards five storeys, filtering daylight through a half-domed structure down to the sanctuary floor, and enclosing two galleries for additional seating during High Holidays. Below street level is a social hall; at roof level, the library looks out on a roof garden.

Opposite, Above Left:
Sixth floor plan
Opposite, Centre Left:
Ground floor plan
Opposite, Right:
Development sketches of interior/street relationship
Opposite, Below: *Design model, street view*
Above: *Design model, aerial view*
Below: *Site cross section*

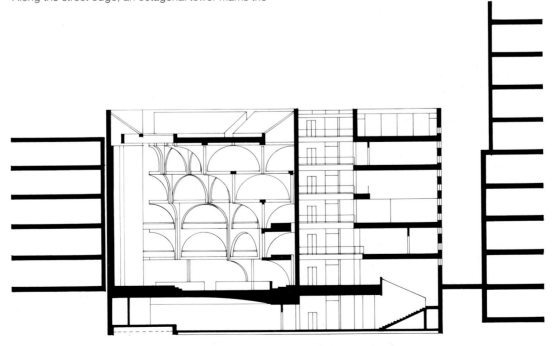

FORD CENTER FOR THE PERFORMING ARTS

VANCOUVER, BRITISH COLUMBIA   1994-95

■ Conceived in the tradition of the great Broadway theatres, this 1,800-seat theatre occupies a compact site located in the middle of a city block. On the street facade, the stone base of the building cuts away to reveal the gently arching volume of the auditorium within. Small metal shingles reflect the changing skies and the urban evening's neon glow.

At the south end of the facade, a five-storey glass cone forms the theatre entrance, parting the opaque street wall and breaking the cornice line of the facade. A glowing pinnacle by night and a vertical window by day, the transparent cone both lights and exposes the sequence of curving, layered lobby spaces within. During the day, the glass cone and a continuous south-facing, vertical window introduce

light and views of the surrounding city to matinée crowds. In the evening, the interior drama of theatre-goers radiates over the street. To the north end of the elevation, an arch framing the stage becomes a live electronic marquee in the skyline.

The public sequence through the theatre begins at the street level entrance lobby and proceeds up a series of dramatic stairs that fill a grand oval atrium. A faceted four-storey mirrored wall rises with the curving stair, fragmenting and reflecting the activity of three upper lobbies served by bars and lounges for the orchestra and balconies. Within the performance hall, the intimate scale of the balcony and dress circle is achieved by a maximum distance from seat to stage of only 27 metres.

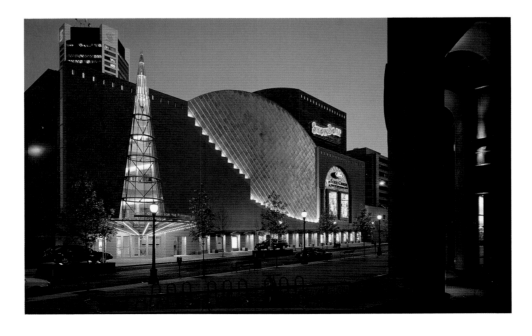

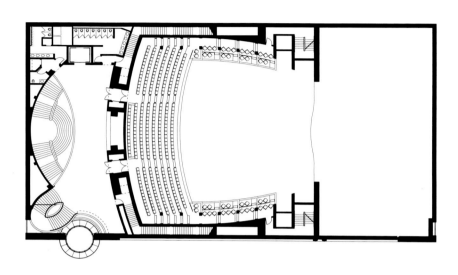

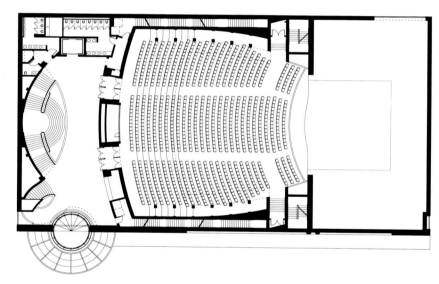

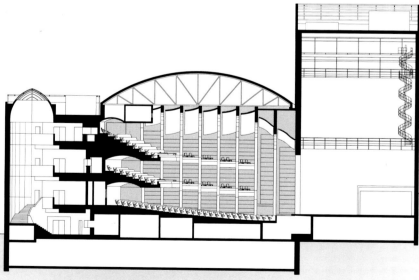

Above: *Orchestra level plan*
Centre: *Ground level plan*
Below: *Longitudinal building section*

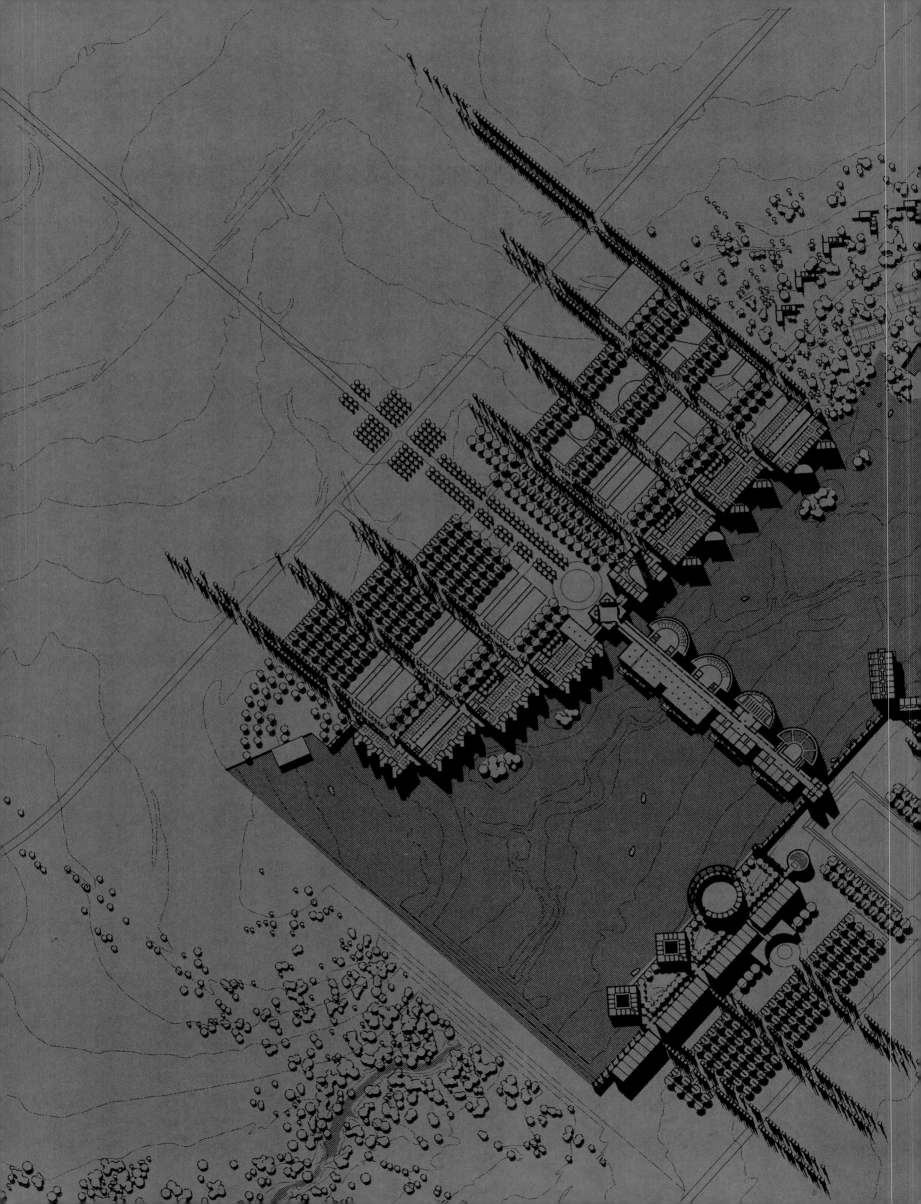

EDUCATION AND RESEARCH

MORGAN HALL

HARVARD BUSINESS SCHOOL, BOSTON, MASSACHUSETTS 1986-92

■ In 1984, the Harvard Business School sought to develop a new master plan to address contemporary servicing issues, car access and future expansion. The Harvard Business School campus was built according to a 1928 master plan by McKim, Mead and White. Won by competition, their design directed campus building projects for more than 50 years.

Originally focused towards the Charles River and Harvard College on the opposite bank, the modern campus is more often approached from parking lots bordering its former back door. The design for future development establishes a new entrance to the campus, integrates car traffic and parking into the campus' pedestrian circulation, and concentrates the faculty offices, which were previously scattered throughout the campus, into Morgan Hall and the adjacent Baker Library.

The first phase of the new master plan constituted renovating and extending Morgan Hall, the original 1928 administration building. A new L-shaped wing joins McKim, Mead and White's building to form a rectangular structure, with an exterior of brick and prefabricated concrete bay and bow windows unifying the new and original Georgian facades. An attic level, first proposed in 1928, was added to both wings. The

building now accommodates 164 faculty offices and work areas for 84 support staff and 78 research assistants.

Situated in the heart of the campus, pedestrian walkways lead to entrances on all four sides of the building. Cross-axes within the building, paved with slate, intersect at a glass-roofed court built around a fourth-century Roman mosaic owned by Dumbarton Oaks, the trustees for Harvard University.

The east and west axes are continuously open to skylights four storeys above. With adjustable mirrors to maximise direct daylighting through the long New England winter, this glass-roofed spine lights the main hall and four levels of support staff areas, while attic offices gain views and daylight through glass dormers.

In close collaboration with the clients, a system was developed for interlocking, L-shaped faculty offices that contain a desk, soft-seating area, meeting/work table, and storage within a maximum affordable area of 23 square metres. Clusters of eight offices with four support staff areas seek to create an efficient but intimate working relationship. To test the concept, a full-scale, fully furnished mock-up was constructed and suggestions from the users were incorporated into the final design.

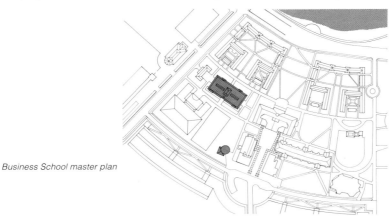

Business School master plan

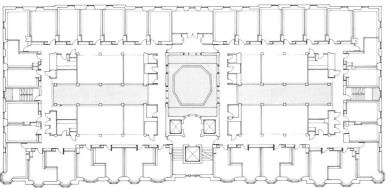

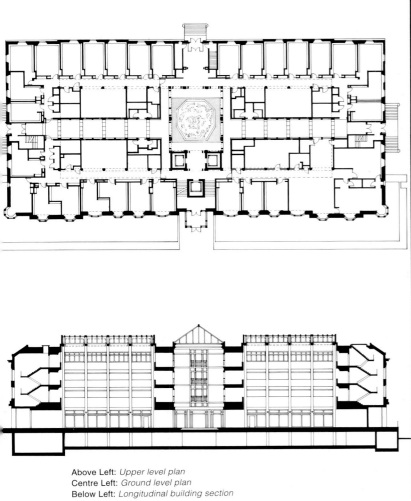

Above Left: *Upper level plan*
Centre Left: *Ground level plan*
Below Left: *Longitudinal building section*

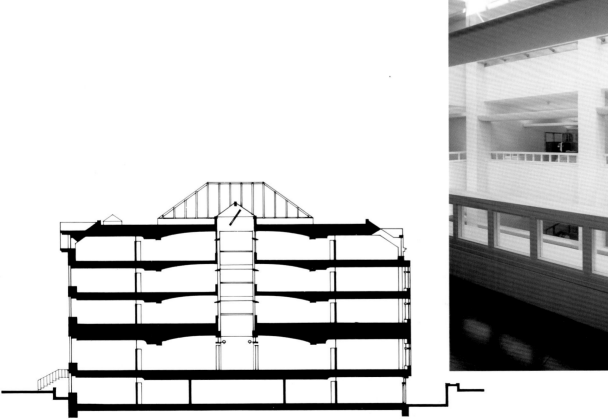

Building cross section

CLASS OF 1959 CHAPEL

HARVARD BUSINESS SCHOOL, BOSTON, MASSACHUSETTS 1986-92

■ The Class of 1959 Chapel is a nondenominational sacred and meditative space. The cylindrical, green oxidised copper drum intersects a glazed interior garden that terraces down into the earth. Biblical plants, flowering trees and water form a transparent oasis in the heart of the campus, and create a quiet transition from daily to spiritual experience. A tower timepiece by artist Karl Schlamminger stands at the entry to the chapel, its gold sphere rising and falling through the 24 hours of day and night.

Inside, the 100-seat sanctuary is contained by undulating banded concrete walls that rise to a height of over 8 metres. Multiple axes encourage any spatial orientation of worship, and since the Chapel opened, exceptional acoustics have regularly drawn instrumental and vocal performers to fill the room with sound.

During the day, light enters the sanctuary from overhead. Within the skylights, large-scale acrylic prisms filled with mineral oil are positioned to refract sunlight and wash the walls with the colours of the visible solar spectrum. A rotating drum supports this array and follows the sun's path; as the sun moves across the sky, glowing patterns slowly move and change across the chapel walls.

Below Left: Cross section through garden and sanctuary
Below Right: Ground level plan

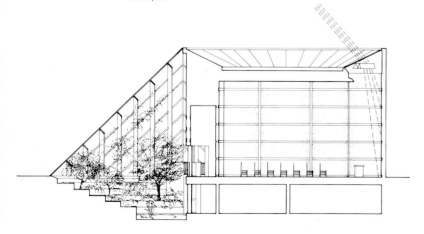

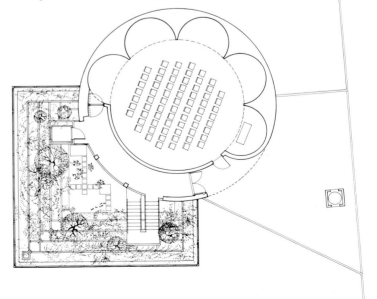

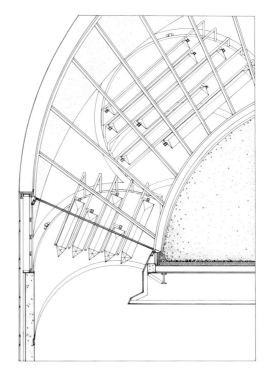

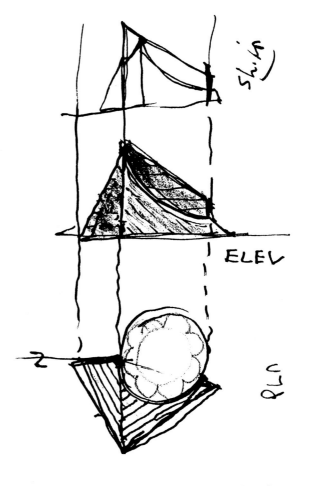

Above Right: *Axonometric section through roof assembly*
Below Right: *Development sketches*

NEVE OFER COMMUNITY CENTER

TEL AVIV-JAFFA, ISRAEL   1989-95

■ Neve Ofer is situated in Abu Kabir, a disadvantaged neighbourhood that is currently beginning to develop. Conceived as a symbol and a support for the community's aspirations, the building defines a central piazza as a focus for internal activities and a connection to an adjacent neighbourhood park. Paved and landscaped, the court is enclosed by a continuous colonnade linking the building's four main areas: a library, an auditorium wing with a 280-seat theatre, and two wings of workshops. A road that originally crossed through the centre of the site is designed as an open pedestrian axis, directly linking different sectors of the neighbourhood with the heart of the community centre.

Banded with local limestone, the building is sedate from the exterior, enclosing a rich and varied core. Within its walls, gallery spaces, activity rooms, offices, a senior citizens club with its own garden, arts and crafts workshops, and a small gym provide day and evening activities for all members of the community. Each wing is lit naturally, with daylight filtered through the arcade and horizontal slots in the heavy exterior wall. The upper workshops are roofed with vaulted skylights.

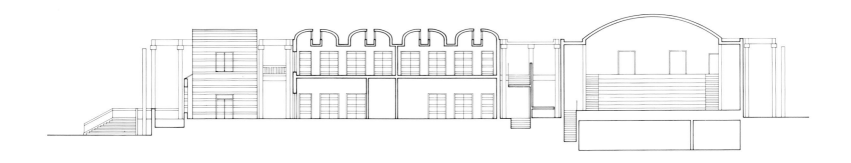

Longitudinal building section

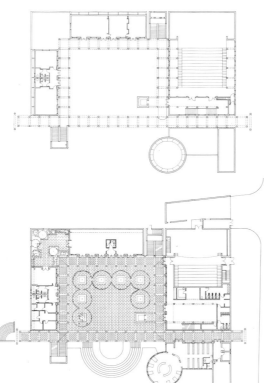

Centre Left: *Upper level plan*
Below Left: *Lower level plan*

ROSOVSKY HALL

HARVARD-RADCLIFFE COLLEGE, CAMBRIDGE,
MASSACHUSETTS 1992-94

■ Rosovsky Hall serves as the home for the Harvard-Radcliffe Hillel student and faculty organisation. Surrounded by the historic Harvard campus and the city of Cambridge, the site neighbours Lowell House and the Fly Club, and faces the Harvard Lampoon and Quincy House.

Three vaulted wings containing a dining room, two congregation spaces, a library, classrooms, and offices surround a circular trellised courtyard. Distinct spaces within are united by the centralised outdoor court whose transparent perimeter joins each room within the whole institution; and the life of the institution with the rest of the campus. Encircled with light at night and enlivened with activity in warm weather, this outdoor gathering space becomes the major formal expression of the building. While virtually open on its public side, it stands slightly above street level and is screened by a peristyle of wisteria vines.

On a diagonal axis with the busy thoroughfare of Mount Auburn Street, the entry tower and the onion-domed tower of the Lampoon building create a new forecourt for this district of the campus. With walls of limestone-coloured precast concrete and brick, and leaded copper, skylit roof vaults, the building devotes its three upper-level skylit rooms to the library and congregation spaces.

Below Left:
Ground level plan
Below Right: *Plan and
elevation sketches*

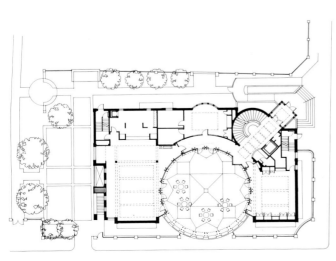

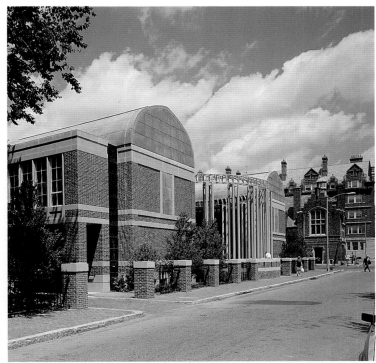

N15   N20
N10   N25   N30
                      N35
S55   N40
S50   HEB Tunnel   Waxahachie,
                    Texas   N45
S45
                              N50
S40   N55
                       S10
        S15   IR 8
S35 S30
          S25   S20   IR 5
              Main Collider
              Ring Tunnel

SUPERCONDUCTING SUPER COLLIDER
WAXAHACHIE, TEXAS 1992-93

■ Located south of Dallas, Texas on flat prairie land, the Superconducting Super Collider Laboratory was designed to house the world's largest and most advanced machine for high-energy physics research. The client, the US Department of Energy and a consortium of universities known as University Research Associates, desired a master plan for the campus, and design guidelines for the experimental and industrial outbuildings required at intervals along the accelerator tunnel's 87-kilometre perimeter.

To anchor the campus on a wide stretch of grazing land, the design focuses on a cooling pond that is one of the functional requirements of the accelerator. On the west side of the pond, offices and laboratories form the private side of the community, planned to grow and expand in layers like a mill town along a river. On the east side, public

functions include an education centre, a hotel and villas for visiting scientists. Joining public and private across the water is a double-height bridge building with cafeterias, meeting rooms, a large auditorium, a library and two experiment control rooms. Transparent and open towards the water and horizon on the south, rounded and dam-like towards the north, this long link provides the opportunity for interaction among all members of the scientific and lay community. Adjustable canopies shade public terraces facing south across the pond. For the construction of the experimental and industrial buildings, corrugated sheet metal was proposed to span vaulted sheds of different sizes.

Work on the Superconducting Super Collider was suspended by the US Congress in 1993.

Opposite, Below Left:
Diagram of observation points and facilities along outer accelerator ring
Below: *Concept sketch of cooling pond elevation*

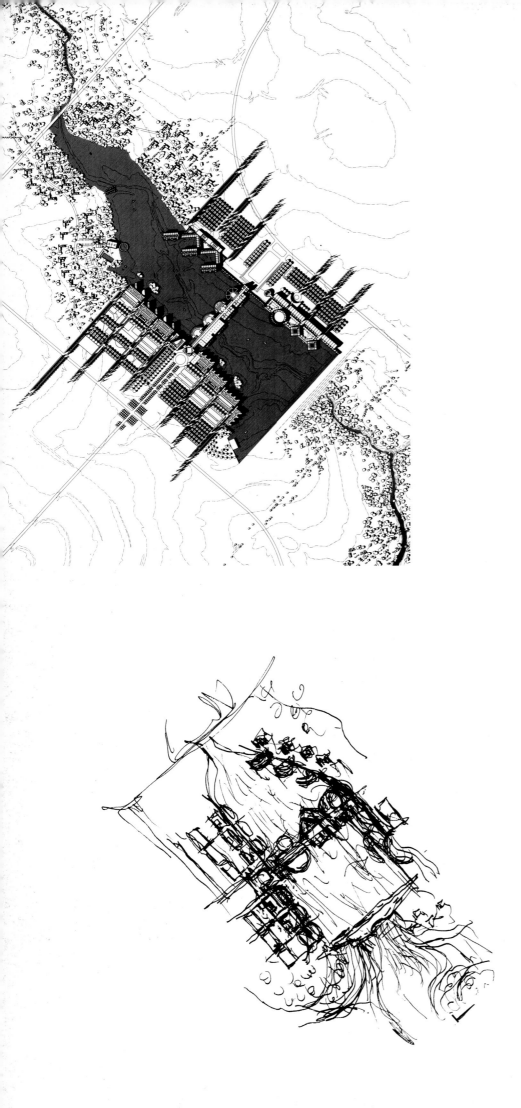

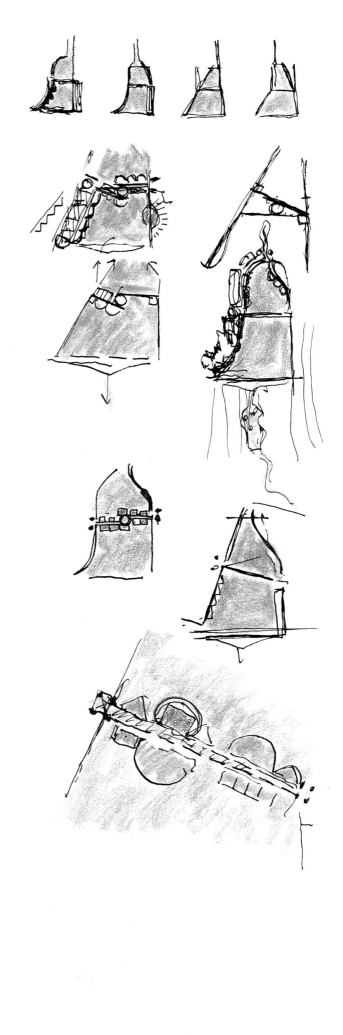

Above Left: *Site plan*
Below Left: *Early site sketch*
Right: *Site development sketches*

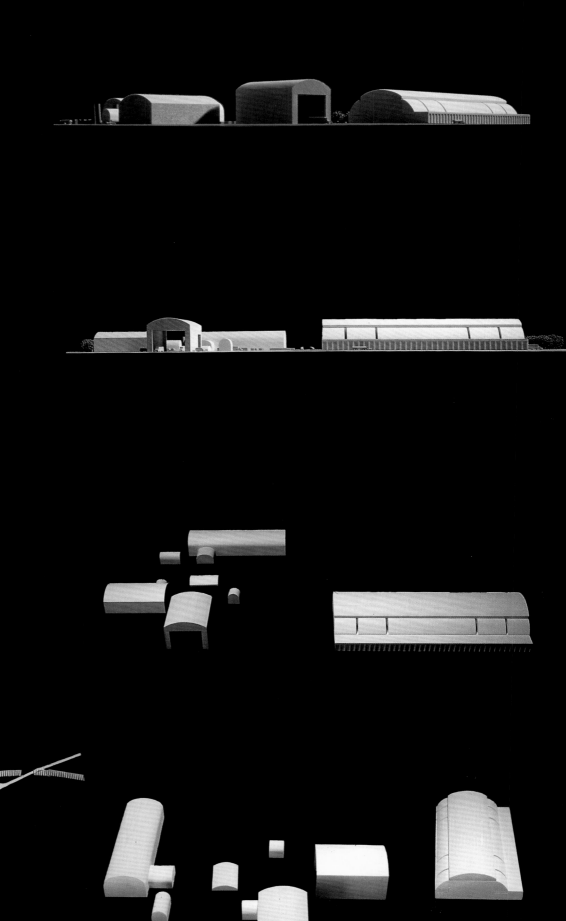

Right: *Industrial outbuildings accommodating detectors and cryogenic facilities*
Below Left: *Accelerator ring landscaping and outbuilding points*

The sense of flow, objects in the water "linked" many buildings

Above Left: *Early concept sketches*
Above Right: *Perspective sketch of bridge building, north facade*
Below Left: *Study sketches of south-facing sunshading*
Below Right: *Perspective sketch of bridge building sunshading*

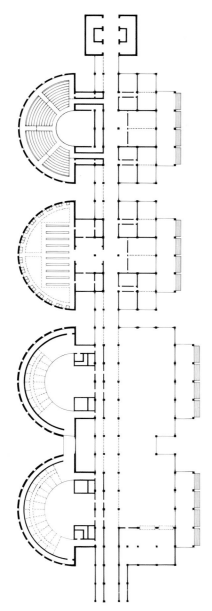

Left: *Lower level plan of bridge building*
Above Right: *Aerial view of design model*
Centre Right: *Detail of design model looking south-west towards bridge building and laboratories*
Below Right: *Detail of design model looking north-west towards laboratories and shaded terraces of bridge building*

SKIRBALL MUSEUM AND CULTURAL CENTER
LOS ANGELES, CALIFORNIA   1986-95

■ The Skirball Museum and Cultural Center stands at the base of the Santa Monica Mountains off the 405 freeway, a midpoint between the Los Angeles Basin and the San Fernando Valley. The 11,600-square-metre building houses a museum of the Jewish-American experience, a conference centre, an educational centre, classrooms and meeting rooms, a resource centre, and a 350-seat auditorium. The 2,500-square-metre communications centre and event hall is scheduled to begin construction in 1997.

Responding to the site's dramatic topography, the building forms a series of longitudinal wings tucked against the steep natural slope. An amphitheatre and the back wall of the communications centre buttress an unstable area of the mountain against mud slides. Courtyards are oriented towards views of the hills and canyon beyond. The main outdoor gathering space, a shaded water court for conferences, events and receptions, is defined by a double-height, trellised arcade. From the courtyard, a stair leads to a sculpture garden and a footpath that curves around the hill. A lookout and meditation pavilion, as yet unbuilt, will serve as a beacon for the complex with a panoramic view.

The building's exposed concrete frame supports stainless steel infill panels that contrast with and reflect the alternating pink granite and warm-coloured concrete bands of the base. Precast concrete trellises, covered in wisteria, extend over outdoor walkways and courtyards. At sunset, the stainless steel vaulted roofs glow against the darkening Santa Monica hills.

Below Left: *Site plan*
Below Right: *Site development sketches*

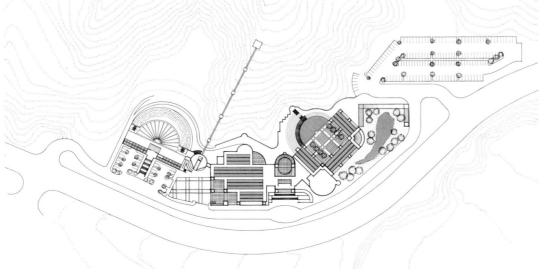

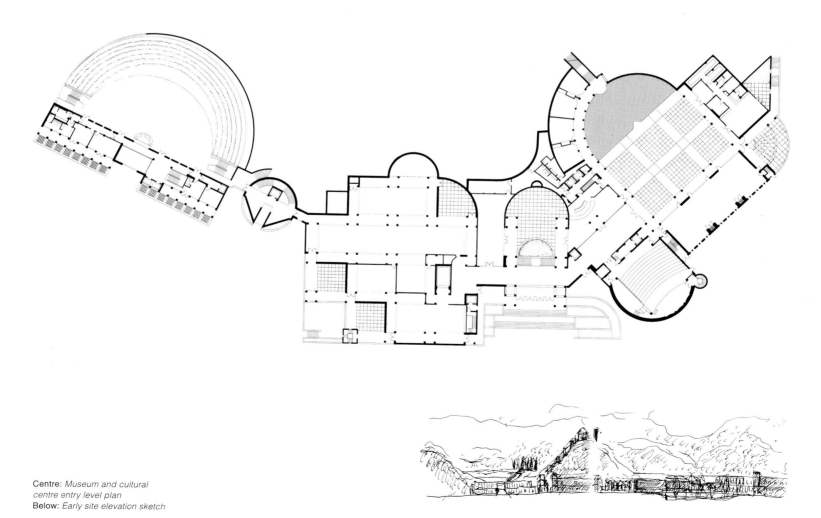

Centre: *Museum and cultural centre entry level plan*
Below: *Early site elevation sketch*

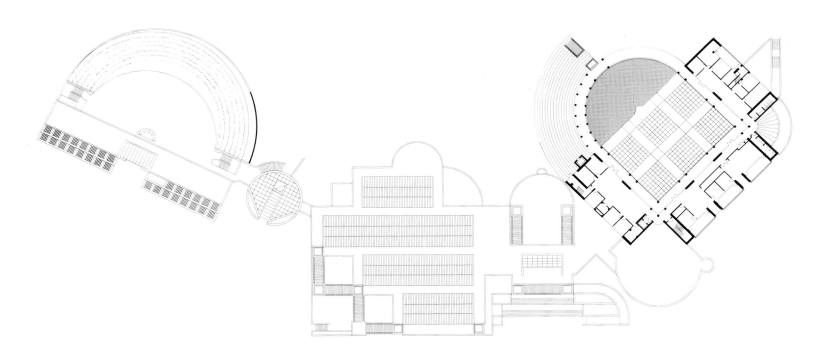

Centre: *Cultural centre upper level plan*
Below: *Early building elevation sketch*

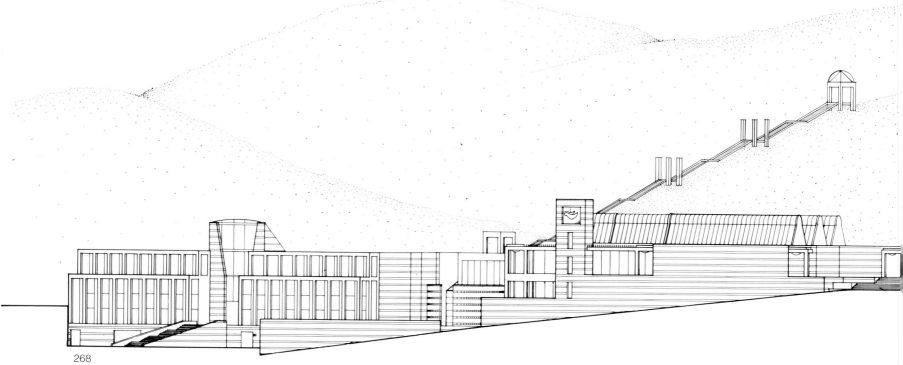

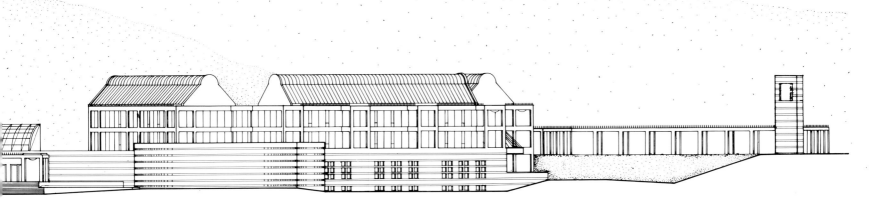

Site elevation

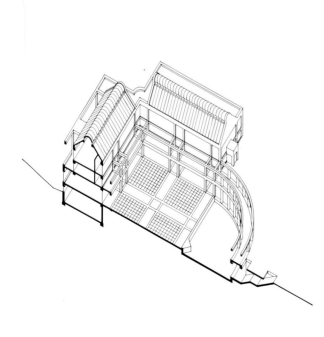

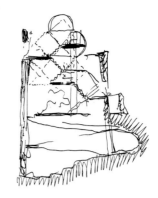

Opposite, Below Left: *Cut-away axonometric through cultural centre water court*
Above Right: *Early section and elevation sketches of children's museum*

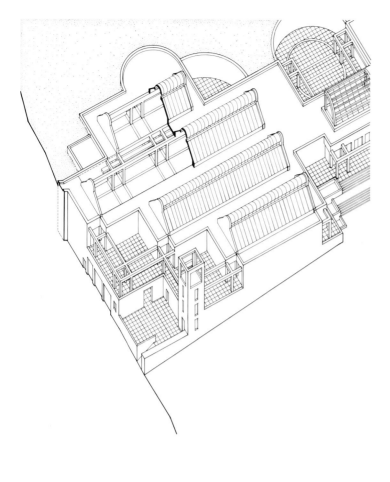

Above Left: *Cutaway axonometric of museum and entry court*

MIXED-USE FACILITIES

COLUMBUS CENTER

NEW YORK CITY   1985-87

■ The result of a competition for the redevelopment of the New York Coliseum site, Columbus Center is situated on a 16,000-square-metre parcel bordering Columbus Circle. Located at the south-west corner of Central Park, the site constitutes a point of transition between the residential scale of the Upper West Side and the more massive commercial scale of Midtown.

The design incorporates an existing 21-storey office structure and, in addition to providing a hotel, apartments, major retail centre and office space, includes the headquarters and several trading floors for Salomon Brothers. This enormous programme is separated into two main towers of 69 and 62 storeys, set on a base that encloses a four-storey garden atrium. Secondary towers meet the cornice height of apartment buildings lining Central Park

West, and engage at their base an open, skylit galleria. A rich network of public spaces is designed to reinforce the civic character of Columbus Circle and to enhance the public life of the street in this section of the city. Extending from Broadway to 58th Street, the galleria forms a gently curving facade along the Circle itself.

Continuously set back to form five-storey daylit gardens, the design provides offices with light, space, and a strong visual connection with Central Park. Arrays of smaller indoor gardens for the two-storey residential units meet the sky with a transparent crystalline crown.

Work on the Center was halted due to the withdrawal of Salomon Brothers from the project, following the downturn of the stock market in October 1987.

Study sketch of Columbus Circle facade

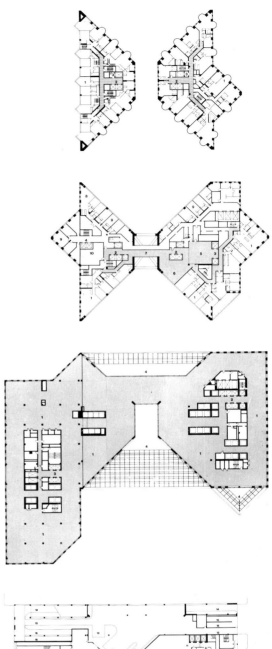

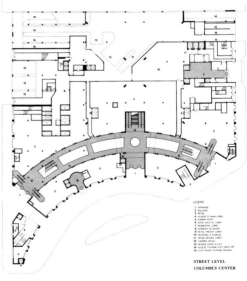

STREET LEVEL
COLUMBUS CENTER

Above left: *Rendered perspective
of public galleria*
Below Left: *Rendered perspective
section looking north through
main entry, galleria, atrium, and
trading floors*
Above Right: *Typical apartment
level plans*
Centre Right: *Typical office level plan*
Below Right: *Street level plan*

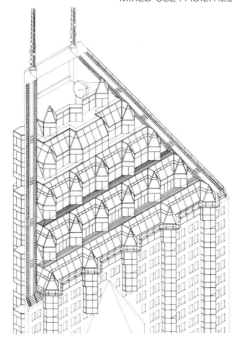

Opposite, Below: *Early concept sketch*
Above Left: *North elevation of design model*
Above Right: *Detail axonometric of north tower crown and roof gardens*
Right: *Sketches of Columbus Circle elevation*

LIBRARY SQUARE

PUBLIC LIBRARY AND FEDERAL GOVERNMENT HEADQUARTERS,
VANCOUVER, BRITISH COLUMBIA   1992-95

■ The result of an international competition, Library Square occupies a city block in an expanding section of downtown Vancouver. The project contains Vancouver's 32,500-square-metre Central Library, a 27,800-square-metre Federal Government Office Tower, retail and service facilities and underground parking for 700 cars.

The building consists of a seven-storey rectangular core containing open book stacks, library services, circulation and the latest data technology. This core is wrapped by an ellipse, a freestanding, precast concrete double shell that holds study alcoves, reading arcades and public walkways with views of the city. At the north-east corner of the site, this curving exterior facade rises into the 21-storey Federal Office Tower.

From either end of the library complex, a public promenade flows from the street around the library's interior core. Enclosed by one face of the library

block, shear and glassy, and the inside face of the arcaded shell holding small cafes and stores, this glazed urban room is flooded with sunlight. An auditorium and meeting rooms are located below the promenade.

Within the library, visitors rise through the centre to collect books and study materials, and traverse light steel bridges to a long curving reading arcade with tables, carrels, and interior and exterior views. Mechanical sub-floors carry all the building services, computer data and air circulation systems, providing continuous, uninterrupted shallow barrel-vaulted ceilings. The rectangular library core is roofed with a garden overlooked by two storeys of Provincial Offices.

The elliptical shell is constructed with an outer facing of large-scale precast concrete elements made with an aggregate of local red granite. In the construction process, these elements served as formwork for the cast *in situ* concrete structure. The office tower is clad in matching precast concrete, with a taut, glazed corner facing east towards the bay.

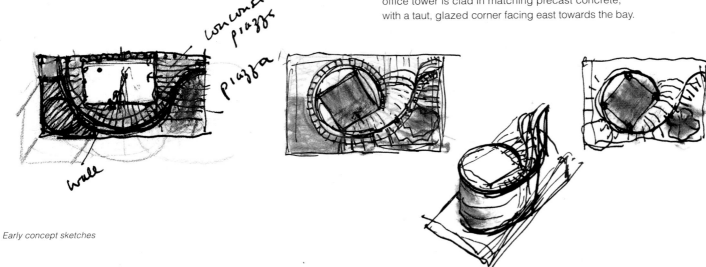

Early concept sketches

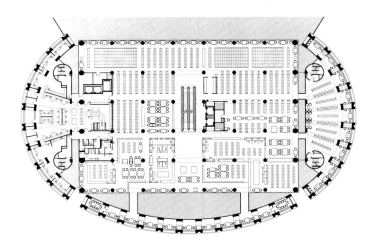

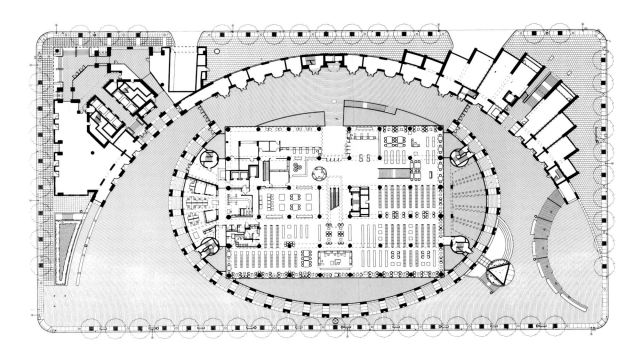

Opposite, Below: *Early studies*
Above: *Fourth level plan*
Centre: *Ground level plan*
Below: *Longitudinal site section
through library*

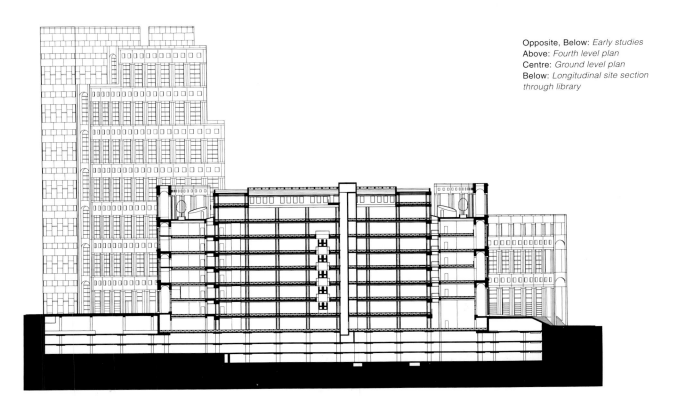

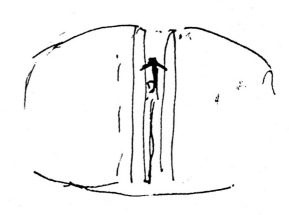

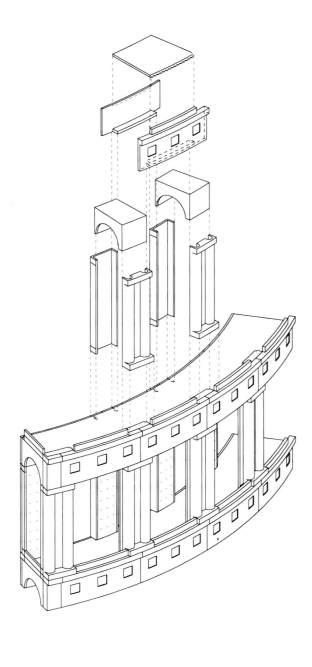

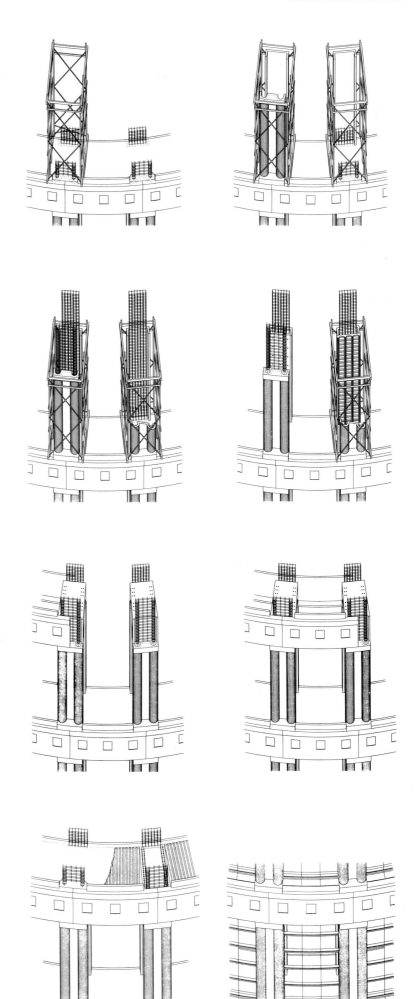

Above Left: *Precast concrete formwork assembly diagram*
Right: *Construction sequence of precast concrete as formwork for cast* in situ *reinforced concrete frame*

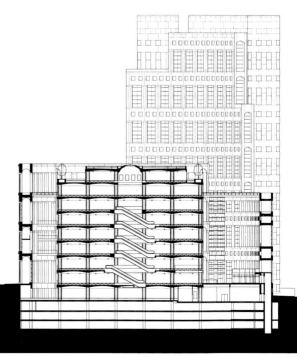

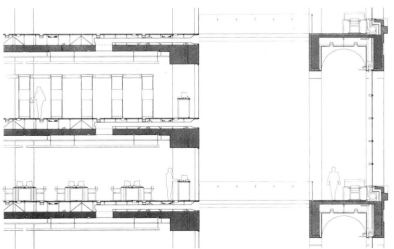

Below Left: *Site cross section through library*
Below Right: *Detail section through library and reading arcade*

CITY DESIGN

KEUR FARAH PAHLAVI

SENEGAL   1975-78

■ Keur Farah Pahlavi was designed as a new industrial harbour, serving nearby phosphate mines and an oil refinery. The site selected for its construction is 160 kilometres north of Dakar, the capital of Senegal. Here, sand dunes stretch approximately 2 kilometres inland from the severe Atlantic coast, where they drop suddenly 6 to 9 metres into an area known as the Niayes. In the Niayes, surface water is captured in a narrow band of lakes and ponds, sandwiched between the dunes to the west and the gently rising plateau of peanut fields to the east. The Niayes is oasis-like: rich in vegetation, palms and other trees.

The city is planned for a population of 200,000 people, many to be employed in the city's refinery, mining and port facilities, others lured from the crowded capital. Under a barter deal with Iran, tankers would deliver Iranian oil for refining, and return with loads of phosphate fertilisers. The city design seeks to provide for future growth, optimal pedestrian circulation, and public transportation in a culture where few own cars, as well as maximal preservation of the extraordinary natural features of the site.

The physical plan of the city follows the line of the Niayes. Commerce, community institutions and recreational facilities constitute the city's central spine, with residential neighbourhoods sloping inwards on either side of a couplet of one-way urban boulevards. The neighbourhoods are served by smaller-scale streets perpendicular to the spine. Where the two road systems intersect, neighbourhood centres with shops and services open towards the central district and are linked together by its roads and parks. Contained on their outer edges by limited-access perimeter roads, the neighbourhoods and central

district are entirely free of fast-moving traffic. The Niayes winds through the city as a lush linear centre, and a pedestrian fabric of paths, markets, squares and bazaars allows residents to travel by foot completely independent of the city's road system. Certain roads extend to the beach, permanently preserving the coast as an open space for recreation.

As the city develops, its central spine will grow along the path of the Niayes. The existing infrastructure, public transportation and road system will thus guide and connect naturally with new development. Phase one is planned several kilometres inland, with growth towards the harbour so that the most dense and diverse activity will occur here, when the city reaches a stage of economic and civic maturity.

The proposed housing is designed to accommodate the traditional Senegalese pattern of living, while at the same time allowing a significant increase in density to preserve land and provide basic infrastructure economically. The typical housing cluster forms an extended family compound, enclosing a series of communal courtyards that generate cross-ventilation and provide outdoor spaces for the many daily outdoor activities. The upper level in each of the two basic housing types is designed to shade the main courtyard from the scorching direct sunlight.

The construction materials are all local: concrete masonry units form the walls; small, prefabricated concrete planks form the floors; and roofs are moulded asbestos cement with laminated coconut pulp for insulation. With the detailed design and prototype units completed, development of the city was interrupted when the Khomeini regime in Iran discontinued its support.

Opposite: *Site plan*
Above: *Aerial view of site looking north-west*

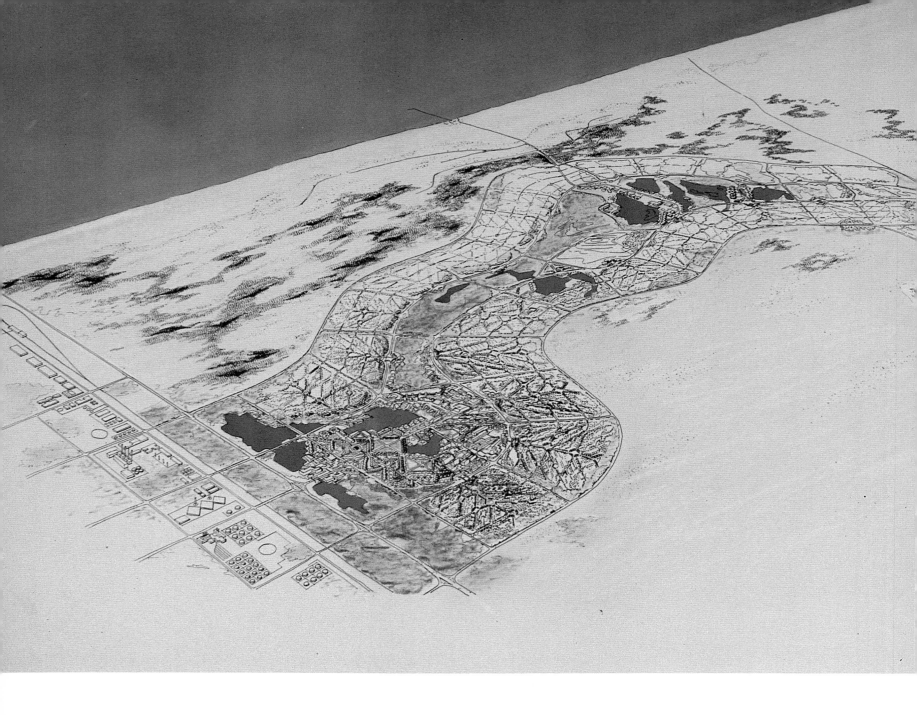

Above: *Aerial perspective site plan*
Below: *Site strategy alternatives
studying relationship between city,
sea, and landscape*

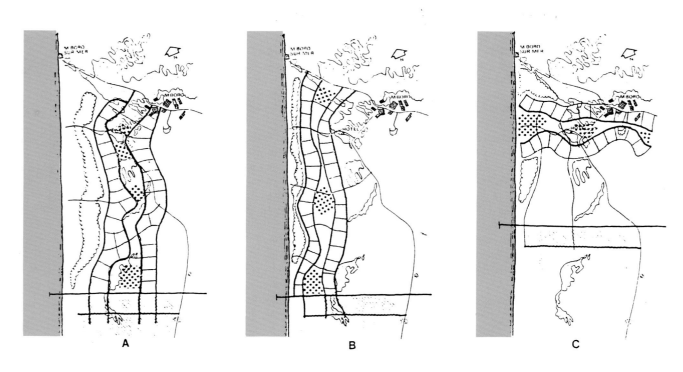

A   B   C

Above Left: *Aerial perspective
of town centre*
Below Left: *Site diagram showing
neighbourhoods and town centres
along Niayes*
Right: *Street section studies of
relationship between building
massing and sunshading*

OLD PORT OF MONTREAL

MONTREAL, QUEBEC   1977-90

■ Montreal's Old Port consists of a series of 19th-century piers and grain elevators, which border the entire Old City of Montreal, extend north along a street of 18th- and 19th-century structures, and culminate in two major civic landmarks. The Place Jacques Cartier slopes up from the edge of the St Lawrence River towards the Courthouse and City Hall, and the historic Bonsecours Market, once forming a civic waterfront. During the 20th century, this city edge was buried behind a series of port warehouses, piers and other industrial activities that container shipping has rendered obsolete in the past decade.

The new design for the Port proposes to reunite the harbour with the Old City and to re-establish the waterfront as a vital urban district. By connecting the outermost edge of each pier, traffic through the area would be diverted to the perimeter of one large waterfront zone encompassing the Old City structures, the piers, and the river. The currently abandoned harbour area would then become a relatively traffic-free network of public open space and mixed-use development.

Because the level of the St Lawrence River fluctuates approximately 4.5 metres seasonally, a 7.5-metre drop exists between the city's edge and the water. Links between the piers would allow the inner harbour water level to be maintained at a higher level than the outer river water, further closing the distance between the water and the activity of the city. The piers, warehouses and grain elevators would be re-used as parks, converted housing, markets, museums and other public facilities to create a vital mix of uses for the district as a whole. Finally, certain portions of the landfill between the piers would be removed to restore the civic stature of the original waterfront buildings and re-establish civic gathering spaces like the Bonsecours Market along the river.

Several alternative designs were developed and presented for public discussion. Of the four alternatives proposed, the design representing minimal engineering and minimal private development was selected. To date, several warehouses have been recycled for public use, and a promenade built along the harbour.

Opposite: *Aerial view of design model*
Above: *Aerial view of site*

Above Left: *View of existing site looking north along original 18th-century waterfront*
Below Left: *Rendered perspective of design proposal reestablishing urban waterfront*
Above Right: *View of existing site looking east towards harbour*
Below Right: *Rendered perspective looking towards revitalised waterfront*

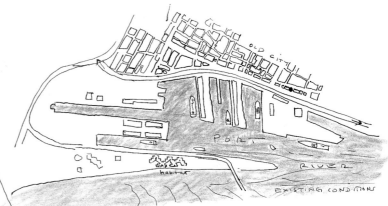

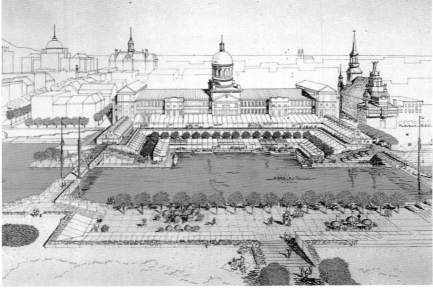

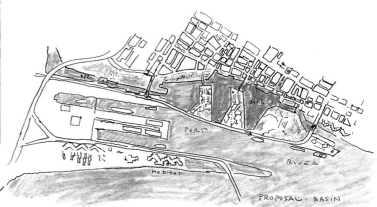

Above Left: *View of existing site looking west towards Bonsecours Market*
Below Left: *Rendered perspective of new civic waterfront with restored market*
Above Right: *Plan sketch of existing site*
Below Right: *Plan sketch of design concept*

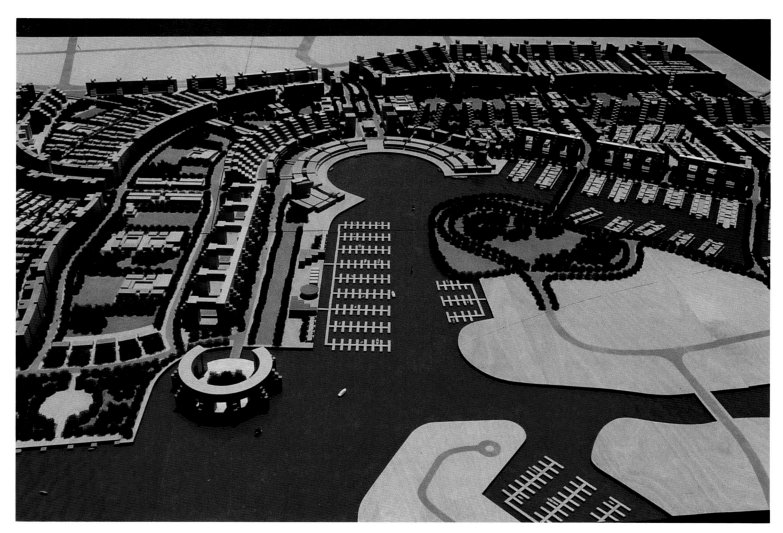

SIMPANG NEW TOWN
REPUBLIC OF SINGAPORE 1994

■ This design for a new town with a projected population of 125,000 was commissioned by the Housing and Development Board of the Republic of Singapore. The site faces the Straits of Johore on the northern coast of Singapore Island, 20 kilometres from Singapore's city centre. An extensive mangrove swamp close to the site will be preserved as a wildlife refuge, and the sandy beaches of the nearby island of Pulau Seletar will provide a spectacular recreation area for the city.

Town planning in Singapore has suffered from a relentless repetition of housing types in neighbourhoods isolated by arterial roadways. The design for Simpang seeks to introduce variety and alleviate the environmental costs of high density, while maintaining Singaporean standards of high efficiency. The design uses building massing and natural site features to create 'built edges' and 'built valleys' that maximise light, air and uninterrupted vistas.

The principal organising devices are a hierarchy of three main streets and an urban linear park that curves through the city. These elements, in turn, are woven together by streets and pedestrian ways running perpendicular to the spine and bringing all dwellings in the town into close driving and walking proximity to the central park, the town centre and the sea front. Most social and educational services are located within or adjacent to the linear park, and the emphasis of all circulation networks is on continuity between pedestrian precincts, with traffic confined to main boulevards.

The central challenge of the design was to develop variety and offer amenities within the great densities specified by the client. Therefore, several types of high-rise buildings line the park, the southern edge of the city and the waterfront. The high-rises capture views and create urban edges with 'urban windows' that preserve continuous circulation and views. Between these high built ridges, low-rise housing is oriented towards gardens and community decks with internal, landscaped views.

Opposite, Above: *Perspective sketch studying variety of high-rise edge housing* **Opposite, Below:** *Site model* **Above:** *Aerial view of urban edge along central park* **Below:** *Perspective sketch of town centre*

Above Left: *Perspective sketch of stepped housing along urban edges*
Above Right: *Perspective sketch of low- and high-rise housing to form 'urban windows'*

Above: *Perspective study of high-rise housing types*
Below: *View of promenade and linear park from harbour*

NEW CITY OF MODI'IN
ISRAEL 1989–

■ The New City of Modi'in is being built on the site of the ancient city of the Maccabees, halfway between Tel Aviv and Jerusalem. The city, planned for an ultimate population of 200,000, is intended to provide alternatives for residents of both the Tel Aviv and Jerusalem metropolitan areas, as well as to alleviate crowding along the coastal plain. The site covers 33 million square metres of treeless, hilly terrain, with rocky escarpments and fertile valleys. A series of valleys runs east to west, and at the centre of the site converges with the *Anaba*, a future nature reserve that stretches 30 kilometres west to the Mediterranean.

Traditional planning in this region would place arterial roads within the valleys, creating isolated neighbourhoods on the hilltops. Modi'in's master plan rejects this precedent of separate, self-contained neighbourhoods and instead proposes joined neighbourhoods and a shared city centre.

Each valley, with a couplet of one-way roads at its edges, will be a long communal district ranging from 50 to 150 metres in width. At least 50 per cent of this area is devoted to parks and playgrounds; the balance accommodates neighbourhood shopping areas, schools, synagogues, clinics and other community facilities. Each valley is planted and thus identified with its own species of tree, to create a Valley of Pines, of Palms, of Jakarandas. The outer edges of the valley boulevards are defined by four-storey apartments and three-and-a-half storey terraced housing follows the natural topography

towards high-rise structures on the hilltops. Each unique in design, the high-rises are constructed to act as landmarks throughout the area and to provide alternative housing with views of the Mediterranean.

The city centre occurs where the valleys and the nature reserve converge. With a series of separate pedestrian streets and traffic-oriented streets, the centre contains public institutions, shopping, housing and offices, and will expand to the north along a broad boulevard, similar in dimension to the Barcelona Ramblas. At the pivotal location where the two valleys and a major highway meet, a large traffic circle circumscribes the intercity bus terminal, the regional train and parking facilities, all of which serve as a transportation hub for commuters to and from the city centre, as well as a point of interface for all regional public transportation systems.

A set of detailed urban design guidelines controls development in all neighbourhoods, and all housing and public buildings in the first neighbourhood have been designed according to 1:500 scale plans. Individual architects and developers then prepare construction documents in accordance with these plans. The entire city, with the exception of schools and community services, is being built by the private sector without subsidy.

Construction commenced in 1993 and there were 9,000 housing units under construction in 1996, to be occupied by the end of the year. Within ten years, the population of Modi'in is expected to reach 100,000.

Opposite: *Aerial view of hillside neighbourhoods and valley under construction*
Above: *Site before construction*

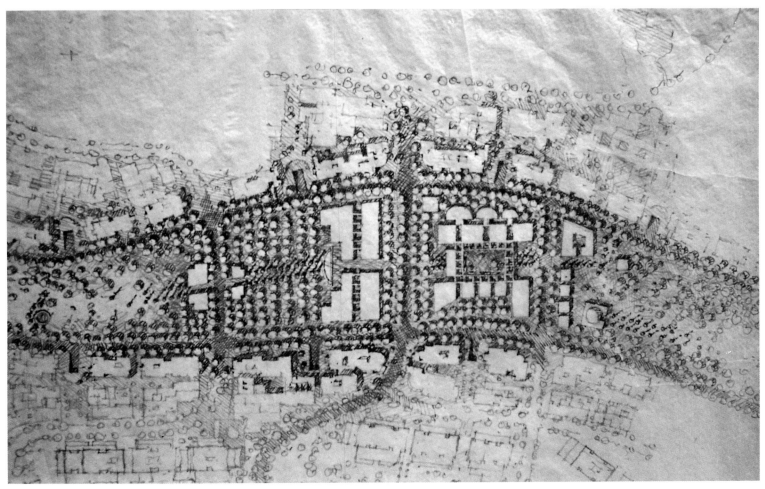

Opposite: *Rendered plan of city, with valleys and Anaba nature reserve converging on city centre*
Above: *Perspective along valley*
Below: *Rendered plan of valley*

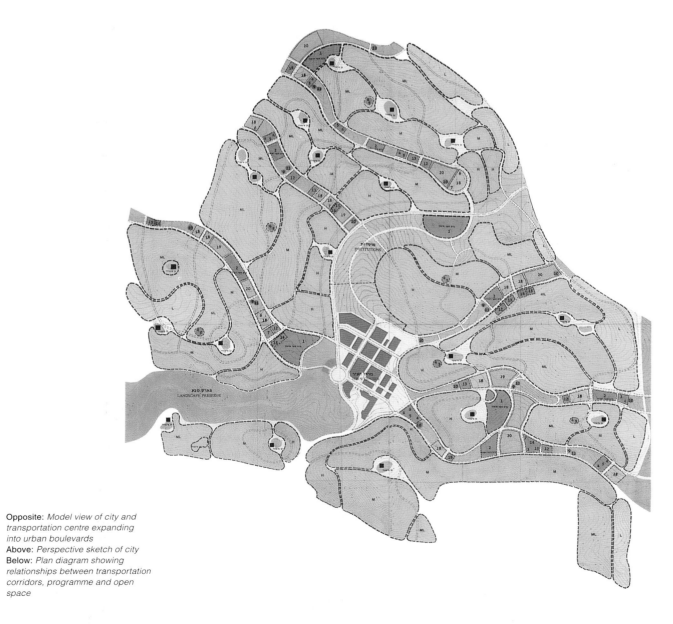

Opposite: *Model view of city and transportation centre expanding into urban boulevards*
Above: *Perspective sketch of city*
Below: *Plan diagram showing relationships between transportation corridors, programme and open space*

EPILOGUE

SCIENCE CENTER AND CHILDREN'S MUSEUM
WICHITA, KANSAS 1994-99

■ Planned to begin construction in 1997, the
Science Center and Children's Museum is located at
the confluence of the Little Arkansas and the
Arkansas Rivers, across the water from downtown
Wichita. Two pavilions organise the interpenetrating
elements of river, park, and museum into a public
place for learning and recreation. Echoing the
institution's mission of scientific and humanistic
education meaningful for people of all ages, the
museum is designed to be expressive of its purpose; to integrate indoor and outdoor spaces;
symbolically to reach out through park and river walk
systems towards the entire city.

The museum programme includes a series of
outdoor exhibits and activities that will be joined to
create a continuous path through the project along
the river's western edge, from the city's northern
museum district to its downtown. Descending into
the water, a museum *agora* forms an outdoor green
to accommodate a variety of community activities,
with a tented area for temporary exhibits set within it.
The 'landside' pavilion, containing the museum
lobby, gift shop, cafeteria, Cyberdome, simulation

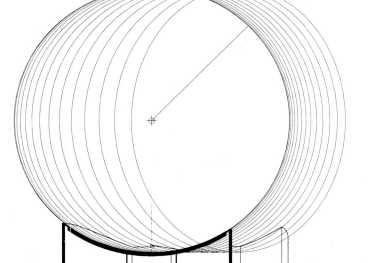

theatre and curatorial wing, curves along the river's
edge and connects across a channel to the 'island'
pavilion of themed exhibition galleries.

Surrounded by water, the galleries are dedicated
to the human experience on earth. The building is
organised into a wide central spine holding community rooms, auditoria and mechanical facilities, with
galleries on either side formed by a series of
undulating structural walls. An innovative system for
data, electrical and mechanical services, and air-
conditioning distribution runs throughout a 60-
centimetre high subfloor, fully accessible to accommodate new service requirements in the future.
Extremely efficient compared to traditional systems,
a displacement air-conditioning system uses the
subfloor as a plenum to distribute air and return it to
mechanical rooms via ducts.

The outer gallery walls, curved and bowed into the
river, rise to support the broad concave roof: a radial
laminated wood beam and mill deck structure.
Draining towards the centre, the curve of the roof is
generated by a torus geometry, in this case with its
imaginary centre in the sky. Across the channel, the
convex curving rooftop of the 'landside' pavilion
forms a vault rising from the land, structured with
laminated beams shaped by a torus with its centre
deep in the earth. At night, the undulating roofs will
be lit to create a floating, twisted plane reflected in
the river. Earthbound and skybound, the two
geometries create a skyline for the museum to be
seen from various parts of Wichita.

DROP the site –
What about the building blocks ?

(Economy of) means.

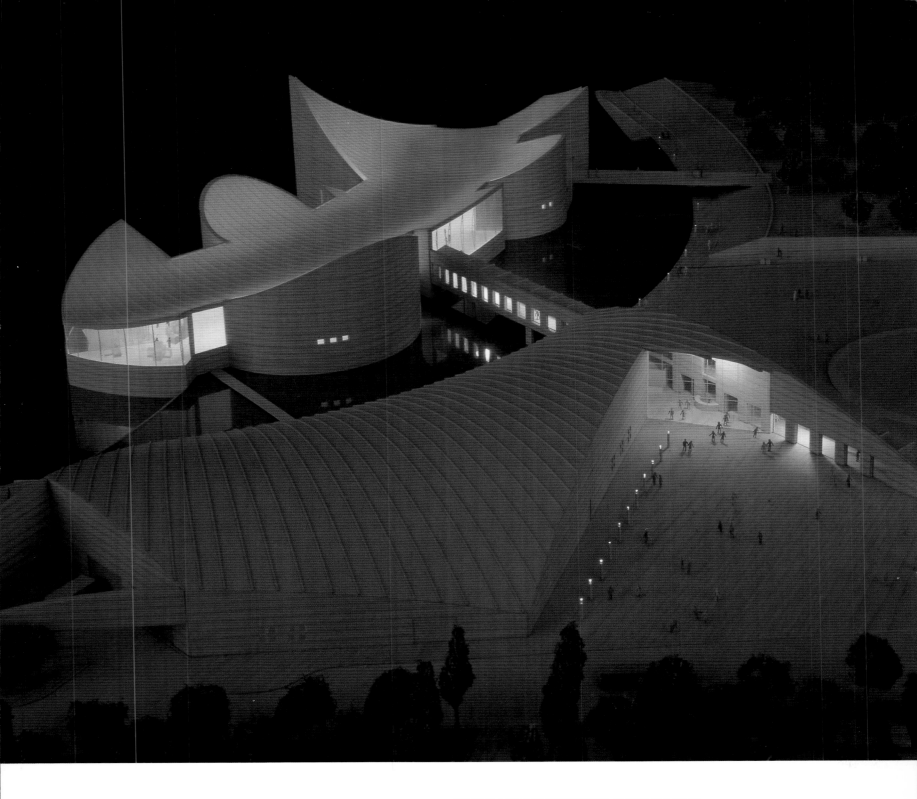

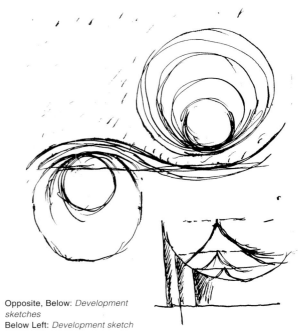

Opposite, Below: *Development
sketches*
Below Left: *Development sketch*

BIOGRAPHY

Born

Haifa, Israel, 1938

Education

Bachelor of Architecture with Honours, McGill
University, Montreal, Quebec, 1961

Professional

Van Ginkel & Associates, Architects/Planners,
Montreal, Quebec, 1961-62

Louis I Kahn, Architect, Philadelphia, Pennsylvania, 1962-63

Canadian Corporation for the 1967 World Exposition, 1963-64

Private Practice

Principal Offices

Montreal, Quebec, 1964-78

Boston, Massachusetts, 1978-present

Branch offices

Jerusalem, Israel, 1970-present

Montreal, Quebec, 1978-present

Toronto, Ontario, 1985-present

Teaching

Visiting Professor, McGill University, 1970

Davenport Professor of Architecture, Yale School
of Art and Architecture, 1971-72

Professor of Architecture and Director, Desert
Research Institute, Ben Gurion University,
Israel, 1975-78

Director of the Urban Design Program, Professor
of Architecture and Urban Design, Harvard
University Graduate School of Design, 1978-84

Ian Woodner Professor of Architecture and Urban
Design, Harvard University Graduate School
of Design, 1984-89

Selected Honours

Lieutenant Governor's Gold Medal, Canada, 1961

Sigma Delta Tau Gold Medal for Distinction in
Design, 1982

Honorary Doctorate of Law, McGill University
(LLD honoris causa), 1982

The Order of Canada, 1986

Mt Scopus Award for Humanitarianism, Hebrew
University, Jerusalem, 1987

Honorary Doctorate in Sciences, Laval University *(ScD honoris causa)*, 1988

Honorary Doctorate in Fine Arts, University of
Victoria *(DFA honoris causa)*, 1989

Richard Neutra Award for Professional Excellence, 1993

Fellow, American Institute of Architects, 1995

Gold Medal, Royal Architectural Institute of
Canada, 1995

Honorary Doctorate in Engineering, Technical
University of Nova Scotia *(honoris causa)*, 1996

Selected Awards

*Moshe Safdie and Associates does not participate in
self-nominated award programmes*

Massey Medal for Habitat '67, Royal Architectural
Institute of Canada, 1968

Award for Excellence for Habitat Puerto Rico, *The
Canadian Architect*, 1969

Award for Excellence for San Francisco State
College Student Union, *The Canadian Architect*, 1969

Award for Excellence for Yeshiva Porat Yosef, *The
Canadian Architect*, 1972

Award for Excellence for Western Wall Precinct
Plan, *The Canadian Architect*, 1973

Urban Design Concept Award for Coldspring
New Town Master Plan, US Department of
Housing and Urban Development, 1980

International Design Award in Urban Design for
Mamilla Master Plan, American Society of
Interior Designers, 1980

Award for Excellence for Quebec Museum of
Civilisation, *The Canadian Architect*, 1981

Merit Award for Coldspring New Town, American
Society of Landscape Architects, Pennsylvania,
Delaware Chapter, 1981

Rechter Prize for Hosh District, The Association
of Architects and City Planners of Israel, 1982

Prix d'Excellence en Architecture for Musée de
la Civilisation, Ordre des Architectes du
Québec, 1988

Governor General's Medal for Architecture for

Quebec Museum of Civilisation, Royal
Architectural Institute of Canada, 1992

Honor Award for the Harvard Business School
Class of 1959 Chapel, Interfaith Forum on
Religion, Art and Architecture of the American
Institute of Architects, 1993

Art and Architecture Collaboration Award for the
Harvard Business School, Class of 1959 Chapel,
Boston Society of Architects, 1993

Excellence Award for Vancouver Library Square,
Power Smart, 1995

Selected Exhibitions

For Everyone A Garden, Baltimore Museum of
Art, National Gallery of Canada, and San
Francisco Museum of Modern Art, 1973-74

Context, a travelling exhibit sponsored by New
York Institute for the Humanities, 1982-85

The National Gallery of Canada, Harvard University Graduate School of Design and National
Gallery of Canada, 1985

Moshe Safdie, Projects: 1979-1989, Harvard
University Graduate School of Design, 1989

The Museums of Moshe Safdie, Tel Aviv University, 1997

*Moshe Safdie Buildings and Projects 1967-1992:
A Retrospective*, organised by The Canadian
Architecture Collection, McGill University (in
planning)

Books by Moshe Safdie

Habitat, Tundra Books (Montreal),1967

Beyond Habitat, John Kettle (ed), The MIT Press
(Cambridge, Mass), 1970. Tr in Japanese,
Kajima Institute Publishing Company Ltd
(Tokyo), 1974

For Everyone A Garden, Judith Wolin (ed), The
MIT Press (Cambridge, Mass), 1974

Habitat Bill of Rights, in collaboration with JL Sert,
N Ardalan, BV Doshi and G Candilis, Ministry
of Housing (Imperial Government of Iran) 1976

Form and Purpose, John Kettle (ed), Houghton
Mifflin Co (Boston), 1982

*The Harvard–Jerusalem Studio: Urban Designs
for the Holy City*, Rudy Barlow and Uri Shetrit

(assistant eds), The MIT Press (Cambridge), and Keterpress Enterprises (Israel), 1986

Beyond Habitat by 20 Years, Tundra Books (Montreal),1987

The Language and Medium of Architecture, Harvard University Graduate School of Design (Cambridge), 1989 (from lecture delivered Nov 15 1989)

Jerusalem: The Future of the Past, Houghton Mifflin Co (Boston), 1989

The City After the Automobile, with Wendy Kohn, Basic Books (New York) and Stoddart Publishing Co Ltd (Ontario), 1997

Selected Articles by Moshe Safdie

'New Forms for City Housing', *C–I–L Oval*, June 1961

'Un Nouvel Aspect d'Habitat Urbain', *Architecture Bâtiment Construction*, July 1961

'A Case for City Living', *Habitat*, Nov 1961

'The Master Plan: Growth, Change and Repetition', *Habitat*, May 1962

'Habitat '67', *Habitat*, Sept-Dec 1965

'Habitat '67', *Bétons du Québec*, no 4, vol 7, Sept 1965, pp9-15

'Why Not Utopia?' Part I: 'Impressions of India' *Habitat*, May-Aug 1966. Part II: 'Proposals and Requirements', *Habitat*, Sept-Dec 1966

'The Urgency of Urban Development', *The Business Quarterly*, June 1966

'Systems, Utopias and the Dynamics of It All', *Modulus 67*

'Anatomy of a Building System', *The Canadian Architect*, Oct 1967

'Post Mortem on Habitat: Anatomy of a System', *Royal Institute of British Architects Journal*, no 74, vol 11, Nov 1967, pp489-94

'The Changing Environment – Hell or Utopia', in *Midway*, University of Chicago Press (Chicago), Summer 1968

'Habitat '67', in Richard Kostelanetz (ed), *Beyond Left and Right: Radical Thought for our Time*, William Morrow and Company (New York), 1968, pp143-46

'The City That Could Be', *The Japan Architect*, July 1970

'Can Technology Rescue the Cities?' in Harold W Helfrich (ed), *Agenda for Survival: The Environmental Crisis – 2*, Yale University Press (New Haven), 1971

'Systems: No Panacea', *The Canadian Architect*, no 16, vol 2, Feb 1971, pp39-40

'On Teaching at Yale', *Yale Magazine*, Feb 1971

'A View of Cities in 2024', *Saturday Review World*, Aug 1974

'Collective Consciousness in Making Environment', in *The Frontiers of Knowledge*, Doubleday & Company, Inc (Garden City, New York), 1975, pp201-34

'Private Jokes in Public Places', *The Atlantic Monthly*, Dec 1981

'Collective Significance', *Harvard Architecture Review*, Spring 1984

'Moshe Safdie on the Columbus Circle Project', *Interiors*, May 1988

'Platform', *Interiors*, May 1988

'Skyscrapers Shouldn't Look Down on Humanity', *The New York Times*, 29 May 1988

'The Tall Building Humanistically Reconsidered', *Mass*, Sept 1988

'Thoughts on the Integration of Design', *The Canadian Architect*, no 34, vol 3, March 1989, p26

'The National Gallery of Canada', *A + U*, vol 240, Sept 1990, pp3-31

'Architecture in Search of Ethic', *The Canadian Architect*, no 36, vol 11, Nov 1991, pp44-45

'Habitat at 25', *Architectural Record*, July 1992

'1995 RAIC Gold Medal Acceptance Speech', *RAIC Update*, no 19, Nov 1995, p9

'From D'Arcy Thompson to the Superconducting Super Collider', in Peter Galison and Emily Thompson (eds), *The Architecture of Science*, The MIT Press (Cambridge, Mass), 1997

Films

Coldspring New Town, National Film Board of Canada, 1973

The Innocent Door, National Film Board of Canada, 1973

Untitled on Bach and Piranesi, with Yo-Yo Ma, directed by François Girard (in progress), 1995

SELECTED BIBLIOGRAPHY

Books

Montreal Museum of Fine Arts, Jean-Noël Desmarais Pavilion, Montreal Museum of Fine Arts (Montreal), 1991

Witold Rybczynski, *A Place for Art: The Architecture of the National Gallery of Canada*, National Gallery of Canada (Ottawa), 1993

Irena Zantovská Murray (ed), *Moshe Safdie: Buildings and Projects 1967-1992*, introduced by Bill Lacy, with essays by Robert Oxman and John Bland, McGill-Queen's University Press (Montreal), 1996

General Articles

'The Canadian Architect Yearbook Award, 1968', *The Canadian Architect*, 1968, pp35-63

James Marston Fitch, review of *Beyond Habitat* in *The New York Times*, 3 Jan 1971, pp6, 25

Reyner Banham, review of *Beyond Habitat* in *Architectural Forum*, no 135, vol 1, July 1971, p10

Myrna Gopnik, and Irwin Gopnik, 'Generative Architecture: Moshe Safdie' *Artscanada*, vols 158, 159, Aug 1971, pp37-39

Christopher Lehmann-Haupt, 'Habitat was not the end of it', review of *Beyond Habitat* in *The New York Times*, 17 Dec 1971, p45

Philip Drew, 'Moshe Safdie', in *The Third Generation: The Changing Meaning of Architecture*, Pall Mall Press (London), 1972

Carl Steinitz et al, *Jerusalem and its Northern Region: Design Proposals for the Next Twenty Years*, Department of Landscape Architecture, Harvard University (Cambridge, Mass), 1982

K Hayakawa, 'Works of Moshe Safdie', *A + U*, vol 137, Feb 1982, pp19-36

Sara Boutelle, review of *Form and Purpose* in *Architecture: The American Institute of Architects Journal*, no 71, vol 13, Nov 1982, p72

Bradford Perkins, review of *Form and Purpose* in *Architectural Record*, no 171, vol 1, Jan 1983, pp77, 79

Michael H Burgoyne, review of *The Harvard–Jerusalem Studio: Urban Designs for the Holy City* in *Middle East Journal*, no 43, vol 2, March 1984, p314

Jim Strasman, 'An Interview with Safdie', *The Canadian Architect*, no 29, vol 2, Feb 1984, pp26-31

'College Union, San Francisco State College', *Process Architecture*, vol 56, March 1985, pp31-33

Wolf von Eckardt, 'Moshe Safdie and the Architecture of Context', *Process Architecture*, vol 56, March 1985, pp78-85

Jun Watanabe, 'The Morality of Architecture', in *Process Architecture*, vol 56, March 1985, pp133-40

Dan Turner, *Safdie's Gallery: An Interview with the Architect*, 1989

Paul Goldberger, review of *Jerusalem: The Future of the Past*, in *The New York Times*, 3 Dec 1989, pp3, 38

Christopher Hume, 'Reading Herod's Purpose', *Landscape Architecture*, no 80, vol 9, 1990, pp39-40

Judy Oberlander, review of *Jerusalem: The Future of the Past*, in *The Canadian Architect*, no 35, vol 8, Aug 1990, p6

Robert Oxman, 'Native Stone: The Architecture of Moshe Safdie', *Architecture of Israel*, vol 8, (reprint), 1992, pp17-27

Bruno Zevi, 'Dynamic Forms', *Architecture of Israel*, vol 13, Aug 1992, pp48-53

Horacio G Levit, 'En el reino de las ideas', *Arquitectura*, Ano 11, no 83, 11 Oct 1995, p4

Ami Ran, 'An Interview with Moshe Safdie', *Architecture of Israel*, no 24, Jan-Feb 1996, pp4, 5, 15

M R Montgomery, 'The Singular Moshe Safdie', *The Boston Globe*, 4 Jan 1996, pp61, 67

Michael Wise, 'The Many Facades of Moshe Safdie', *The Forward*, 19 April 1996, pp9-10

Murat Soygenis, 'Profil/Sylesi: Moshe Safdie', *Arredamento Dekorasyon*, April 1996 pp70-86 and cover

Michael Webb, 'Moshe Safdie: An Architect Who Bridges Two Worlds', *Korean Architect*, no 142, June 1996, pp87-93

Articles on Projects

Robert Fulford, 'Visit', *Maclean's*, vol 38, 8 Aug 1964 *(Habitat '67)*

Oscar Newman, 'Habitat '67: A Critique', *The Canadian Architect*, no 9, vol 10, Oct 1964, pp37-64

'Habitat '67', *Kenchiku*, vol 5, May 1965, pp71-90

Norman Edwards, 'Habitat '67: Montreal – An Assessment . . .' *Architectural Association Journal (Arena)*, vol 81, July 1965, pp45-51

Walter Rooke, 'Habitat Pioneers in Design and Methods', *Heavy Construction News*, no 10, vol 16, 22 April 1966, pp8-14

'Expo '67', *Time*, no 87, vol 25, 24 June 1966, pp11, 12 *(Habitat '67)*

'Expo '67', *Architecture Canada*, vol 43, July 1966, pp29-52 *(Habitat '67)*

'Montreal's Expo '67', *Fortune*, no 74, vol 5, Oct 1966, pp169, 174 *(Habitat '67)*

'Building a City with King Kong Blocks', *Progressive Architecture*, Oct 1966, pp226-37

(Habitat '67)

'Habitat '67', *Construction Moderne*, no 83, vol 5, 1967, pp50-57

'Habitat and After', *Architectural Forum*, no 126, vol 4, May 1967, pp34-51

'Expo '67', *Architectural Design*, vol 37, July 1967, pp337-47 *(Habitat '67)*

'Habitat '67 – An Approach to High-Density Living', *Construction News*, no 7, vol 6, Dec 1967, pp2-9

David Jacobs, 'A Box is not a Home', *Horizon*, no 19, vol 1, Dec 1967, pp70-73 *(Habitat '67)*

August E Komendant, 'Post-Mortem on Habitat', *Progressive Architecture*, vol 49, March 1968, pp138-47

'More Safdie', *Architectural Design*, vol 39, Jan 1969, pp37-42 *(Habitat Puerto Rico, Habitat New York)*

Phyllis Birkby, 'Beyond Habitat', *Design and Environment*, no 1, vol 4, Dec 1970, pp60-63 *(Habitat Israel)*

Douglas Davis, 'New Architecture: Building For Man', *Newsweek*, 19 April 1971, pp78-90 *(Habitat '67)*

'Habitat à Porto-Rico', *Architecture d'Aujourd'hui*, vol 44, Dec 1971, pp46-63 *(Habitat Puerto Rico)*

Andrew Tobias, 'Someday we may live in Lefrak City', *New York Magazine*, 12 March 1973, pp36-42 *(Battery City Park)*

Israel Shenker, 'Moshe Safdie', *Horizon*, no 15, vol 1, Dec 1973, pp54-63 *(Habitat '67)*

'A Perspective of Modern Canadian Architecture', *Process Architecture*, vol 5, 1978 *(Mamilla Center, Yeshiva Porat Yosef)*

Tom Paskal, 'Montreal's Waterfront District: Focus of a Planning Brainstorm', *Habitat*, no 21, vol 4, 1978, pp34-39 *(Old Port of Montreal)*

'Jerusalem Complex', *Progressive Architecture*, no 59, vol 2, Feb 1978, p41 *(Mamilla Center)*

Mildred F Schmertz, 'Three Projects by Moshe Safdie in Jerusalem', *Architectural Record*, no 163, vol 4, April 1978, pp103-14 *(Mamilla Center, Western Wall Precinct, Yeshiva Porat Yosef)*

Alan Blanc and Sylvia Blanc, 'Rebuilding Jerusalem: The Work of Moshe Safdie's Practice', *Building Design*, vol 421, 10 Nov 1978, pp30-31 *(Western Wall Precinct)*

Kunihiko Hayakawa, 'Coldspring New Town, Baltimore, Maryland', *A + U*, no 99, Dec 1978, pp13-22

'New Town for Senegal', *Urban Design International*, no 1, vol 1, Nov 1979, pp22-25 *(Keur Farah Pahlavi)*

'Colegio Hebreo "Maguen David" School Complex – Mexico City, Mexico', *A + U*, vol 137, Feb 1982, pp26-27 *(Colegio Hebreo 'Maguen David')*

'Mamilla – Jerusalem, Israel', *A + U*, vol 137, Feb 1982, p34 *(Mamilla Center)*

'National Museum of Civilisation – Québec, Canada' *A + U*, vol 137, Feb 1982

'Yeshiva Porat Joseph – Jerusalem, Israel', *A + U*, no 137, Feb 1982, pp19-22

Philip Johnson and John H Burgee, 'In Competition: Beverly Hills, California, Civic Center', *Skyline*, Nov 1982, pp4-6

'Safdie: Van Leer Residence + Western Wall Plaza, Jerusalem, Israel', *Space Design*, vol 229, Oct 1983, pp58-59

'A Private House in Alabama', *Architectural Record*, no 171, vol 13, Nov 1983, pp128-31 *(Callahan Residence)*

Mildred F Schmertz, 'Purpose and Place', *Architectural Record*, vol 171, Nov 1983, pp124-31 *(Van Leer Residence)*

Hugh Desrosiers and Daniel van Ginkel, 'The Montreal Vieux-Port, Third Option Desnoyers Mercure and Moshe Safdie', *Section A*, no 2, vol 1, Feb 1984, pp8-14

Charles Giuliano, 'A New Museum for Canada', *Art News*, no 83, vol 4, April 1984, pp13-16 *(National Gallery of Canada)*

'Hebrew Union College', *Process Architecture*, vol 56, March 1985, pp61-65

'Western Wall Precinct', *Process Architecture*, vol 56, March 1985, pp52-57

Jean Sutherland Boggs, 'The Designing of a National Gallery of Canada, Ottawa', *The Burlington Magazine*, vol 127, April 1985, pp201-07, 209

'Hebrew Union College Cultural Center, Los Angeles', *A + U*, vol 194, Nov 1986, p8 *(Skirball Museum and Cultural Center)*

Nathalie Grenon, 'New York: Columbus Center Versus Coliseum', *L'Arca*, vol 6, May 1987, pp16-27

Jun Watanabe, 'Columbus Center Proposed by Moshe Safdie is Going to be Realized', *A + U*, vol 202, July 1987, pp7-9

Brendan Gill, 'The Sky Line: On the Brink', *The New Yorker*, no 63, vol 38, 9 Nov 1987, pp113-125 *(Columbus Center)*

'Triumph of an "Outcast"', *Maclean's*, 23 May 1988, pp31, 33 *(National Gallery of Canada)*

Trevor Boddy, 'The National Gallery of Canada, Ottawa', *The Canadian Architect*, no 33, vol 6, June 1988, pp28-49

Joseph Baker, 'Street-wise in Montreal', *The Canadian Architect*, no 33, vol 7, July 1988, p43 *(Montreal Museum of Fine Arts)*

'Toronto Ballet Opera House: Three Winning Submissions', *The Canadian Architect*, no 33, vol 8, Aug 1988, pp24-39

Roger du Toit and Mark Franklin, 'Toronto Ballet Opera House', *The Canadian Architect*, no 33, vol 8, Aug 1988, pp24-39

Robert Campbell, 'National Gallery that is a Symbol of National Pride', *Architecture: AIA Journal*, vol 77, Sept 1988, pp98-103 *(National Gallery of Canada)*

Witold Rybczynski, 'Art for Art's Sake', *Saturday Night*, no 103, vol 10, Oct 1988, pp70-76 *(National Gallery of Canada)*

Mildred F Schmertz, 'Collective Significance', *Architectural Record*, vol 176, Oct 1988, pp120-29 *(National Gallery of Canada)*

Aldo Castellano, 'Order Midst Complexity', *L'Arca*, vol 25, March 1989, pp40-47 *(Ballet Opera House)*

Richard L Castro, 'Museum of Civilisation, Québec City', *The Canadian Architect*, no 34, vol 3, March 1989, pp18-27

Witold Rybczynski, 'Since Habitat', *Small Talk: A Housing Newsletter*, no 7, vol 2, Aug 1990, pp6-7

Dennis Sharp, ' The National Gallery of Canada: Fortuitous Triangular Amalgam', *A + U*, no 240, Sept 1990, pp33-36

Lony Gershoni, 'Modi'in New City', *Architecture in Israel*, 1991, pp10-15

'Monumental Complexity', *The Canadian Architect*, no 6, vol 37, June 1992, pp28-31 *(Montreal Museum of Fine Arts)*

Bronwen Ledger, 'A Public Affair', *The Canadian Architect*, no 7, vol 37, July 1992, pp21, 39 *(Vancouver Library Square)*

Heidi Landecker, 'Unquiet Union', *Architecture: AIA Journal*, no 8, vol 81, Aug 1992, pp68-73 *(Montreal Museum of Fine Arts)*

'Il Colosseo a Vancouver: Library Square', *L'Arca*, vol 63, Sept 1992, pp64-67 *(Vancouver Library Square)*

Jonathan Hale, 'A Building Boom at Harvard', *Progressive Architecture*, no 74, vol 2, Feb 1993, p19 *(Morgan Hall, Class of 1959 Chapel, Rosovsky Hall)*

'Circles of the Mind', *The Economist*, no 1, May 1993 *(Superconducting Super Collider Laboratory)*

Elizabeth S Padjen, 'Business Unusual', *Harvard Magazine*, May-June 1993, pp52-61 *(Class of 1959 Chapel, Morgan Hall)*

Ami Ran, 'Ottawa City Hall – Flowing from Light to Water', *Architecture of Israel*, vol 17, Jan 1994, pp46-55

Donald Albrecht, 'Boundaries of Light', *Architecture*, no 5, vol 83, May 1994, pp70-75 *(Morgan Hall, Class of 1959 Chapel, Rosovsky Hall)*

Tracey Metz, 'Jerusalem: And the Walls Came Tumbling Down', *Architectural Record*, Aug 1994, pp14-15 *(Mamilla Center, Damascus Gate Precinct)*

Carlo Paganelli, 'La Microcittà', *L'Arca*, vol 89, Jan 1995, pp12-15, 20 *(Ottawa City Hall)*

Trevor Boddy, 'Civic Lessons', *The Canadian Architect*, no 40, vol 2, Feb 1995, pp13-22 *(Ottawa City Hall)*

'Ottawa City Hall', *The Canadian Architect*, no 40, vol 2, Feb 1995, pp16-18

Fritz de Wit, 'David's Village in Jerusalem – Wordt nu Snel Voltooid', *Cobouw* (Den, Netherlands), 16 June 1995, p7 *(David's Village, Mamilla)*

Paul Goldberger, 'Passions Set in Stone', *The New York Times Magazine*, 10 Sept 1995, section 6, pp42-7, 56, 58, 76, 77 *(Jerusalem projects)*

Christopher Thomas, 'Canadian Colossus', *Architecture*, no 10, vol 84, Oct 1995, pp72-79 *(Vancouver Library Square)*

Diane Haithman, 'Take the 405 to Utopia', *Los Angeles Times Calendar*, 19 Nov 1995, *p3* *(Skirball Museum and Cultural Center)*

Witold Rybczynski, 'A Sight for Sore Eyes', *Saturday Night*, March 1996, p82 *(Vancouver Library Square)*

Michael Webb, 'Moshe Safdie: An Architect Who Bridges Two Worlds', *Korean Architect*, no 142, June 1996, pp84-171 *(20+ projects)*

'On the Boards', *Architecture*, no7, vol 85, July 1996, pp46-47 *(Wichita Science Center and Children's Museum)*

Karen Stein, 'City on a Hill', *Architectural Record*, Aug 1996, pp94-101 *(Skirball Museum and Cultural Center)*

In 1990, the Canadian Architecture Collection at McGill University in Montreal established the Moshe Safdie Archive. The Archive, containing all drawings, models, sketchbooks and papers from 125 design projects, is open to the public and catalogued in Moshe Safdie: Buildings and Projects 1967-1992, *McGill/Queen's Press (Montreal), 1996, also on CD-ROM. A complete bibliography is available at the Archive, and project information and photographs at the CAC web site:*

http://blackader.library.mcgill.ca/cac/safdie

CHRONOLOGICAL LIST OF BUILDINGS AND PROJECTS

Thesis
'A Three-Dimensional Modular
Building System'
McGill University, Montreal, Quebec
Project
1958-61

**San Francisco State College
Student Union**
San Francisco, California
Client: College Union Council, San
Francisco State College
Project
1967-68

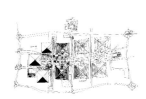

City for Palestinian Refugees
Giza, Egypt
Project
1962

Habitat New York I
New York City
Client: Carol Haussamen Foundation
Project
1967-68

Habitat '67
Montreal, Quebec
Client: Canadian Corporation for the
1967 World Exposition
Associate Architects: David, Barott,
Boulva
Built
1964-67

Habitat New York II
New York City
Client: Carol Haussamen Foundation
Project
1967-68

Molson Center
Montreal, Quebec
Client: Molson Development Ltd
Project
1966

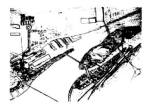

Cité des Iles
Montreal, Quebec
Client: City of Montreal and Central
Mortgage and Housing Corporation
Project
1968

Canadian Pavilion
Osaka, Japan
Client: Government of Canada
Competition
1967

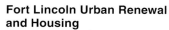

**Fort Lincoln Urban Renewal
and Housing**
Washington, DC
Client: Redevelopment Land Agency
Project
1968

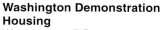

**Washington Demonstration
Housing**
Washington, DC
Client: Redevelopment Land Agency
Project
1967

Indian Carry Resort
Saranac Lake, New York
Client: Indian Carry Associates
Project
1968-69

Tropaco Resort
St Thomas, US Virgin Islands
Client: Armour Enterprises
Project
1968-69

Habitat Puerto Rico
San Juan, Puerto Rico
Client: Development Corporation
International
Project
1968-71

St George's School
Montreal, Quebec
Client: St George's School
Project
1969

Low Density Housing System
Puerto Rico
Client: Development Corporation of
Puerto Rico
Project
1969

Habitat Israel
Jerusalem
Client: Ministry of Housing,
Government of Israel
Project
1969-70

Eberts Residence
North Hatley, Quebec
Built
1969-71

Manchat Housing Master Plan
Jerusalem
Client: Ministry of Housing, Govern-
ment of Israel/ARIM
Built
1969-95

Uniment Systems
Sarnia, Ontario
Client: Polymer Corporation
Systems, Ltd
Project
1970

Merkava Tank
Client: General Israel Tal, Israel
Defense Force
Completed 1970s

Yeshiva Porat Yosef
Old City, Jerusalem
Client: Yeshiva Porat Yosef
Associate Architect: David Best
Partially built
1970–

Habitat Rochester
Rochester, New York
Client: Urban Development Corpora-
tion, City of Rochester and FIGHT
Project
1971

Pompidou Center
Paris
Client: Ministry of Culture,
Government of France
With 14 students from Safdie's design
studio at Yale School of Art and
Architecture
Competition, Second Prize
1971

**Misgav Ladach, Institute for
Sephardic Studies**
Old City, Jerusalem
Client: Hebrew University
Project
1971-74

Van Leer Residence
Jerusalem
Built
1972-76

Youth Wing, Rockefeller Museum
Jerusalem
Client: The Jerusalem Foundation
Built
1971-74

Coldspring New Town
Baltimore, Maryland
Client: City of Baltimore, Department
of Housing and Community Development; FD Rich Housing Corporation
Partially built
1972-81

Block 38 Housing
Old City, Jerusalem
Client: Corporation for the Redevel-
opment of the Jewish Quarter
Built
1971-77

Landmark Square
Stamford, Connecticut
Client: FD Rich Housing Corporation
Built
1972-86

Battery Park City
New York City
Client: Samuel Lefrak Development
Project
1972

Mamilla Center
Jerusalem
Client: Karta/Central Jerusalem
Development Corporation, Ladbroke,
Al-Rov, Ltd
Associate Architect for Master Plan:
Gilbert Weil
In progress
1972-99

Habsystem Housing Study
Client: FD Rich Housing Corporation
Project
1972-73

Western Wall Precinct
Old City, Jerusalem
Client: Municipality of Jerusalem and
the Corporation for the Redevelopment of the Jewish Quarter
Project
1972–

Private Residence
Old City, Jerusalem
Built
1972-73

Nicoforia Hotel
Jerusalem
Project
1973-74

Park Heights Urban Renewal
Baltimore, Maryland
Client: City of Baltimore,
Department of Housing and
Community Development
1973-75

Housing for the Inuit Community
Frobisher Bay, Northwest Territories
Client: Government of the Northwest
Territories
Project
1974-77

Cyril Stein Residence
Jerusalem
Built
1973-76

Desert Research Institute
Sde Boker, Israel
Client: Ben Gurion University
Project
1974-79

Caesarea Heights
Caesarea, Israel
Client: Vered Association
Project
1973-76

Bronfman Amphitheater
Old City, Jerusalem
Client: The Jerusalem Foundation
Project
1974-82

Sde Boker Housing
Sde Boker, Israel
Client: Sde Boker Seminary
Built
1973-78

Judith's Residence
Chicoutimi, Quebec
Client: The Thalidomide Foundation
of Canada
Built
1975-77

Rabbinical Supreme High Court
Jerusalem
Client: Ministry of Public Works,
Government of Israel
Project
1973-79

Dung Gate Restoration
Old City, Jerusalem
Client: Corporation for the Redevel-
opment of the Jewish Quarter
Built
1974-85

Bar Ilan University Master Plan
Tel Aviv
Client: Bar Ilan University
1974-77

New City of Keur Farah Pahlavi
Republic of Senegal
Client: Government of Senegal and
Government of Iran
Associate Architects: Desnoyers,
Mercure, Gagnon, Sheppard
Project
1975-78

Hosh District Restoration
Old City, Jerusalem
Client: Corporation for the Redevel-
opment of the Jewish Quarter
Built
1976-78

Old Port of Montreal Master Plan
Montreal, Quebec
Client: Minister of State for Urban
Affairs, Government of Canada
Joint venture with Desnoyers,
Mercure, Gagnon, Sheppard
Partially built
1977-90

Habitat Tehran
Elahieh, Tehran, Iran
Client: The Special Bureau
of Her Imperial Majesty,
The Shahbanou of Iran
Project
1976-78

Atrium on the Plaza
Kansas City, Missouri
Client: Atrium Associates
Built
1978-80

Hedra Yeshiva Restoration
Old City, Jerusalem
Client: Corporation for the Redevel-
opment of the Jewish Quarter
Built
1976-84

Callahan Residence
Birmingham, Alabama
Built
1978-81

**Yad Vashem Children's Holocaust
Memorial**
Jerusalem
Client: Yad Vashem Museum
Built
1976-85

Powerhouse Hotel
Baltimore, Maryland
Client: Boston Properties
Competition
1979

Hebrew Union College
Jerusalem
Client: Hebrew Union College
Built; final phase in progress
1976–

Caesarea World Monument
Caesarea, Israel
Project
1979

Blood Transfusion Centers
Republic of the Ivory Coast
Client: Confarin Cryusan AG
Associate Architects: Desnoyers,
Mercure, Gagnon, Sheppard
Project
1977-78

Ramle Urban Renewal
Ramle, Israel
Client: Ministry of Housing,
Government of Israel
Project
1979-80

Koch Residence
Dover, Massachusetts
Project
1979-80

Kibbutz Idmit
Idmit, Israel
Client: Kibbutz Idmit
Built
1980-82

North Station District Master Plan
Boston, Massachusetts
Client: Boston Redevelopment
Authority
1979-81

Ardmore Habitat
Singapore
Client: Robin Development (PTE) Ltd
Associate Architects: RDC Architects
Built
1980-85

Bar Ilan University School of Economics
Tel Aviv
Client: Bar Ilan University
Built
1979-88

Cambridge Center
(1, 3 and 4 Cambridge Center,
Cambridge Marriott Hotel)
Cambridge, Massachusetts
Client: Boston Properties
Built
1980-88

Bar Ilan University Dormitories
Tel Aviv
Client: Bar Ilan University
Partially built
1979-84

Parcel D-10
Boston, Massachusetts
Client: Joint venture, Boston Proper-
ties and The Rouse Corporation
Competition
1981

Gateway Office Complex
Republic of Singapore
Client: Far East Trading Company
Associate Architects: RDC Architects
Competition
1980-81

Robina New Town Master Plan
Gold Coast, Queensland, Australia
Client: Robina Land Corporation
PTY, Ltd
Project
1981-82

Post Office Square
Boston, Massachusetts
Client: Boston Properties
Project
1980-81

Robina Hotel-Casino Complex
Gold Coast, Queensland, Australia
Client: Robina Land Corporation
PTY, Ltd
Project
1981-82

Rowes Wharf
Boston, Massachusetts
Client: First City Development
Corporation of Boston
Project
1981-82

Kilby Street Office Building
Boston, Massachusetts
Client: Boston Properties
Competition
1982-83

Quebec Museum of Civilisation
Quebec City, Quebec
Client: Ministry of Culture,
Government of Quebec
Associate Architects: Belzile,
Bransard, Gallienne, Lavoie; Sungur
Incesulu; Desnoyers, Mercure
Built
1981-87

International House
Los Angeles, California
Client: UCLA
Project
1982-84

**Tampines Condominium
Development**
Republic of Singapore
Client: Robin Development (PTE) Ltd
Associate Architects: RDC Architects
Project
1981-88

Centennial Housing
Aspen, Colorado
Client: Centennial Partners
Built
1982-86

Park on the Bayou
Houston, Texas
Client: Robin Developments
(PRE Corp)
Project
1982

Shoval Kibbutz Housing
Shoval, Israel
Client: Kibbutz Shoval
Built
1982-86

Beverly Hills Civic Center
Beverly Hills, California
Client: City of Beverly Hills
Competition
1982

**Colegio Hebreo Maguen David
School Complex**
Mexico City, Mexico
Client: Colegio Hebreo Maguen
David
Associate Architects: Isaac Abadi
Husni & Associates
Built
1982-89

National Museum of Man
Hull, Quebec
Client: Canada Museums Construc-
tion Corporation
Competition
1982-83

National Gallery of Canada
Ottawa, Ontario
Client: Canada Museums Construc-
tion Corporation
Joint venture with Parkins Partnership
Associate Architects: Desnoyers,
Mercure
Built
1983-88

Private Residence Renovation
Cambridge, Massachusetts
Built
1984

Supreme Court of Israel
Jerusalem
Client: Yad Hanadiv
Competition
1986

Harvard Business School Master Plan
Boston, Massachusetts
Client: Harvard University Business School
1984-92

United Nations African Headquarters
Addis Ababa, Ethiopia
Client: United Nations
Associate Architects: Desnoyers, Mercure
Competition
1986

Kohlberg Residence
Beit Yannai, Israel
Project
1985-86

Esplanade Apartments
Cambridge, Massachusetts
Client: Capital Partners, Inc
Built
1986-89

Columbus Center
New York City
Client: Boston Properties, Salomon Brothers
Associate Architects: Emery Roth and Sons, PC
Project
1985-87

Morgan Hall
Harvard Business School,
Boston, Massachusetts
Client: Harvard University Business School
Built
1986-92

Montreal Museum of Fine Arts
Montreal, Quebec
Client: Musée des Beaux-Arts de Montréal
Joint venture with Desnoyers, Mercure, Lemay, Leclerc
Built
1985-91

Class of 1959 Chapel
Harvard Business School,
Boston, Massachusetts
Client: Harvard University Business School
Built
1986-92

Yeshiva Aish Hatorah
Old City, Jerusalem
Client: Yeshiva Aish Hatorah and Corporation for the Redevelopment of the Jewish Quarter
Built
1985-94

Skirball Museum and Cultural Center
Los Angeles, California
Client: Hebrew Union College
Built
1986-95

Steeplechase Park
Coney Island, New York
Client: Stephen Shalom
Project
1987

Ottawa City Hall
Ottawa, Ontario
Client: City of Ottawa
Joint venture with Murray & Murray
Associates
Built
1988-94

Pisgat Ze'ev
Jerusalem
Client: Shikun Vepitvach
Project
1987-89

**The Milkin Foundation
Headquarters**
Los Angeles, California
Client: The Milkin Foundation
Project
1989

**Headquarters for Ministry
of Transportation**
Hull, Quebec
Client: Pierre Bourque & Fils
Project
1987-89

Hull Housing
Hull, Quebec
Client: Pierre Bourque & Fils
Project
1989

Ballet Opera House
Toronto, Ontario
Client: The Ballet Opera House
Corporation
Associate Architects: Bregman &
Hamman
Project
1987-90

Wittington Place
Toronto, Ontario
Client: Westnor Limited
Competition
1989

Israel Trade Fair Center
Tel Aviv
Client: Municipality of Tel Aviv
Project
1987-93

Munari Silver Designs
Client: Cleto Munari
1989

Beit Clal Conference Center
Pomona, New York
Client: Clal National Jewish Center
for Training and Leadership
Project
1988

New City of Modi'in
Modi'in, Israel
Client: Ministry of Housing,
Government of Israel
In progress
1989–

Neve Ofer Community Center
Tel Aviv-Jaffa, Israel
Client: The Tel Aviv Foundation
Built
1989-95

National Museum of Scotland
Edinburgh, Scotland
Client: The National Museums of
Scotland
Competition
1990

Labatt's Center
Toronto, Ontario
Client: CN Real Estate/Labatt joint
venture
Joint venture with Bregman &
Hamman
Competition
1990

Elwyn Rehabilitation Center
Jerusalem
Client: Elwyn Foundation
Built
1990-96

Gateway to Israel
Science Museum, Hotel and Resi-
dential Mixed-Use Complex
Tel Aviv
Client: City of Tel Aviv and
Joseph Buchman
Project
1990

Pantages Place
Toronto, Ontario
Client: Livent, Inc of Canada
In progress
1990–

Windsor Casino
Windsor, Ontario
Client: Bally's and Canadian Pacific
Hotels
Competition
1990

Hertzlia Seashore Housing
Hertzlia, Israel
Project
1991

Queen's University Library
Kingston, Ontario
Client: Queen's University
Competition
1990

Eilat Resort Complex
Eilat, Israel
Client: Shamrock Corporation
Project
1991

Museum of Contemporary Art
Stuttgart
Client: State of Baden-Württenberg
Competition
1990

**Yad Vashem Holocaust Transport
Memorial**
Jerusalem
Client: Yad Vashem Museum
Built
1991-94

Museum of Industrial Design, Architecture and Contemporary Art
Munich
Client: State of Bavaria
Competition
1992

Sinai Temple
Chicago, Illinois
Client: Sinai Temple
Competition
1994

Superconducting Super Collider Laboratory
Waxahachie, Texas
Client: US Department of Energy and University Research Associates
Project
1992-93

Ford Center for the Performing Arts
Vancouver, British Columbia
Client: Livent, Inc of Canada
Associate Architects: Downs/ Archambault and Partners
Built
1994-95

Rosovsky Hall
Harvard College, Cambridge, Massachusetts
Client: President and Fellows of Harvard College and Hillel Foundation of Cambridge
Built
1992-94

Science Center and Children's Museum
Wichita, Kansas
Client: The Science Center, Inc
Associate Architects: Schaefer Johnson Cox Frey & Associates
In progress
1994-98

Boca Raton Museum Center
Boca Raton, Florida
Client: Boca Raton Museum of Art
Project
1992-95

Damascus Gate Precinct
(Peace Square)
Jerusalem
Client: The Jerusalem Foundation, Municipality of Jerusalem
Project
1994–

Library Square
Public Library and Federal Government Headquarters
Vancouver, British Columbia
Client: City of Vancouver
Joint venture with Downs/ Archambault and Partners
Built
1992-95

Airside Terminal, Ben Gurion Airport
Lod, Israel
Client: Israel Airport Authority
Joint venture with TRA Ltd
In progress
1995-2000

Simpang New Town
Republic of Singapore
Client: Housing and Development Board of the Republic of Singapore
Project
1994

Tomb of Prime Minister Yitzhak Rabin
Jerusalem
Client: Ministry of the Interior, Government of Israel
Built
1996

Rabin Center
Tel Aviv, Israel
Client: Rabin Center Foundation
In progress
1996–

Hebrew College
Newton Massachusetts
Client: Hebrew College
In progress
1996–

West Jerusalem Master Plan
Jerusalem, Israel
Client: Israel Land Authority
In progress
1996–

STAFF LIST

We wish to acknowledge the invaluable contribution of all those who have constituted this office over the past thirty-two years. We apologise for any inadvertent omissions.

Moshe Safdie and Associates, Inc, Boston
1978-present (including New York office, 1986-88)
Principals
Isaac Franco, William Gillit, Jan Heesplink, Philip Matthews, Joseph Morog, Paul Nakazawa, Tosh Taketomo, Allen Terry
Associates
Kent Duffy, Gene Dyer, Rainer Goeller, Michael Guran, James Herold, John Ingwersen, Ken Janson, Alex Krieger, Michael McKee, Hugh Phillips, David Rinehart, Ron Steffek
Senior Staff
Michael Baenen, Mariela Liu Baker, Stephen Baker, Donald Ball, Bruce Brook, Thomas Canfield, Christopher Chan, Nelson Chen, Anthony De Pace, Polly Dithmer, William Fleissing, Stephen Irvine, Drake Jacobs, Jeff Jacoby, Wendy Kohn, Jonathan Kahn Leavitt, Amir Man, Weiya Noble, Paul Norris, Marcus Rector, Michal Ronnen Safdie, Govind Sohoni, Carl von Stetton, Hugh Sullivan, Donna Viscuglia, Ray Warburton, Cynthia Westerman
Architects and Support Staff
Kika Adler, Paul Alt, Yossi Amir, Timothy Archibald, Imadiel Ariel, Miriam Avins, Dayo Babalola, Darae Baghai, David Bailey, Luis Baldo, Alberto Balestrieri, Les Banasik, Derek Barcinski, Robert Barringer, Roy Barris, Susan Bassett, Jim Bazios, Elizabeth Beal, Nathalie Beauvais, Francesca Beehan, Joan Berg, Jay Berman, Daniel Bernstein, David Blair, Liza Bornstein, Gail Boyajian, Barbara Boylan, Uwe Brandes, Andrea Brue, Robert Bulger, David Burnett, Steven Canter, Daniel Castro, Shannon Champion, David Chen, David Collins, Kenneth Cooper, Nondita Correa, Timothy Costello, Collette Creppeel, Jarunza Cunningham, Benedict Curatolo, Kai Cutter, Steven Davis, Sylvie Debaisieux, Nancy de Girolamo, Margarita de la Iglesia, Julian de Metz, Mark Denton, Joan Devereaux, William Dewson, Sylvia Dickey, Luce Dionne, Tanya Donelly, Robert Drake, Oreste Drapaca, Steven Drucker, Debra Edelstein, Gregory Etter, Mathew Falcone, Robin Falls, Laurie Fanger, Deborah Fennick, Maura Fernandez-Abernethy, Kristina Field, Amy Finch, Judith Fletcher, Carl Frenning, Kristine Frongillo, Ginette Fulham, William Gallagher, Benjamin Garcia, Robert Gebhardt, Mark Gerwing, James Gilmer, Brian Girard, Sharon Glassman, Marcus Gleysteen, Mary Glock, Chris Goad, Mark Gordon, Ramsey Gourd, Oscar Grauer, Marlene Gray, Lisa Green, Shana Greenblata, Mark Griguts, Richard Grisard, Salome Grisard, Nancy Grotevont, Michaela Haberland, Amy Hahn, Robert Han, Jennifer Hands, Colleen Harka, Suzanne Harriman, Joan Harris, Nina Harrison, Thea Havican, Amnon Haviv, David Hernandez, John Hill-Williams, Nancy Hines, James Ho, Amy Jo Hofner, Herman Howard, Shawn Howell, Elizabeth Howey, Caroline Hu, Scott Huetteman, Christine Hyland, Jeung Seol Hyun, Suzanne Ingraham, Barbara Ingves, Patricia Intrieri, Diona Ioan, Calvin Irving, Susan Israel, Carole Jackson, Lisa Jackson, Peter Jelley, Awilda Jimenez, Carrie Johnson, Michael Joyce, Glen Kachkowski, Ravit Kaplan, Jeanne Kavanagh, Allison Kehne, Maximilian Keller, Alicia Kennedy, George Kennedy, Jennifer Kennedy, Steven Kersey, Michael Kim, Sarah Kimball, Keiran King, Andrew Kinoshita, Marjory Klein, Gary Kleinschmidt, Judith Kopeloff, Roel Krabbandam, Rolondo Kraeher, Yasmin Kuhn, Helen Kurz, Jeff Lackney, Martha Laguess, John Lam, Dor Langbaum, Celine Larkin, Arnold Lee, Erwin Lee, Jenny Lee, Ray-yu Lee, Samuel Lee, Beni Levy, Jou Min Lin, Marleen Lipsick, Deborah Little, David Litz, Felicia Lopes, Sharon Ludman, Lea Ann Lupfer, Carolyn Lushin, John MacGillivray, Shawn Mahoney, Stephen Mak, Dan Malamoceanu, Ronald Mar, Evan Markiewicz, Christine Marks, Kristen Marschke, Nancy Martin, Stephanie

Mashek, Amy Masters, Veronica Mayer, Jae McCabe, Shirley McDougall, Thomas McLaughlin, Neil McNulty, Andrea Meaney, Edmundo Medieros, Andrew Miao, Richard Miche, Margaret Minor, Peter Mitsakos, Anne Mock, Jonathan Moeller, Serafin Moniz, Thomas Morog, Joyce Morrow, Timothy Moynihan, Lewis Muhlfelder, Jeff Murphy, David Narcizo, Pamela Nener, Doreve Nicholeff, Robert Nichols, Paul Noms, Robert Noreau, Laura Norton, Andres Ogarrio, Benjamin Olson, Aris Ottaqnian, Barbara Paddick, Elaine Paul, Georgine Pennington, Julie Perkins, Bogdan Pestka, Lynn Pilon, John Pohorylo, Beverly Politano, Rhonda Postrel, Florrie Povirk, Patricia Progin, Sarah Radding, Helen Rainone, Ehud Rapoport, Gabrielle Reese, Isabel Renteria, Taina Rhodin, David Rib, Daphne Allen Rice, Kristine Richard, Edward Richland, Mark Rios, Elly Rodriguez, Tamar Rosenblum, Alison Rowell, Richard Rundell, Taal Safdie, Kimberly Salerno, Donna Savchunk, Barbara Scaltolini, Jonathan Scamman, Peter Schlesinger, William Schuneman, Stephen Schreiber, John Schwartz, Brian Scott, Heather Seligman, Ann Sellars, Robin Sen, Caroline Shaw, Shlomo Shay, Scott Shell, John William Sherman, Uri Shetrit, Alona Shiftan-Nitzan, Frank Shirley, Barbara Sicovs, Jonathon Siegal, Michael Silver, Neil Simpson, Robert Mindara Singh, Ellen Sierra, Gary Smith, Shelah Smith, Margaret Sobieski, Nancy Sokol, Collette Sparks, Steven Starkie, Barbara Stein, Neil Stempel, David Stern, Roger Stigliano, Amy Stockman, Norris Strawbridge, Mark Strong, Mary Sullivan, Dale Takeda, Reanna Tang, Austin Tang, William Taormino, Abby Tassel, Terrance Teague, Timothy Techler, Raul Teran, Mark Tobler, Gary Tondorf, Casserine Toussaint, James Tsakirgis, Nnema Ugwegbu, Adrian Ulrich, Robin Upton, Karin Varnik, Anthony Ventre, Senen Vina-De-Leon, Adrian von Ulrich, Mary Waitu, Maureen Ward, Jun Watanabe, Roger Weaver, Wendy Weeton, Nancy Wilkins, Nell Willis, Geraldine Woodruff, Ralph Wolfe, Judi Wong, Michael Zakain, Ronald Zeytoonian, Gideon Ziv, Dena Zyroff

Moshe Safdie Architecte, Montréal
1964-78
Associates
Isaac Franco, William Gillitt, Sarina Katz, Pierre Larose, Philip Matthews, Alfred Meyer, George Pollowy, David Rinehart
Architects and Support Staff
Stephen Aber, Raul Almeida, Bruce Anderson, Mercedes Aupy, Robert Awad, Martine Badeaux, Emily Bambiger, Leszek Banasik, Thomas Barrington, M Baygin, Guy Beaulieu, Cinq-Mars Belanger, Henry Benouaich, Stephane Bergeron, A Berlinski, Julie Blatt, R Bourgouin, Raymond Catchpole, George Challies, Georges Chalut, J Chechik, Suzan Cole, Annie Cronzon, Theodore Davidson, Sergio de Almeida, Arnaud de Tassigny, Stephen Dent, Tanja Hahn-Dorsey, Susan Doubilet, Neil Downey, John Dundon, Claude Durand, Jeremiah Eck, S Eden, Norman Edwards, Stanca-Maria Enachescu, Yaira Ephrati-Wisenthal, Steve Flamer, John Giannou, Monique Glassen, Melvyn Glickman, Stephan Gottlieb, Helen Gregus, Michael Grossman, Jean Guillemette, Ramesh Gulatee, Michael Guran, Barry Habib, Jay Hanson, Richard Hansen, Rodney Hatanaka, Dani Hausmann, Kunihiko Hayakawa, Edward Hord, Elizabeth Hume, Emil Johnson, Nizamuddri Khan, Herike Komendant, Dennis Walter Krause, Monica Laanela, James Lefebvre, Gilles Lemaire, Robert Leschhorn, Jo-Anne MacIntyre, Iraj Madjzub, Roy Mahabir, Nikolai Marinov, Terence Mason, Marianne McKenna, Jacob Molho, Bruno Moos, Bernard Morrain, Andrew Morrison, Lucille Mosckovakis, Marc Munan, Earl Murphy, Heather Nicholls, Richard Nordhaus, Richard O'Dwyer, Aris Ohanian, Keith Oliver, George Oommen, Anthony Ostrowski, Georges Parent, Isaac Percal, Joao Pimenta, Eva Porgesz, Margaretha Porteu de la Morandiere, William Postlethwaite, Louis Poupon, Diane Prevost, Sandra Prevost, Peter Roper, Janusz

Rosinski, Morton Rossberg, Arthur Rubinstein, Witold Rybczynski, George Saheb, Joseph Salgado, Edward Sattarthwaite, Robert Schell, Jeff Schlesinger, David Schouela, Vernon Sexton, Moshe Shaki, Stuart Sharpe, Arshalom Schwartz, Jennifer Simpson, Yasuyaki Takaguchi, E Takeda, Simon Tang, Bruce Taylor, D Tolmatch, Olga Ventura, Gay Walley, Robert Welch, Stuart Wilson, Allen Wiseman, Debra Yacoulis-Trachewsky

Moshe Safdie Architects, Ltd, Jerusalem
1970-present
Principals
Zahi Halberstadt, Dan Lansky, Bernard Marson, Eylon Meromi, Carlos Prus, Richard Rabnett, Uri Shetrit
Associates
Avraham Assaf, Miron Cohen, Gene Dyer, Stanley Field, Irit Kohavi, Haim Leshem, Yehuda Pereg, Eli Reisz, Ofer Sashitzky
Senior Staff
Samy Amzallag, Adrianna Barboy, David Ben Basat, Avi Ben Gur, Gabi Cohen, Lior Couriel, Suri Drucker, Razia Gilboa, Maria Greenberg, Haim Lotner, Claudio Lusthaus, David Mitchell, Jacob Molho, Marcus Rector, Eli Reisz, Gilbert Sayada, Gilbert Weil
Architects and Support Staff
Uriel Adiv, Shlomit Almagor, Eitan Alon, Miriam Aluel, Sigalit Amikam-Cohen, Ofer Amir, Aliza Arens, Merav Atar, Eilat Atias, Dafna Avni, Karin Bahajian, Barbara Baker, Robert Barringer, Iris Ben David, Gidon Ben Mordechai Halevi, Eitan Ben Zvi, Ari Berman, Dalit Binyamin, Merav Block, Steve Blumis, Aviva Braun, Aharon Brom, Stacey Brooks, Dani Brosh, Paul Cadville, Gil'ad Cahana, Dianna Cahn, Lili Calev, Silvia Campanys, Alfredo Cheriti, Tamar Clay, Einat Cohen, Howard Cohen, Ilan Cohen, Irena Cohen, Shlomit Cohen, Leor Curiel, Isabel Damelin, Yoav David, Eli Davidov, Steve Davies, Yossi Dayan, Sharon Ditish, Dalia Dotan, Avener Drori, Naftali Duetsch, Zvi Dunsky, Signalit Eilati, Livnah Engelhart, Laurie Fanger, Tali Feldman, Michal Firestone, Caroline Fluck, Helena Flusfeder, Shmuel Freidberg, Leah Friedman, Leah Frumer, Inoje Fumikatsu, Sara Ganzel, Gaila Gavish, Zehava Gavrielli, Ziona Gershstein, Amos Gidron, Yonat Gilboa, Gabi Goldshmidt, Erica Goldstein, Diana Gonzales, Eitan Goodman, Donna Estes Greental, Ron Gross, Alfredo Gruto, Mark Guralnick, Nira Hassin, Amnon Haviv, Dorit Hook, Alfonso Hosta, Eddie Itzcovitz, Abdal Kadar, Meir Kaiserman, Arik Katz, Elite Kedan, Leora Keter, Yeuda Kimellman, George Kleinman, Joe Kolbe, Ofer Kolker, Cathy Kones, Mark Krugly, Sara Lancry, Joanna Layman, Batsheva Lerman, Ruth Lerman, Rachel Lev, Ilana Levine, Sarit Levy, Shawn Lewis, Ruthi Liberty, Gary Lichtblau, Garcia Lipstein, Batsheva Livni, Cindy Lopez, Haim Lotner, Elazar Malichi, Daniel Manuel, Amir Mann, Shulamit Maper, Inbal Marciano, Ziona Margolit, Alfons Hosta Matev, Devora Mayer, Carmiel Michaeli, Zahi Milman, Lyn Milstone, Adua Mintz, Leora Mirvish, Yoel Mizrahi, Avi Mizrahi, Oleg Moldovsky, Edna Monetz, Eran Mordohovicz, Tami Mordohovicz, Shoshi Nahum, Yael Naor, Haim Netzach, Meir Nugrian, Michal Openheim, Ester Or, Paul Orentlicher, Gracia Lopez Patino, Sharon Perlman, Sharon Poran, David Posen, Eytan Poznansky, Elsa Ralev, Bram Ratner, Deganit Rauchwerger, Chen Raz, Moshe Raz, Zali Reshef, Koby Ristig, Orit Ronen, Alla Rozinsky, Jonathan Seigel, Eyal Sha'ar, Chaim Shachar, Ezra Shalom, Roni Shanit, Arie Shapira, Rachel Shapira, David Sharki, Tamar Shender, Debbie Shlo, Amir Shoham, Aharon Silberstein, Louis Sokolovsky, Domenec Cadevall Sole, Amitai Solo, Zvi Szkolnik, Shuli Tanami, Yehuda Tolkovsky, Gail Trachtenberg, Micha Vaknin, Rami Vimer, Cecile Visny, Henry Walsch, Mary Waltie, Leonid Weitzman, Miriam Wenzelbaum, Aya Wolhd, Wehudit Ya'acobi, Roni Yalon, Vered Yamin, Perach Yankelowitz, Etti Yosef, Melanie Yufa, Yitzhak Zaude, Yoni Zinkover, Leora Zion